The Market for Virtue

The Market for Virtue

THE POTENTIAL AND LIMITS OF CORPORATE SOCIAL RESPONSIBILITY

David Vogel

BROOKINGS INSTITUTION PRESS
Washington, D.C.

To Virginia

ABOUT BROOKINGS
The Brookings Institution is a private nonprofit organization devoted to research, education, and publication on important issues of domestic and foreign policy. Its principal purpose is to bring the highest quality independent research and analysis to bear on current and emerging policy problems. Interpretations or conclusions in Brookings publications should be understood to be solely those of the authors.

The Library of Congress has cataloged the hardcover edition as follows:
Vogel, David.
The market for virtue : the potential and limits of corporate social responsibility / David Vogel.
    p.   cm.
Includes index.
ISBN-13: 978-0-8157-9076-1 (hardcover : alk. paper)
ISBN-10: 0-8157-9076-7 (hardcover : alk. paper)
1. Social responsibility of business. 2. Business ethics. 3. Virtue. I. Title.
HD60.V64 2005
658.4'08—dc22   2005015005

ISBN-13: 978-0-8157-9077-8 (pbk. : alk. paper)
ISBN-10: 0-8157-9077-5

9 8 7 6 5

The paper used in this publication meets minimum requirements of the American National Standard for Information Sciences—Permanence of Paper for Printed Library Materials: ANSI Z39.48-1992.

Typeset in Sabon

Composition by OSP, Inc.
Arlington, Virginia

Printed by R. R. Donnelley
Harrisonburg, Virginia

Contents

Preface to the Paperback Edition   vii

Preface to the First Edition   xix

1   The Revival of Corporate Social Responsibility   1

2   Is There a Business Case for Virtue?   16

3   What Is the Demand for Virtue?   46

4   Corporate Responsibility for Working Conditions   75
in Developing Countries

5   Corporate Responsibility for the Environment   110

6   Corporate Responsibility for Human Rights   139
and Global Corporate Citizenship

7   Beyond the Market for Virtue   162

Notes   175

Index   207

Preface to the
Paperback Edition

Since the completion of *The Market for Virtue* in the spring of 2005, a number of changes have occurred in the area of corporate social responsibility (CSR). Some demonstrate the potential of CSR; others illustrate its continuing limitations. In what follows, I review some of these developments and consider their implications for the conclusions reached in this book.

Corporate Responsibility and Consumer Demand

Although consumer purchases remain primarily informed by price, quality, and convenience, there are some signs that the market for responsibly produced products is growing. Sales of Fair Trade coffee in the United States continue to increase. They have tripled since 1999, making Fair Trade coffee the fastest-growing segment of the specialty coffee business.[1] More than 35,000 retailers and restaurants now carry it, an increase of 60 percent in three years. In Great Britain, consumer awareness of the Fair Trade brand doubled to 50 percent between 2003 and 2005, and sales of all Fair Trade products, including coffee, bananas, chocolate, and flowers, increased by 51 percent between 2003 and 2004.[2]

1. Jennifer Alsever, "Fair Prices for Farmers: Simple Idea, Complex Reality," *New York Times*, March 19, 2006, Business Section, p. 5.
2. Clare Goff, "Almost Famous," *Ethical Corporation* (June 2005): 9.

More firms have also started to feature their social practices in their marketing.[3] American Apparel—which sold $250 million of casual clothing in 2005, all manufactured in Los Angeles—has made its sweatshop-free production part of its company image and brand. Timberland has launched a new footwear packaging initiative that will work as a "nutritional label," telling consumers about the community and environmental impacts of the company's manufacturing. The British retailer M&S has begun a major advertising campaign that informs consumers how its products are sourced and made; the firm has also developed a line of ethically labeled products. American Express, the Gap, Giorgio Armani, and Nike-owned Converse have all joined with Irish rock star Bono to sell a line of products bearing the Product RED logo; the sales proceeds will be used to address health problems in developing countries.

The potential marketing appeal of "ethical" products has prompted three large corporations to purchase smaller brands closely identified with CSR. The British confectionary firm, Cadbury Schweppes, has bought Green & Black, which sells Fair Trade and organic chocolate; the French cosmetics giant L'Oréal has purchased the Body Shop; and Colgate-Palmolive now owns Tom's of Maine, which makes natural personal care products. It remains to be seen to what extent these corporate acquisitions will expand the market for ethical products or whether their new ownership will undermine some of the distinctive social and environmental practices of the acquired firms.

Activists continue to pressure corporations to behave more responsibly, though some of their focus has shifted from overseas labor practices to domestic ones. In the spring of 2005, a coalition of fifty organizations, which included labor unions, environmentalists, and community organizations, joined together to launch the most coordinated public relations campaign ever mounted against a retailer.[4] Their target was Wal-Mart, whose brand was recently ranked as the sixth-most valuable in the world. The firm's critics argued that the company's business model of low prices had led to low wages, poor working conditions, inadequate health care benefits, suburban sprawl, and the destruction of independent merchants. Wal-Mart's public relations problems, along with increased community

3. Poulomi Saha and Tobias Wedd, "Brave Branding," *Ethical Corporation* (March 2006): 10–11.
4. Lisa Roner, "Watching Wal-Mart," *Ethical Corporation* (May 2005): 16–17.

opposition to its opening of new stores, have slowed the firm's sales growth and helped depress the price of its shares.[5]

Like Nike, Shell, and other highly visible firms accused of irresponsible CSR practices, Wal-Mart has responded by changing some of its policies. The company has made some modest improvements in its health care programs, and it played a much-appreciated role in the rapid delivery of supplies to those affected by Hurricane Katrina. However, Wal-Mart's most visible embrace of "good corporate citizenship" involves a series of environmental initiatives.[6] These include selling a line of organic cotton baby clothes in Europe and Japan, sourcing its wild-caught fish from sustainable fisheries certified by the Marine Stewardship Council, pledging to reduce its greenhouse gas emissions, reducing packaging waste, building more energy-efficient stores, and encouraging suppliers to "green" their products and packaging. The firm plans to spend $500 million annually to introduce environmental technologies into its more than 5,000 stores around the world. Although these commitments have failed to appease the company's social critics, its belated "greening" has received mixed reviews from the environmental community. Some have been skeptical of its commitments, while others believe that Wal-Mart's sales volume and leverage over its suppliers could have far-reaching environmental impacts and could encourage similar moves by other retailers.[7]

Another firm whose CSR practices have been in the media spotlight, Whole Foods, illustrates the continued difficulty of defining what it means to be a responsible company. The company and its CEO and founder John Mackey have acquired nearly iconic status within the CSR community. With its slogan, "Whole Foods, Whole Planet, Whole People," the grocery chain has developed a reputation as a progressive trendsetter, its natural and organic products placing it at the forefront of America's green lifestyle revolution. Whole Foods's dramatic growth—it is now a Fortune 500 corporation—has often been cited as proof that CSR can and does pay.

But while the firm has made healthier foods more accessible—though certainly not more affordable as witnessed by its nickname "Whole Paycheck"—it has also driven many independent natural foods retailers out of

5. Daniel McGinn, "Wal-Mart Hits the Wall," *Newsweek*, November 14, 2005, pp. 42–43.

6. Jonathan Birchall, "Wal-Mart Picks a Shade of Green," *Financial Times*, February 7, 2006, p. 9.

7. Lisa Roner, "An Environmental Epiphany?" *Ethical Corporation* (December 2005): 23–24.

business and promoted the corporate consolidation of organic agriculture. Like Wal-Mart and American Apparel, Whole Foods is also aggressively antiunion. According to one critic, "It's a bleak commentary on the current social climate when a management team that spews some of the most backward antiunion rhetoric this side of the last 150 years is still considered socially responsible by liberal investors and others spellbound by any company that combines talk of all things sustainable with record profits."[8]

Corporate Responsibility for the Environment

Further evidence from the environmental front underscores the need for caution in assessing the societal impact of CSR. Toyota's hybrid Prius has been among the most commercially successful green products, notwithstanding its substantial price premium. Although hybrids, which can run on batteries as well as on gasoline, make up only 3 percent of Toyota's worldwide sales, the success of the Prius has given the firm a reputation as an environmental innovator and encouraged other automotive manufactures to expand production of hybrid vehicles. However, notwithstanding their green reputation, increased sales of hybrids will do little to improve the fuel economy of America's vehicle fleet, let alone reduce gasoline consumption.[9] Hybrid technologies are frequently used to boost the horsepower and acceleration of larger vehicles rather than to improve their fuel efficiency, and hybrid sports utility vehicles are markedly less fuel efficient than many automobiles that run on gasoline. Moreover, the efficiency gains of all hybrids tend to diminish substantially when they are driven on highways, as their batteries quickly become exhausted.

In part inspired by Toyota's example, several firms have launched or expanded environmental initiatives, which often include investments in green technologies. General Electric's (GE's) widely publicized "ecoimagination" program consists of seventeen products, including wind power and more-efficient jet engines and power generators.[10] The company plans to more than double its environmental research budget by 2010 and

8. Mark Harris, "Welcome to 'Whole-Mart,'" *Dissent* (Winter 2006): 66.

9. For skepticism about hybrids, see Holman W. Jenkins Jr, "Dear Valued Hybrid Customer..." *Wall Street Journal*, November 30, 2005, p. A19; Holman W. Jenkins Jr, "Prius Follies, Take Two," *Wall Street Journal*, December 14, 2005, p. A21; Jamie Lincoln Kitman," Life in the Green Lane," *New York Times*, April 16, 2006, Week in Review, p. 12.

10. Jeffrey Immelt, "GE Looks Out for a Cleaner Profit," *Financial Times*, July 1, 2005, p. 8.

expects sales of ecoimagination-tagged products to increase by a similar amount. Such investments and products clearly blur the line between normal business opportunities that are driven by shifts in consumer demand and CSR. Ironically, while GE's environmental commitments have been primarily driven by business considerations, they have not impressed Wall Street: GE's stock has been stagnant for two years and is worth considerably less than it was when Jack Welch retired in September 2001. Nonetheless, as the largest company to claim a competitive advantage in going green, GE is likely to encourage other firms to follow suit.[11]

A growing number of institutional investors, including the members of the Investor Network on Climate Risk, which controls $3 trillion in investment capital, have become more aware of and interested in the financial implications of companies' responses to the risks and opportunities associated with global climate change and a more carbon-constrained environment.[12] Ceres, a coalition of investors and environmentalists, periodically ranks 100 global corporations on their strategies for curbing greenhouse gases.[13] However, the results of such efforts to affect share prices remain limited: no appreciable differential in share prices has yet occurred between greener firms and industry laggards.[14] ExxonMobil, whose single-minded commitment to fossil fuels and strong opposition to the Kyoto Protocol has made it the bête noire of the environmental community, remains the most profitable major oil company. During the last five years, its shares outperformed those of Shell and BP, two companies that have increased their investments in renewable energy.[15]

Global Corporate Citizenship

The impact of corporate practices on developing countries in the areas of the environment and human rights remains an important dimension of CSR. In February 2006, eight jewelry companies, collectively accounting for 14 percent of retail gold sales, endorsed a national campaign called No

11. Fiona Harvey, "Giant Expects Its Example to Be Followed," *Financial Times*, July 1, 2005, p. 8.

12. Ken Stier, "Investing in Climate Change," *Ethical Corporation* (June 2006): 23.

13. Claudia Deutsch, "Study Says U.S. Companies Lag on Global Warming," *New York Times*, March 22, 2006, p. C3.

14. Stier, "Investing in Climate Change."

15. Jay Mouawad, "The New Face of an Oil Giant," *New York Times*, March 30, 2006, pp. C1–C2.

Dirty Gold. It commits them to monitor the environmental practices of the firms that produce and process gold, 80 percent of which is fabricated into jewelry.[16] This effort is designed to head off a consumer backlash that is due to increased public awareness of the negative environmental and social impacts of gold mining, especially in developing countries. A number of retailers and mining firms have also established the Council for Responsible Jewelry Practices.[17] Its long-term goal is to develop environmental and health standards for every stage of the process of creating and selling jewelry, which then will be subject to independent third-party verification.

Both efforts are modeled on an earlier initiative among diamond miners, exporters, and retailers to identify, track, and prohibit the sale of so-called conflict diamonds harvested by private armies waging civil wars in Africa.[18] As a result of the five-year-old United Nations–backed Kimberley Process, named after the South African city where this accord was reached, the export of illegal diamonds mined from West Africa has measurably declined, though the certification system does not appear to be foolproof; some African gems, especially alluvial diamonds, continue to be exported and sold.[19]

More broadly, the global mining industry, concerned about its poor environmental reputation, has been working to strengthen the effectiveness of the International Council of Mining and Metals, which describes itself as "the responsible face of mining."[20] The council recently developed a Cyanide Code, which provides guidelines for the safe application of this poison in gold mining.

The mining firm Freeport-McMoRan, which has frequently been criticized by human rights activists for its close relationship with Indonesia's repressive military, took the unprecedented step of asking a nongovernmental organization (NGO), the International Center for Corporate Accountability, to conduct an independent audit of its vast Papuan min-

16. Kirk Johnson, "With This Ethical Ring I Thee Wed," *New York Times*, April 6, 2006, p. E1, E7.

17. Peter Davis, "Chains of Responsibility," *Ethical Corporation* (September 2005): 35–36.

18. Nicol Degli, "A Positive Example of Co-operation on Conflict Stones," *Financial Times*, June 18, 2005, p. 4.

19. Ron Lieber, "Between a Rock and a Hard Place," *Wall Street Journal*, February 4–5, 2005, p. B1.

20. Rebecca Bream, "Digging Deep: Mining Faces Up to the Cost of Presenting a Cleaner Image to the World," *Financial Times*, January 17, 2006, p. 13.

ing complex.[21] The center's lengthy report, which was made public in the fall of 2005, represents a major achievement for the corporate responsibility movement: no other global mining or oil company has agreed to such extensive disclosure of its social and environmental practices. The report exhaustively reviews Freeport's human rights policies, military links, tribal employment, use of contract labor, and community development efforts. Unfortunately, the firm's operations subsequently became the site of violent protests, precipitated by the decision of government security forces to prevent people who live near the mine from panning the mine's waste for gold.[22] Some Indonesian politicians are now demanding that the firm pay higher taxes to compensate for the environmental damage caused by its extensive operations, especially in light of the fact that gold prices have reached a twenty-five-year high. Student activists want the firm to leave Indonesia.

Other CSR initiatives by companies in extractive industries have also produced disappointing results. Shell's efforts to improve its environmental practices and promote community development in Nigeria's Niger Delta have been overshadowed by increased violence and civil unrest. As a result, Shell has been forced to periodically remove its personnel from the region, and Nigeria's oil exports have been reduced by 20 percent.[23] Even more sobering is the fate of one of the most promising examples of global corporate responsibility described in *The Market for Virtue*, a partnership involving ExxonMobil, the World Bank, various NGOs, and the government of Chad, widely regarded as one of the world's most corrupt. In an attempt to break the pattern by which resource-rich countries squander their royalty payments, the government of Chad was forced to agree to commit virtually all its revenues from oil exports to poverty reduction or place them in a future generations fund. But in December 2005 Chad took advantage of increased oil prices to break its agreement with the World Bank, which had helped finance the country's $4.2 billion oil

21. Aaron Bernstein, "Freeport's Hard Look at Itself," *Business Week*, October 24, 2005, pp. 108–9. For an extensive discussion of the social and environmental impact of the firm's mining operations in Indonesia, see Jane Perlez and Raymond Bonner, "Below a Mountain of Wealth," *New York Times*, December 27, 2005, p. 1, A14.

22. Jane Perlez, "Indonesians Protest U.S, Mine," *San Francisco Chronicle*, March 17, 2006, p. A12.

23. Lydia Polgreen, "Blood Flows with Oil in Poor Nigerian Villages," *New York Times*, January 1, 2006, p. 1; Dino Mahtani and Carola Hoyos, "Nigeria Security Alert after Shell Attacks," *Financial Times*, January 17, 2006, p. 4.

pipeline.[24] It scrapped the future generations fund and channeled monies designated for social programs to the military. Both of these examples underline the difficulty that global firms face in operating responsibly in developing countries in the absence of support from local governments and civil society.

On a more hopeful note, the Extractive Industries Transparency Initiative, the partners of which have been working to reduce corruption and bribery in the businesses of oil, gas, and mining, has persuaded nearly twenty countries, including Angola, Azerbaijan, Equatorial Guinea, Ghana, the Kyrgyz Republic, and Nigeria, to audit and disclose the royalty payments they receive.[25] However, to date only Nigeria and Azerbaijan have implemented these disclosures. Seven oil companies—BP, ChevronTexaco, ExxonMobil, Statoil, Repsol, Total, and Anglo-American—stung by criticisms of the misuse of their royalty payments, have also agreed to make public their payments to governments, though so far their disclosures have been limited. The global impact of the EITI has been limited further by the failure of any member of OPEC, any country in Latin America, as well as China and India, to endorse it. Nor have any state-owned oil companies agreed to disclose their payments to governments. Nonetheless, some human rights activists are encouraged by the fact that payments and revenues are beginning to be published, suggesting some progress toward greater transparency and accountability in this critically important dimension of business-government relations.[26]

Signs of increased public interest in the impact of global firms on human rights are also visible in the campaign for withdrawal from the Sudan, initiated in response to widely publicized human rights abuses in Darfur.[27] Although American firms have been barred from doing business in the Sudan since 1997, more than 100 non-American firms continue to operate there, including Total, Toyota, Siemens, Ericsson, PetroChina, Sinopec, Alcatel, and ABB. More than half of China's foreign oil reserves

24. Lydia Polgreen, "Chad Backs Out of Pledge to Use Oil Wealth to Reduce Poverty," *New York Times*, December 3, 2005, p. A15; See also, Chip Cummins, "Exxon Oil-Fund Model Unravels in Chad," *Wall Street Journal*, February 28, 2006, p. A4.

25. Peter Davis, "Extracting Transparency Promises," *Ethical Corporation* (May 2005): 35–36.

26. Alan Beattie, "Deal Signed to Expose Bribery in Extractive Industries," *Financial Times*, March 18, 2005, p. 5.

27. Carla Fried, "How States Are Aiming to Keep Dollars Out of Sudan," *New York Times*, February 19, 2006, Business Section, p. 5.

are located in the Sudan, and the Oil and Natural Gas Corporation of India has recently increased its investments in that war-torn country, which holds 6.3 billion barrels of proven oil reserves.[28]

American investors own shares in many of these firms, either directly or through international mutual funds. The national Sudan Divestment Task Force, along with human rights activists, religious organizations, and African and African-American student groups, has been pressuring universities and state and local governments to divest, especially from those companies that provide revenues or arms to the Sudanese government. To assist in the divestment campaign, several ethical investment advisory bodies are compiling databases of companies involved in Sudan, and one bank, Northern Trust, has established six Sudan-free index funds for its institutional clients. These efforts, which echo the campaign that was aimed at American and British firms doing business in apartheid South Africa two decades ago, have been increasingly effective. Several major universities, including Harvard, Yale, Brown, Stanford, and the University of California, have sold their shares in some firms with substantial investments in the Sudan, as have a growing number of cities and states. In December 2005, the nation's largest public pension fund, the California Public Employees Retirement Plan, called upon ABB, Alcatel, and Siemens to cease their business operations in the Sudan. The firms refused, and the pension fund managers are considering their next step.

So far, the impact of the divestment campaign has been primarily symbolic. It has not affected the share prices of any targeted firms, nor have any major global firms agreed to withdraw. However, activists are encouraged by the fact that earlier efforts targeting businesses in Sudan appeared to have some effect. In 2002, before the start of the Darfur conflict, Talisman Energy of Canada withdrew from the Sudan after divestments by American and Canadian investors caused a 35 percent decline in its share price.[29] In addition, the current divestment campaign has clearly worried the government of Sudan, which has publicly denounced it.

Does Virtue Pay?

The Market for Virtue argues that although CSR may provide benefits to some firms in some areas—by protecting or improving their reputation,

28. Carola Hoyos, "China and India Fill Void Left by Rights Campaigners," *Financial Times*, March 1, 2006, p. 3.

29. Sam Graham-Felsen, "Divestment and Sudan," *Nation*, May 8, 2006, p. 5.

for example, or helping them attract, motivate, and retain employees—
these benefits are often elusive and rarely affect their financial performance. Rather the benefits and costs of a company's CSR programs and
policies are typically overshadowed by normal business risks and opportunities. A recent issue of *Business Week* provides further evidence favor-
ing skepticism about the business case for CSR.[30] The magazine features
a list of the fifty best financial performers in the United States, based on
ten measures of long-term growth and earnings. Not only do few of these
firms have above-average social or environmental performance, but
nowhere in the twenty-page article is there any mention of business benefits, opportunities, or risks related to CSR.

The growth of socially responsible investment (SRI) funds under management in the United States has slowed during the past year. The performance of such funds has also lagged slightly behind that of all mutual
funds, though some individual SRI funds have done extremely well.[31]
Similarly, since their inception, two major ethical stock indexes, the
FTSE4Good Index (which began in 2001) and the Dow Jones Sustainability Index (which began in 1999), have underperformed the market by
3 percent and 8 percent, respectively.[32]

Nonetheless, the debate continues over whether virtue pays. One influential meta-analysis of 52 academic studies conducted between 1972 and
1997 found a positive correlation between CSR and financial performance.[33] A British study of the performance of 451 firms in the FTSE All
Share Index, which was published in February 2006, reached the opposite
conclusion: it reported that the average return for the least socially responsible companies was 24 percent higher than the average for the most ethically minded firms and 17 percent higher than the average for the market.
According to one of the British study's authors, "If the sole objective is to
maximize returns, it is still worth looking at corporate and social responsibility (CSR) indicators, but in a negative way—invest in funds with the
lowest scores because they will generate the highest returns."[34]

30. Dean Foust, "The Best Performers," *Business Week*, April 3, 2006, pp.
64–100.

31. Richard Beales," Putting a Price on Integrity," *Financial Times*, August 9,
2006, p. 4.

32. Stier, "Investing in Climate Change."

33. Marc Orlitzky, Frank Schmidt, and Sara Pynes, "Corporate Social and
Financial Performance: A Meta-Analysis," *Organizational Studies* 24, no. 3
(2003): 403–11.

34. Ed Monk, "It Pays to Be Bad," *FTAdvisor* (*Financial Times*), March 29,
2006 (www.ftadviser.com/?m=11173&amid=92790).

Beyond the Market for Virtue

The Market for Virtue concludes by arguing that an important short-coming of CSR is its failure to appreciate the critical role of public policy in promoting more-responsible corporate behavior. Too often, there is a disjuncture between a company's voluntary CSR programs and commitments and its political activity. A classic example was William Ford's commitment to reduce Ford's environmental impact, while the company lobbied against the strengthening of federal standards for fuel economy. However, there are encouraging signs that some companies are beginning to recognize the limits of CSR and the need for more responsible public as well as private policies.

According to the 2006 annual report of Human Rights Watch, several international firms have concluded that self-regulation and codes of conduct are not only often ineffective but can place more responsible firms at a competitive disadvantage in international competition.[35] For example, after Swiss gold refineries responded to public pressure by suspending purchases of "tainted gold" from African countries controlled by warlords, within two months the center of gold refining moved from Switzerland to Dubai. Not surprisingly, there is increasing business support for legally enforceable standards that would apply to all firms—unlike voluntary standards that primarily apply to visible ones that are headquartered in the United States and Europe.

Starbucks, which provides health care benefits for all employees who work at least twenty hours a week—and which now spends more on health care than on coffee—has publicly supported national health care legislation. Wal-Mart has backed the raising of the minimum wage, and Nike has endorsed internationally binding labor standards. For its part, Levi Strauss has supported the inclusion of labor provisions in all trade agreements ratified by the United States and has worked with the Guatemalan government to enact more stringent labor laws.

More significantly, several companies, some of which have made impressive progress in reducing their own carbon emissions, have indicated their willingness to support some form of regulation of greenhouse gases in the United States.[36] In some cases, their ability to make voluntary

35. Gay Dinmore, "Business 'Sees Gain in Binding Standards on Human Rights,'" *Financial Times*, January 9, 2006, p. 4. See also, Kenneth Roth, "Rules on Corporate Ethics Could Help, Not Hinder, Multinationals," *Financial Times*, June 21, 2005, p. 15.

36. John Fialka, "Big Businesses Have New Take on Warming," *Wall Street Journal*, March 28, 2006, p. A4; John Carey, "Global Warming: Suddenly the Cli-

reductions in a cost-effective manner has persuaded them that mandatory reductions in carbon emissions are economically feasible. Some firms are worried that the uncertainty of future public policies makes long-term planning difficult. Convinced that carbon constraints are inevitable, these firms want the government to set clear and reachable goals sooner rather than later. Other firms are concerned that the lack of U.S. regulation will reduce their ability to remain competitive in the race toward greener energy innovations. Among the firms now backing some form of carbon regulation are Wal-Mart, General Electric, DuPont, and Goldman Sachs, as well as several utility companies. Whether they will be as effective in affecting public policy as they have been in ameliorating their own environmental impacts remains unclear.

During the last year, I have made numerous presentations at CSR conferences and at universities throughout the United States and Europe. In light of the fact that my book questions so much of what has been said and written about CSR, I have been pleasantly surprised by the reactions of academics, practitioners, and advocates of CSR. A reviewer on a CSR website wrote, "*The Market for Virtue* hits like a jolt of strong coffee the morning after a spirit-filled cocktail party . . . CSR and SRI supporters would benefit by deeply considering [its] sober arguments, which tend to temper undue enthusiasm."[37] In a review for the *Stanford Innovation Review*, Matthew Hirschland, a director of Business for Social Responsibility, wrote that my book "details many of the challenges and questions raised after two decades of work by civil society organizations, governments, and companies redefining the relationship between business and society."[38] Encouraged by this response, I look forward to additional research into what CSR has and has not been able to achieve, as well as analyses of the relationship between CSR and public policy.

---

mate in Washington Is Changing," *BusinessWeek online,* June 27, 2005 (www.businessweek.com/magazine/content/05_26/b3939111.htm).

37. William Baue, Book Review—*The Market for Virtue: The Potential and Limits of Corporate Social Responsibility*, August 31, 2005, (www.Social-Funds.com/news/article.cgi/1793.html).

38. *Stanford Social Innovation Review*, (Spring 2006): 75–76.

Preface to the
First Edition

When I was in graduate school in the late 1960s and early 1970s, there was considerable public and academic interest in the subject of corporate responsibility. In 1978 I published *Lobbying the Corporation: Citizen Challenges to Business Authority,* which chronicled the emerging politicization of consumers and investors in the United States. In subsequent years, my research interest shifted to other areas more in the mainstream of political science. I did, though, continue to follow both academic research and popular writing on corporate social responsibility (CSR).

About five years ago I became aware of a major revival of CSR. Reading through the large and steadily growing volume of books, articles, and reports on this subject, I was struck by the weakness of many of the claims about the potential of CSR to make firms more virtuous. I began writing an essay to critically evaluate the business, academic, and professional literature on corporate social responsibility and in the process realized that, in addition to criticizing the arguments of others, I needed to offer my own analysis of what CSR could and could not accomplish. Hence, thanks to the encouragement of Christopher Kelaher at the Brookings Institution Press, an extended literature review grew into this book.

In discussions with colleagues and those outside academia unfamiliar with CSR, I discovered that they had a rather different view of this subject. Their typical response was: Corporate social responsibility? Does such a thing exist?

So I find myself writing for at least two audiences. For those who think that the contemporary reemergence of CSR heralds a major transformation in the social role and values of business, I hope to provide a view that is somewhat closer to reality. And for those who believe corporations cannot behave more responsibly in the absence of more government regulation, I hope to show that they are unnecessarily pessimistic. CSR is real and substantive and deserves to be taken seriously by anyone interested in politics, business, or the relationship between the two. For those unfamiliar with but interested in this subject, I hope this book serves as a useful overview of the contemporary reemergence of CSR and some of the ongoing issues surrounding its impact and role.

This has proven a difficult topic about which to write. The amount of material in books, scholarly essays and papers, newspaper and magazine articles, reports, and conference proceedings, to say nothing of websites, is enormous—far beyond the capacity of anyone to absorb. The quality of writing on CSR is highly uneven, and much of it has a strong normative bias, making its value difficult to assess. And its quantity keeps growing. A substantial portion of the material I refer to was published quite recently, often as I was completing the final draft of the manuscript.

I am a political scientist who primarily studies public policy. There are a limited number of governmental institutions, their output takes the form of discernible laws and regulations, and much of their decisionmaking process is relatively transparent. By contrast, there are literally thousands of businesses with a wide range of social and environmental policies, and their decisionmaking processes are rarely public. Moreover, while there is a rich tradition of public policy analysis that evaluates the costs, benefits, and impact of government decisions, nothing comparable exists for the realm of "private policy" in which CSR is located.

My analysis makes no claim to be exhaustive or conclusive. I have omitted much, and I am sure that at times I have been either insufficiently critical or too critical of both firms and nongovernmental organizations (NGOs). I have attempted to present a coherent and informative overview and analysis of the potential and limits of CSR in the hope that it will both contribute to public discussion and improve the quality of future studies of this important subject. In particular, there is a dearth of research on CSR's actual impact on the social and environmental problems it has sought to address. And while much has been written about the business benefits of CSR, there have been relatively few analyses of its costs, or of the relationship between the two.

CSR is very much a moving target. It is now much different than it was five or ten years ago, and it will continue to evolve. It remains to be seen how prescient my analysis will prove. But I do want to confess a bias that comes from following the subject for more than thirty years. The argument I hear most in response to skeptics of the potential of CSR (such as myself) is that as a new generation of more socially committed managers moves into positions of responsibility, we can expect corporations to become increasingly responsible.

I remember first hearing this claim at a conference I attended at Princeton in 1970. Then the argument was that as the sixties generation moves into positions of responsibility, companies will act more responsibly. I believe my skepticism of this claim has proven well founded. The Wall Street scandals of the 1980s, many of which involved this generation, hardly suggested that we had entered a new era of business morality, let alone corporate social responsibility.

I remain skeptical. Important social and political forces encourage firms to behave more responsibly, and they have accomplished much more than almost anyone would have predicted a decade ago. But there are also important restraints on more responsible business behavior. CSR has played a part in and will continue to influence the practices of some companies, but little is to be gained by exaggerating its accomplishments or potential.

I am pleased to acknowledge the contributions of Susan Aaronson, David Baron, Budd Cheit, Cary Coglianese, Ariel Colonomos, Magali Delmas, Neil Gunningham, Robert Kagan, Peter Kinder, David Levine, Jeremy Moon, Dara O'Rourke, Forest Reinhardt, Christine Rosen, and John Ruggie, who took the time to read my original essay or all or a portion of various drafts of the book manuscript and to offer suggestions for improving it. Needless to say, they bear no responsibility for the final product.

I also want to express my appreciation for the comprehensive and thoughtful comments of the three reviewers for the Brookings Institution Press, as well as the very helpful editorial suggestions of Mary Kwak and Janet Mowery, my editors at the press. It was a pleasure working with them. I also benefited from the comments I received when I presented my analysis at workshops at the Stanford Business School and the London School of Economics, as well as at a conference on trans-Atlantic business ethics held at Escade Business School in Barcelona, and at a public lecture sponsored by the Corporate Responsibility Initiative of the Center for

Business and Government at the Kennedy School of Government at Harvard University. Dara O'Rourke, David Victor, Jeremy Moon, David Baron, Matt Christensen, Peter Kinder, Elliot Schrage, S. Prakash Sethi, John Ruggie, and Ariel Colonomos facilitated my research by generously giving me access to unpublished papers and other not readily accessible material.

My deepest professional debt is to my research assistant and graduate student Michael W. Toffel, now finishing his doctorate in Business and Public Policy at the Haas School of Business. Not only did he help me collect research material, check references, and read over countless drafts of each chapter, but our frequent conversations continually challenged me to clarify and strengthen my analysis. I also wish to express my appreciation to Brionna Garner for her editorial assistance.

As always, my greatest personal debt is to my wife, Virginia, who has managed to bear with me through the personal and professional challenges of writing this book. Her patience has been inexhaustible and her emotional support indispensable.

CHAPTER 1

The Revival of
Corporate Social Responsibility

What does it mean to be a virtuous company? Are companies becoming more virtuous? Is there a market for virtue? Consider some of the changes in business that have taken place since the beginning of the 1990s.

—Nike, along with numerous other American and European firms that produce or sell apparel, footwear, sporting equipment, and toys, monitors working conditions in its supplier factories in developing countries.

—Ikea requires its rug suppliers in India to prohibit the employment of children and provides families with financial assistance to help keep their children out of the labor market.

—Starbucks, as well as many other major coffee distributors and retailers, sells coffee bearing the Fair Trade label, which guarantees coffee producers an above-world-market price for their products.

—Home Depot, along with major retailers of wood products in the United States and Europe, no longer sells products harvested from old growth or endangered forests.

—British Petroleum, along with scores of other major firms in the United States and Europe, has significantly reduced its greenhouse gas emissions.

—Shell, along with many other major international extractive industry firms, has adopted policies to address human rights and environmental abuses associated with its investments in developing countries.

—Citibank, along with other major financial institutions, has developed criteria for assessing the environmental impact of its lending decisions in developing countries.

—PepsiCo, along with more than a dozen oil companies and consumer goods manufacturers, has withdrawn its investments from Burma because of human rights concerns.

—McDonald's has adopted the European Union's restrictions on the use of growth-promoting antibiotics for its suppliers of beef and chicken in the United States.

—Chiquita has implemented stringent environmental practices for its suppliers of bananas in Central America.

—Timberland allows its employees to take one week off with pay each year to work with local charities.

These are all examples of corporate social responsibility (CSR) or business virtue—that is, practices that improve the workplace and benefit society in ways that go above and beyond what companies are legally required to do.[1] What do these activities signify? Do they support Jeffrey Hollender's claim that "Corporate Social Responsibility [is] . . . the future of business. It's what companies have to do to survive and prosper in a world where more and more of their behavior is under a microscope"? Or, as argued by Joel Bakan, does corporate social responsibility amount to nothing more than a "new creed" designed to mask the fact that "the corporation . . . [remains] designed to valorize self-interest and invalidate moral concern"? Alternatively, is corporate social responsibility "[not] merely undesirable but potentially quite dangerous," as columnist Martin Wolf claims, because it can "distort the market by deflecting business from its primary role of profit generation"?[2]

The Market for Virtue examines these claims by analyzing the forces driving CSR and their impact on current and future business behavior. There are many reasons why some companies choose to behave more responsibly or virtuously in the absence of legal requirements. Some are strategic, others are defensive, and still others may be altruistic or public-spirited. The leadership of many of the businesses spearheading the contemporary CSR movement—a group that includes the Body Shop, Marks & Spencer, Patagonia, Starbucks, Statoil, Interface, and BP—may be genuinely motivated by a commitment to social or environmental goals. Not every business expenditure or policy need directly increase shareholder value, and many of the benefits of CSR are difficult to quantify. But in the final analysis, CSR is sustainable only if virtue pays off. The supply of corporate virtue is both made possible and constrained by the market.

Consequently, this book focuses on the market forces that encourage and limit the practice of corporate social responsibility or business virtue. Among the most important dimensions of such "civil regulation" are consumer demand for responsibly made products, actual or threatened consumer boycotts, challenges to a firm's reputation by nongovernmental organizations (NGOs), pressure from socially responsible investors, and the values held by managers and other employees.[3]

How effective are such forces? Based on the record since about the early 1990s, we can conclude that there is a market for virtue. Corporate social responsibility may be, in the words of the *Economist,* "the tribute that capitalism everywhere pays to virtue."[4] Nonetheless, it has led many firms to make important changes in their social and environmental practices, not only in the United States and Europe but also in the developing world. As John Ruggie, a former United Nations official active in this field, observes, "Although it remains contested, the principle is taking hold that transnational firms . . . ought to be held accountable not only to their shareholders, but also to a broader community of stakeholders who are affected by their decisions and behavior."[5]

But there are important limits to the market for virtue. The main constraint on the market's ability to increase the supply of corporate virtue is the market itself. There *is* a business case for CSR, but it is much less important or influential than many proponents of civil regulation believe. CSR is best understood as a niche rather than a generic strategy: it makes business sense for some firms in some areas under some circumstances. Many of the proponents of corporate social responsibility mistakenly assume that because some companies are behaving more responsibly in some areas, some firms can be expected to behave more responsibly in more areas. This assumption is misinformed. There *is* a place in the market economy for responsible firms. But there is also a large place for their less responsible competitors.

CSR reflects both the strengths and the shortcomings of market capitalism. On the one hand, it promotes social and environmental innovation by business, prompting many firms to adopt new policies, strategies, and products, many of which create social benefits and some of which even boost profits by reducing costs, creating new markets, or improving employee morale.[6] Perhaps most important, it enables citizens to both express their own values and possibly influence corporate practices, by "voting" their social preferences through what they purchase, whom they are willing to work for, and where they invest. This politicization of the market can also help shape public debate and public policy.

On the other hand, precisely because CSR is voluntary and market-driven, companies will engage in CSR only to the extent that it makes business sense for them to do so. Civil regulation has proven capable of forcing *some* companies to internalize *some* of the negative externalities associated with *some* of their economic activities. But CSR can reduce only some market failures. It often cannot effectively address the opportunistic behaviors such as free riding that can undermine the effectiveness of private or self-regulation.[7] Unlike government regulation, it cannot force companies to make unprofitable but socially beneficial decisions. In most cases, CSR only makes business sense if the costs of more virtuous behavior remain modest. This imposes an important constraint on the resources that companies can spend on CSR, and limits the improvements in corporate social and environmental performance that voluntary regulation can produce.

What Is Corporate Social Responsibility?

Many ambiguities surround the concept of CSR, including what business practices count as responsible behavior. Activities associated with corporate virtue typically represent firms' efforts to do more to address a wide variety of social problems than they would have done in the course of their normal pursuit of profits. But some companies may label as "CSR" initiatives they were planning as part of their normal business activities— reducing energy use, for example—while for others a business decision may have multiple causes, some more narrowly market-driven and others reflecting social pressures or ethical concerns.

Thus, not surprisingly, there is no consensus on what constitutes virtuous corporate behavior. Is sourcing overseas to take advantage of lower labor costs responsible? Are companies morally obligated to insist that their contractors pay a "living wage" rather than market wages? Are investments in natural resource developments in poor countries with corrupt governments always, sometimes, or never irresponsible? Are environmental expenditures necessarily welfare-enhancing? Is it irresponsible to produce weapons or nuclear power or to make money from gambling? More broadly, is it ever responsible for companies to use their shareholders' resources to provide public goods if doing so makes them less profitable? Or are corporations acting most responsibly when they seek to maximize shareholder wealth?

Similar questions arise when rating individual firms. Should Wal-Mart be considered a responsible company for providing consumers with low-priced goods or an irresponsible one for paying its employees low wages and driving out independent merchants? Was Monsanto's introduction of genetically modified seeds a contribution to sustainable agriculture or a threat to public health and ecological integrity? Should BP be praised for recognizing the problem of global climate change or criticized for its continued development of fossil fuels? Is McDonald's a responsible firm because it uses environmentally friendly packaging or an irresponsible one because it contributes to mass agricultural production? Is Union Oil acting responsibly by improving working conditions on its pipeline construction project in Burma or irresponsibly by continuing to do business in a country with a repressive military government?

As if these questions were not difficult enough, CSR's multidimensional nature further complicates the task of evaluating firms. Companies, like individuals, do not typically exhibit consistent moral or social behavior. They may behave better in some countries than in others or have more responsible environmental policies but less responsible labor practices. Hewlett-Packard, for example, might be considered responsible by some because of its environmental and community development initiatives, while other observers might label the company irresponsible for abandoning HP's long-standing policy of guaranteeing job security. Many of the same firms that have improved their social practices in developing countries have also cut back on health benefits to employees and retirees in the United States. Enron undertook a number of commendable social and environmental initiatives, while also defrauding its investors.

Finally, just as corporations need not engage in CSR in order to produce social benefits, not everything firms do in the name of CSR should be considered responsible.[8] Some firms have undermined the welfare of poor families—and of poor children in particular—by attempting to prohibit child labor. Some decisions made in response to NGO and consumer pressures may have increased, not reduced, the potential for harm to the environment—consider Shell's decision to dispose of its Brent Spar oil platform on land. In short, voluntary regulation can be as welfare-distorting as either government regulation or the pursuit of shareholder value without adequate legal or social constraints.

Despite these ambiguities, the term "corporate social responsibility" remains a useful one, if for no other reason than that it is employed so frequently. Nonetheless, the reader should feel free to imagine quotation marks every time he or she encounters the word "responsible" or its synonyms "ethical," "virtuous," or "social."

Behind the Resurgence of Corporate Social Responsibility

Some of the principles and practices of corporate social responsibility date back more than a century, but a major resurgence of interest in this dimension of corporate behavior took place in the United States during the 1960s and 1970s. Many contemporary strategies of civil regulation were developed during this period, including voluntary codes of conduct, social audits, public interest proxy resolutions, social investment funds, assessments and rankings of corporate social and environmental performance, and more generally the use of corporations as sites for political activity.[9] The protests and boycotts directed against Dow Chemical around 1970 prefigure those that targeted Nike and Shell in the 1990s, while the campus-led campaign pressuring firms to divest from South Africa during the 1970s parallels contemporary civic challenges to corporations with investments in Burma and Sudan.

But since the early 1990s, the importance of CSR has grown considerably. A recent search on Google for "corporate social responsibility" found more than 30,000 sites. More than 15 million pages on the World Wide Web address dimensions of corporate social responsibility, including more than 100,000 pages on corporate websites. Amazon lists 600 books on the subject. More than 1,000 corporations have developed or signed codes of conduct governing dimensions of their social, environmental, and human rights practices, and more than 2,000 firms now issue reports on their CSR practices. In the mid-1980s there were a handful of social mutual funds in the United States. In 2005 there are more than 200, and since 1995 their assets have increased tenfold.

International organizations, such as the United Nations, the World Bank, and the Organization for Economic Cooperation and Development (OECD), actively promote CSR, as do several European governments and the European Union. Numerous organizations and publications regularly monitor, report, and rate aspects of corporate social performance, and several give awards to companies they consider to be the most virtuous. Many leading business schools in both the United States and Europe offer courses on CSR. Numerous academic and professional conferences address the subject, the largest of which attract several hundred participants. Many NGOs now devote a significant portion of their resources to monitoring and pressuring corporations. In response, most large and brand-sensitive corporations have established internal systems to manage stakeholder relations, including their interaction with NGOs. As the *Economist* has observed: "CSR is thriving. It is now an industry in itself, with full-time staff, websites, newsletters, professional associations and massed armies of consultants. This is to say nothing of those employed by the NGOs that started it all."[10]

The Growing Reach of CSR

In addition to having become more institutionalized, the contemporary resurgence of CSR is distinctive for its new focus and for its spread around the world. Substantively, CSR continues to address domestic corporate policies such as community relations, environmental practices, and diversity, but its primary focus is now the conduct of global corporations, especially in developing countries. In particular, corporate responsibility for the labor and human rights practices of their supply chain partners has become among the most salient dimensions of contemporary CSR. And the geographic center of gravity of CSR has shifted from the United States to Europe, in particular to Great Britain.

While some of the earliest examples of corporate responsibility date from nineteenth-century Britain, corporate responsibility was disproportionately if not almost exclusively an American phenomenon through the 1980s. This reflected in part the American reliance on corporations to deliver social services, such as pensions and medical care, that are primarily provided by the government in other capitalist countries. It also reflected the strategies of the U.S. civil rights and antiwar movements, which focused much of their political activity on pressuring corporations to integrate their retail operations and workplaces, stop producing war materials, and withdraw from South Africa.

Today more conferences on this subject are held in London than any other city, and the London-based *Financial Times* and *Economist* cover CSR more extensively than the New York–based *Wall Street Journal, Fortune,* or *Business Week.* Since the mid-1990s, many of the most important publications on CSR, including influential critiques, have come from British-based organizations and individuals.[11] *Ethical Corporation* and

AccountAbility Forum are published in Britain, and UK-based Greenleaf and Earthscan are the major publishers of books on the subject. While ethical investment funds and advisers are more likely to be American, largely because of the larger size of U.S. capital markets, ethical consumerism is much more widespread in the United Kingdom.

Interest in CSR has also spread to the European continent. "Ethical" mutual funds, as well as ethical indexes and rating services, now exist in every European country and capital market. Socially labeled products have a larger market share in much of Europe than in the United States. Fair Trade coffee labeling began in the Netherlands; Rugmark, a human rights label for carpets, was developed in Germany; and eco-marketing has been especially influential in northern Europe. In France, historically a country in which morality and capitalism were regarded as separate spheres, corporate social responsibility has become increasingly salient in the business and investment community.[12]

On many dimensions, European companies are now more engaged in CSR than their American counterparts.[13] European firms are more likely than U.S. firms to have signed on to the UN Global Compact, which in 2001 established a set of global norms for responsible corporate conduct; they are also more likely to have adopted the nonfinancial reporting standards of the Global Reporting Initiative (established in 1997), to issue detailed and comprehensive social reports, and to have their social reports audited.

The Links between CSR, Globalization, and Regulation

What explains the growing importance of CSR since the early 1990s? Much of the answer is linked to the expansion of global and national markets. At the international level, the trend is driven by the growth of world trade and investment. At the national level, it reflects increasing privatization and economic deregulation. While these developments have produced many economic benefits, they have also generated dissatisfaction with some of the consequences of globalization and liberalization—as reflected most dramatically in the demonstrations mounted by protesters at many international business and political meetings.

For some critics of globalization, corporations are the most powerful institutions on the international stage. Because of their global scope and influence, such observers argue, multinational businesses can no longer be effectively monitored or controlled by national governments.[14] These critics also see little effective international regulation. Civil regulation represents an effort to fill the governance gap between the law and the market. It represents a dimension of what political scientists have characterized as a process of "global regulatory privatization . . . through a growing reliance on markets and market based strategies" and regulatory mechanisms that do not derive their authority from governments. [15] Civil regulation constitutes a "soft" form of regulation in that it does not impose legally enforceable standards for corporate conduct. [16]

By applying pressure directly to companies, activists and organizations seek to foster changes in business practices that national governments and international law are unlikely or unwilling to bring about. Often these initiatives seek to export more stringent standards from developed to developing countries. In a sense, much civil regulation represents a private, market-based version of "trading up."[17] It seeks to influence business practices in developing countries by leveraging the preferences for more stringent corporate practices shared by activists—and to some degree by consumers, employees, and investors—in the developed world. Most NGOs and many supporters of CSR might prefer that global firms be governed by more effective and extensive regulation at both the national and international levels, and many favor the use of trade policies to restrict imports of irresponsibly produced products. But to the extent that neither expansion of public authority appears likely or politically feasible, then civil regulation represents a second-best alternative.

Growing interest in making global capitalism more humane may be the most visible link between globalization and the rise of CSR, but it is not the only one. Globalization has not only stimulated interest in civil regulation; by creating global brands, it has also given this strategy added bite. Large multinational firms are more vulnerable than ever to pressures from consumers and activists throughout the world.[18] Many NGOs have taken advantage of this vulnerability—and of new communications technologies, such as the Internet—to target such companies by organizing or threatening boycotts and demonstrations or more generally by "naming and shaming" them into changing their policies. Global brands provide a market-based vehicle for activists in one country to affect corporate practices in another, a strategy that effectively bypasses the WTO's restrictions on governmental trade sanctions.

CSR can also represent an alternative to government action at the national level, particularly in the United States. Virtually every NGO demand, ranging from reducing carbon emissions to protecting forests to reducing the use of antibiotics in beef and chicken, could in principle be addressed through additional government regulation. But because the increased political influence of business has made the enactment of such regulations more difficult, many activists have chosen to lobby executives instead of politicians. Getting some large corporations to change their policies is often easier than changing public policy.

But this does not mean that government and civil regulation operate in isolated spheres. Firms facing civil pressures may seek government regulation to create a more level playing field or, alternatively, adopt socially responsible practices in order to avoid state intervention. In some cases, civil regulation has facilitated the expansion of government regulation, and in others it has impeded it.

Governments may also promote CSR as an indirect form of regulation. The Apparel Industry Partnership, for example, a coalition of companies, NGOs, and universities that seeks to improve working conditions overseas, emerged from a Clinton administration initiative. But governments in Europe have been far more active in this field—possibly because of their stronger traditions of business-government cooperation. Britain has had a minister for corporate responsibility since 2000, and a reform of company law has expanded company nonfinancial reporting requirements. Six European governments require that pension funds consider social practices in making investment decisions, and six countries in Europe have mandatory social or environmental disclosure requirements for firms that operate in their countries or are listed on their stock exchanges.[19]

The Rise of the Business Case for CSR

Globalization and liberalization may explain why interest in CSR among Western governments and NGOs has grown. But why are so many major corporations following suit?

CSR has attracted at least some corporate adherents by taking a more expansive view of business's potential contribution to society. Many executives want to believe that their companies *can* play a more constructive role in addressing a wide range of social and environmental problems and take considerable pride in their CSR initiatives, not all of which are undertaken in response to NGO demands. Such executives participate in organizations like the World Business Council for Sustainable Development, which was established by 170 companies from thirty-five countries following the UN-sponsored environmental summit of 1992 in Rio de Janeiro. The UN Global Compact has more than 1,300 corporate signatories. Other national and international business organizations active in promoting CSR include the International Business Leaders Forum, the Business Leaders Initiative on Human Rights, the Conference Board, Business in the Community, and San Francisco–based Business for Social Responsibility.[20]

However, the most important driver of corporate interest in CSR is the argument that good corporate citizenship is also good business. Oceans of ink have flowed to support the claim that corporate virtue delivers financial rewards. For example, a report for the Global Corporate Citizenship Initiative undertaken by the consulting firm Arthur D. Little concludes:

> Companies that take corporate citizenship seriously can improve their reputations and operational efficiency, while reducing their risk exposure and encouraging loyalty and innovation. Overall, they are more likely to be seen as a good investment and as a company of choice by investors, employees, customers, regulators and joint venture partners. . . . The range of business benefits that can result should be sufficient to make *any* forward-thinking organization see increasing corporate citizenship as an integral part of good business management.[21]

Similarly, a recent corporate report maintains: "If we aren't good corporate citizens as reflected in a Triple Bottom Line that takes into account social and environmental responsibilities along with financial ones—eventually our stock price, our profits and our entire business could suffer."[22] More broadly, the growing use of the term "sustainability" in connection with business performance reflects the belief that financial, social, and environmental goals can all be pursued at the same time. According to the Dow Jones Sustainability Index, an influential ethical fund index, corporate sustainability is "a business approach that creates long-term shareholder value by embracing opportunities and managing risks deriving from economic, environmental and social developments."[23]

Since the late 1990s, the primary message of the numerous books, articles, and reports published on CSR is not simply that more responsible firms can also be profitable. Nor are they primarily interested in showing how behaving more responsibly can make a firm more profitable. Rather, many proponents of CSR have a broader and more ambitious agenda:

they want to both encourage and herald a new era of business practices driven by linking financial goals and social purposes.[24] As Michael Hopkins predicts in *The Planetary Bargain*, "In time, it will not be possible to conduct business without being socially responsible. . . . New rules or corporate laws may well be unnecessary, because corporations will see for themselves—and many have seen this already—the need to behave more responsibly in the social arena."[25]

Corporate Social Responsibility and Its Critics

Notwithstanding the growing popularity of CSR, it is not without its critics. Writing in 1973, during the most recent previous period of heightened interest in corporate responsibility, Neil Chamberlain concluded that "every business . . . is in effect 'trapped' in the business system it helped create. . . . Hence the dream of the socially responsible corporation that, replicated over and over again, can transform our society is illusionary."[26] Nearly thirty years later, Milton Moskowitz wrote in the fifteenth-anniversary issue of *Business Ethics*, "Looking over the history of corporate social responsibility, I can see it has consisted of 95 percent rhetoric and five percent action."[27] This negative assessment is echoed in a 2004 publication by the UK-based NGO Christian Aid entitled *Behind the Mask: The Real Face of Corporate Social Responsibility*, as well as by critics of business such as David Korten, who believe global competitive pressures are increasingly driving corporations to become less responsible, not more.[28]

Others criticize CSR for the opposite reason: they argue it has made corporations too risk-averse and redirected management time and financial resources away from the corporation's core economic mission.[29] According to Arthur Laffer, "What corporate social responsibility really means, in my view, is irresponsibility. The modern corporation is meant to be a vehicle to create wealth for its shareholders, and that is what CEOs must always keep in mind."[30]

The first group of critics regards CSR as a flawed concept because it fails to appreciate the importance firms continue to place on maximizing shareholder value; the second regard CSR as flawed because it encourages companies to neglect that very same goal.[31] Clearly, both criticisms cannot be valid. In fact, neither is.

The argument that companies cannot be expected to behave more responsibly reflects two misconceptions. First, it assumes that all those who manage companies only care about one objective: maximizing profit. But managers, like any other group of individuals, have diverse preferences. Some managers sincerely want their companies to promote civic purposes as well.[32] Their ability to achieve nonfinancial objectives can be constrained by competitive pressure, but this does not make their personal commitments unimportant or inconsequential: they can and do matter. One striking business development over the past two decades has been the emergence of social entrepreneurship—the practice of starting companies whose purpose is to achieve social or environmental goals. The fact that many of these "companies with a conscience" have also been profitable suggests that it *is* possible for some firms to achieve both financial and nonfinancial objectives and that the two can reinforce one another. Similarly, some consumers, employees, and investors also have objectives other than financial self-interest

Second, this criticism mistakenly assumes that it cannot be in a business's financial interest to act more responsibly. But many companies have been effectively pressured by activists, consumers, employees, and investors to make significant changes in corporate policies. These targeted firms have done so not so much because their managers are public-spirited, though some may be, but because the managers of many highly visible firms believe that it is in their firms' interest to be responsive to these pressures. In other words, civil regulation has frequently changed the strategies firms pursue to maximize shareholder value.

If some critics of CSR from the left do not take the rhetoric of CSR seriously enough, then some conservative critiques of CSR take it too seriously. It is, of course, possible to find companies that publicly proclaim their commitment to objectives such as sustainable development, the reduction of global poverty and inequality, and human rights, and place them on a par with the creation of shareholder value. But if these firms actually took such nonfinancial objectives too seriously, then presumably investors—virtually all of whom only care about financial returns—would respond by selling their shares. In fact, this has rarely occurred.

More responsible firms are not necessarily more profitable, but neither are they less so. Most of the resources companies have devoted to CSR since the mid-1990s have been guided by the belief that such expenditures are in their shareholders' interest. The managers who authorized these expenditures may have occasionally been mistaken, but that does not distinguish investments in CSR from any other business strategy or decision.

Scope and Plan of the Book

The rest of this book combines statistical evidence and case studies to analyze CSR's true potential and limitations. It examines some of the most salient dimensions of contemporary CSR: efforts to improve labor conditions and promote human rights in developing countries, and efforts to improve environmental performance globally. It does not address corporate governance issues, which are associated with very different legal and political dynamics.

However, it is worth noting that some of the recent failures of corporate governance, accompanied in some cases by civil and criminal proceedings against corporations and senior executives, hardly suggest that we are entering a new era of good corporate conduct. Arguably, the net social losses stemming from the financial frauds at the beginning of the twenty-first century outweigh the net social benefits from many CSR initiatives. The substantial increases in senior executive compensation since the early 1990s—many given to executives irrespective of their contribution to the creation of shareholder value—far exceed the additional resources companies have devoted to CSR over a similar time period.[33]

It is difficult to generalize about trends in business ethics or corporate responsibility. Both are multidimensional and continually changing. At any given time, some firms and managers are behaving badly on some dimensions and better on others. This has been true since the origins of capitalism and will likely remain true: there have always been more and less responsible firms. Consequently, the objective of this study is not to determine whether corporations or managers are finally behaving "better." Its goal is more modest: to assess the impact of civil regulation, or the market for virtue, on important corporate policies and practices that are associated with contemporary definitions of corporate social responsibility.

Toward this end, chapter 2 places the business case for CSR in historical perspective and puts it to the test. This chapter asks and answers a critical question: does virtue pay? Its central conclusion is that the business case for CSR has little empirical basis. Chapter 3 examines the business case in greater detail by analyzing three critical drivers of CSR—namely, pressures from consumers, employees, and investors. The results of this analysis are more nuanced. While few consumers, investors, and employees are actually willing to "vote" for CSR in the marketplace, CSR does make business sense for a subset of companies. Specifically, the business case for virtue is strongest for firms that have made CSR part of their strategy for attracting and retaining customers, employees, and investors, and for highly visible global companies that have been targeted by activists. Most firms, however, fall into neither category.

Chapters 4 through 6 turn from the demand for virtue to business's ability and willingness to supply it. These chapters focus on three broad areas: corporate policies toward manufacturing and agricultural workers in developing countries; corporate environmental performance; and business responses to concerns about the impact of foreign investment on human rights and economic development in the developing world. These areas do not exhaust contemporary definitions of CSR, which also include policies in areas as specific as drug distribution and pricing and as broad as corporate philanthropy and community relations. But they are among its most important and visible dimensions. They are also sufficiently representative and important to permit an informed assessment of the potential and limits of the market for virtue.

The concluding chapter assesses the overall impact of civil regulation on corporate practices and then explores the critical relationship between corporate responsibility and public policy. It argues that while civil regulation has forced some improvements in corporate practices, for it to have greater impact public regulation must also be strengthened. The scope of CSR needs to be broadened to include the role of business in shaping public policy.

CSR is a global phenomenon, but this book primarily examines developments in the United States and Europe because these regions continue to play a leadership role. Because its focus is on the contemporary revival of CSR, it emphasizes developments since the early 1990s.

CHAPTER 2

Is There a

Business Case for Virtue?

It is impossible to exaggerate the significance of the contemporary claim that there is a business case for corporate responsibility, business ethics, corporate citizenship, environmental stewardship, pollution control, sustainable development, and the like. To be sure, improving the bottom line is not the only possible reason for CSR. Many executives genuinely care about conducting their businesses in ways that are more environmentally sustainable, that respect human rights, and that foster economic development. Self-regulation can also reduce the likelihood of more government regulation or place a firm in a better competitive position if and when new regulations emerge. Some of the benefits of CSR to a firm, such as higher employee morale or a better reputation, never appear on a balance sheet. For profitable firms, CSR can represent a civic-minded allocation of discretionary resources. But while profitability may not be the only reason corporations will or should behave virtuously, it has become the most influential.

According to the business case for CSR, firms will increasingly behave more responsibly not because managers have become more public-spirited—though some may have—but because more managers now believe that being a better corporate citizen is a source of competitive advantage. A more responsibly managed firm will face fewer business risks than its less virtuous competitors: it will be more likely to avoid consumer boycotts, be better able to obtain capital at a lower cost, and be in a better position to attract and retain committed employees and loyal customers. Correspondingly, firms that are unable or unwilling to recognize this new competitive reality will find themselves disadvantaged in the marketplace: both "responsible" and "sophisticated" investors will regard their shares as too risky; the value of their brands and thus their sales will decline as a result of media exposure, public protests, and boycotts; and the morale of their employees will suffer.

Unfortunately, there is no evidence that behaving more virtuously makes firms more profitable. This finding is important because, unless there is a clear business case for CSR, firms will have fewer incentives to act more responsibly. Conversely, the fact that CSR also does not make firms *less* profitable means that it is possible for a firm to commit resources to CSR without becoming less competitive. In brief, there is a place in the business system for responsible firms, but the market for virtue is not sufficiently important to make it in the interest of all firms to behave more responsibly.

This chapter begins by documenting the contemporary importance of the links between ethics and profits. It then places the relationship between ethics and profits in historical perspective, explaining why they have recently become more influential. The remainder of the chapter reviews the evidence about the actual links between ethics and profits. It presents an overview of academic research on the relationship between CSR and profitability, examines the relative financial performance of social mutual funds, and explores other evidence about the business case for CSR.

Old-Style Corporate Responsibility: Doing Good to Do Good

The business case for corporate responsibility is not new, though its current emphasis is. Historically, the relationship between virtue and profits was understood to be more indirect. The 1953 New Jersey Supreme Court case that legitimated corporate philanthropy was brought by a shareholder who complained that Standard Oil of New Jersey had misused "his" funds by making a contribution to the engineering school of Princeton University. This gift came to typify much corporate philanthropy. It was not unrelated to the purposes of the company: Standard Oil needed well-trained engineers, and its gift to Princeton could be expected to increase their number. But in one sense the shareholder who sued the firm's managers was probably right: this gift was unlikely to make Standard Oil more profitable, since those engineers could just as easily work for its competitors. In effect, Standard Oil was providing a collective court held that the allocation of such a gift was within the scope of management discretion.

Many firms took advantage of this ruling. By the 1960s, corporate philanthropy had become part of the widely accepted definition of being a good corporate citizen. Allocating some portion of pretax profits, typically via a corporate foundation, had become the expected and common practice of large firms. However, the link between these gifts and the interest of shareholders was indirect, in many cases much more so than that between Standard Oil's shareholders and Princeton University. Corporate philanthropy went well beyond higher education, supporting civic institutions in communities where the firms had employees (often through United Way) and cultural activities in the firms' headquarters community. Many of these expenditures reflected the firm's "enlightened" self-interest as it was broadly understood; only infrequently did these gifts reflect a strategy to increase shareholder value.

The importance attached to corporate philanthropy as an expression of corporate citizenship during the 1960s and 1970s is suggested by the emergence of a "5 percent club," so named because its members donated at least 5 percent of their pretax earnings. Many of the firms widely regarded as the leaders in corporate responsibility during this period, such as Levi Strauss, Dayton-Hudson, Cummins Engine, Atlantic Richfield, and Control Data, were members. Many cities established similar clubs, requiring minimum donations to philanthropy of 2 to 5 percent of pretax earnings. While there was substantial peer pressure among corporations to become more philanthropic, no one claimed that such firms were likely to be more profitable than their less generous competitors. And it certainly did not occur to any management scholar that correlating a firm's membership in any of these "clubs" with its financial performance would demonstrate that corporate philanthropy "pays."

According to a study of businesses' urban affairs programs between 1967 and 1970, the most important motivation for their establishment was "enlightened self-interest." David Rockefeller, the chairman of Chase Manhattan Bank, whose firm was a local and national leader in these programs, stated, "Our urban affairs work is good for Chase Manhattan in a strictly business sense. Our efforts are aimed at creating a healthy economic and social environment that is vital to the existence of any corporation." Other executives explained their participation on the grounds that business required both skilled manpower and social stability in order to survive. In light of the ghetto riots that were then sweeping so many

American cities, "it was only common sense to try to solve social problems that could threaten their future."[1]

But the benefits generated by these urban programs went to the business community or to society as a whole rather than to the firms that had committed resources to them. These programs reflected, in the words of the Committee for Economic Development, a "broad recognition that corporate self-interest is inexorably involved in the well-being of the society of which business is an integral part."[2] For all his rhetoric about the interests of "business," Rockefeller did not believe that Chase's extensive urban initiatives would improve its earnings compared to those of other NYC banks. Significantly, only one-eighth of the 201 executives surveyed around 1970 viewed their urban affairs programs as a potential source of profits.[3] Indeed, it is precisely these kinds of enlightened expenditures that prompted Milton Friedman to write the now classic 1970 *New York Times* article in which he argued that the only responsibility of managers was to increase shareholder value.[4] Friedman had no quarrel with corporate social policies or programs that benefited shareholders—a category in which he included contributions to the community where the firm's employees resided. What he objected to were expenditures that benefited "society." And in the late 1960s there was no shortage of business initiatives that appeared to violate his criteria.

The New World of CSR: Doing Good to Do Well

Were Friedman now to revisit this subject, he would find much less to concern him. Virtually all contemporary writing on CSR emphasizes its links to corporate profitability. The typical business book on CSR consists either of examples of companies that have behaved more responsibly and thus have also been financially successful, or advises managers how to make their firms both responsible and profitable. Many of their titles and dust jackets tout the responsibility-profitability connection. Thus *Cause for Success* describes "10 companies that have put profit second and come in first." The experience of these firms, its dust jacket says, illustrates "how solving the world's problems improves corporate health, growth, and competitive edge." The subtitle of *The Sustainability Advantage* is "several business case benefits of a triple bottom line," and *Walking the Talk* is subtitled "the business case for sustainable development." *Corporate Citizenship* presents "successful strategies for responsible companies," and *The Bottom Line of Green Is Black* puts forward "strategies for creating profitable and environmentally sound businesses." For its part, *Profits with Principles* offers "several strategies for delivering value with values."[5]

The message of Chris Laszlo's *The Sustainable Company* is that "an integrated economic, social, and environmental approach leads to more enduring shareholder value. . . . It is a long-term strategy, uniquely relevant to the twenty-first century, in which responsible social change can become a source of innovation and profits rather than added cost." A widely used textbook on CSR, Sandra Waddock's *Leading Corporate Citizens*, analyzes "responsible practices and the associated bottom line benefits." *Companies with a Conscience*, now in its third edition, describes twelve companies whose experiences "prove" that "caring capitalism . . . is not only decent, it is also profitable." *Building Reputational Capital* presents "strategies for integrity and fair play that improve the bottom line." According to *Faith and Fortune: The Quiet Revolution to Reform American Business*, "the business case for doing the right things has become so compelling that companies that do good will also do well."[6]

Writing about corporate environmental policies in the *Harvard Business Review*, Stuart Hart argues that "the more we learn about the challenges of sustainability, the clearer it is that we are poised at the threshold of an historic moment in which many of the world's industries may be transformed." He criticizes managers for looking at their environmental policies in too narrow terms: "Greening has been framed in terms of risk reduction, reengineering or cost cutting. Rarely is greening linked to strategy or technological development, and as a result, most companies fail to recognize opportunities of *potentially staggering proportions*" (italics added). Hart concludes: "The responsibility for ensuring a sustainable world falls largely on the shoulders of the world's enterprises," and that, "in the final analysis, it makes good business sense to pursue strategies for a sustainable world."[7] In another influential *HBR* article, Amory Lovins, L. Hunter Lovins, and Paul Hawken predict that "the companies that first make [the change to environmentally responsible practices] will have a competitive edge." The authors add, "Those that don't make that effort won't be a problem because ultimately they won't be around."[8]

The business case for CSR is also widely accepted by many corporate executives. According to a 2002 survey by PricewaterhouseCoopers, "70 percent of global chief executives believe that CSR is vital to their companies' profitability."[9] Another survey reports that 91 percent of CEOs believe CSR management creates shareholder value.[10] As one corporate report put it in 2004, "If we aren't good corporate citizens as reflected in a Triple Bottom Line that takes into account social and environmental responsibilities along with financial ones—eventually our stock price, our profits and our entire business could suffer."[11] According to a KPMG study of 350 firms, "More big multinational firms are seeing the benefits of improving their environmental performance. . . . Firms are saving money and boosting share performance by taking a close look at how their operations impact the environment. . . . Companies see that they can make money as well."[12]

Trends in corporate philanthropy illustrate the extent to which "doing well" and "doing good" have become more closely linked. Michael Porter has urged companies to connect their philanthropic expenditures "to areas that improve their long-term competitive potential."[13] In fact, U.S. corporations are increasingly "adopting strategic philanthropy" by linking their philanthropy to their business missions.[14] A Council on Foundations study based on interviews with 225 corporate chief executives and 100 "next-generation" CEOs reports that, "seventy-one percent felt that a company must determine the benefits to the business of each cause it supports."[15]

The popularity of cause-related marketing is another illustration of the growing links between corporate social and financial objectives. Such marketing typically features promotions in which a portion of the purchase price of a product or service is donated to a social cause: it essentially links marketing and corporate philanthropy. Besides the obvious public relations benefits, one of the most important measures of its success is increased sales. One of the first cause-related marketing efforts was initiated by American Express in 1983 in connection with the restoration of the Statue of Liberty. The firm promised that over a three-month period it would contribute to this civic enterprise a portion of the amount consumers charged to their American Express cards. The results of the campaign made marketing history. AmEx card use increased 28 percent, new card applications rose 17 percent, and $1.7 million dollars was raised for the Statue of Liberty and Ellis Island.[16] Cause-related marketing has since grown significantly, from $125 million in 1990 to an estimated $828 million in 2002. In 2004 this figure increased to $991 million.[17]

The change in the rationale for and focus of socially responsible investing (SRI) also reflects the increased links between profits and corporate responsibility. When the concept of socially responsible investing first emerged, its purpose was to enable individuals or organizations opposed to particular kinds of businesses or business activities on moral or political grounds to avoid purchasing shares in these companies. For example, some religious institutions and organizations established policies that excluded investing in firms that produced or sold liquor, tobacco, and in some cases military weapons.

Social investment first became politicized during the late 1960s, but its purposes initially remained the same: to enable investors to reconcile their portfolios with their consciences. In 1971 the Pax World Fund was formed as an investment vehicle to register public and investor opposition to the war in Vietnam by avoiding shares in defense firms. Subsequently, activists seeking to end racial segregation in the Republic of South Africa as well as Portuguese control of Angola and Mozambique waged a determined and in many cases successful effort to pressure universities, public sector pension funds, churches, and foundations to divest themselves of their shares of companies with investments in southern Africa. The Calvert Social Investment Fund, established in 1982, excluded shares in companies with investments in South Africa and defense firms, as well as companies that "made money out of environmental degradation. . . . that failed to respect human rights (and that) trampled on the rights of indigenous peoples around the world."[18]

But these initial efforts to politicize share selection did not assume that a more "responsible" portfolio would perform better or even as well as a less responsibly managed one. The students who demanded that their universities sell their holdings in firms with investments in South Africa or firms with defense contracts did not believe that this investment strategy would financially benefit their institutions. Rather, they sharply *attacked* their universities for financially benefiting from their "unethical" holdings in firms that made weapons and had investments in South Africa. Nor did those who excluded defense stocks from their portfolios to protest the war in Vietnam believe that this strategy would make their investments perform better.

Advocates of social investment now claim that it makes financial as well as moral sense. According to the director of research for Calvert Asset Management, "We believe that a company that pollutes the environment or mistreats its workers can get away with it for a while. But eventually it's going to come back to haunt them."[19] One purpose of promoting greater transparency in business conduct is precisely to enable investors to take advantage of the positive relationship between corporate social performance and financial success. Judy Henderson, a member of the directorate of the Global Reporting Initiative, states that a transparent reporting framework provides a competitive advantage "because discerning investors now recognize that a company managed according to interests broader than those of only shareholders is more likely to profit over the long term." She adds, "Corporations with a stakeholder focus have been shown to enjoy greater sales and value growth than companies with narrow shareholder focus."[20] In that same vein, the title of a report by the Global Compact on "connecting financial markets to a changing world" confidently asserts that companies that care will come out on top: *Who Cares Wins*.[21]

The strategy of many social investment funds has changed to reflect this more businesslike approach to SRI. While most ethical funds continue to exclude investing in some firms on the basis of their core business, virtually all also seek to identify and then invest in the firms with the best CSR practices. The increased use of positive screening has an economic as well as a political purpose: positive screening reflects the belief that more responsible firms are also likely to have superior financial performance.[22]

A belief in the business benefits of CSR is particularly influential in Europe. Influenced by the work of Michael Porter, who argues that more stringent environmental standards can improve the competitiveness of a nation's businesses, the European Union has repeatedly stressed the business benefits of CSR.[23] The business case for CSR informs the European Union's influential White Paper on Corporate Social Responsibility. It also is a central motif in conferences sponsored by the EU and its affiliates, where presentations emphasize the benefits of CSR to both investors and companies.[24] Advocates of social and environmental disclosure requirements for companies in Europe believe that they will help the capital markets identify more responsible firms and help predict which firms are likely to be more competitive.

Academic studies have also taken an interest in the relationship between ethics and profits. The first such study was published in 1972; there are currently more than 120 and new ones keep appearing.[25] The rationale for many of these studies is clear: to legitimate a broader conception of the firm's role and responsibilities by integrating it with a narrower financial conception. As Margolis and Walsh insightfully observe:

> Empirical evidence of a positive causal relationship moving from social performance to financial performance also promises, for some, a solution to endless debate about the social role and responsibilities of the firm. . . . Those who construe a narrow economic role for

the firm would embrace a financial rationality for socially responsible practices, and those with a broader conception of the firm's responsibilities would not need to appeal to an alternative construal of the firm's purpose to justify expansive responsibilities.[26]

Such a "solution" clearly appeals to those who study and teach business and society and business ethics at business schools: it places what they teach and study much closer to the mainstream of business education and practice.

The influence of the business case for CSR also has affected the strategies of some NGOs. While many NGOs remain indifferent or hostile to the financial objectives of business, some have developed more cooperative relationships with firms, often helping companies to reconcile their business missions with other objectives, notably environmental quality.[27] They frequently urge firms to behave more responsibly on the grounds that doing so is also good business. The antiwar activists who, during the 1960s, pressured Dow Chemical to stop producing napalm, framed their argument exclusively in moral terms: they neither knew nor cared whether producing napalm would affect Dow's earnings. In contrast, the contemporary environmental activists who are working with Dow to reduce its carbon emissions argue that doing so will make Dow more profitable by lowering its costs. Many socially oriented investors articulate their interest in sustainable environmental practices or human rights issues in similar terms: they ask corporations to act more responsibly on the grounds that doing so is in the best interests of their shareholders, in part by reducing business risk.

The New Business Environment

Never before has the claim that corporate virtue can and should be profitable enjoyed so much currency or influence. Two factors help account for this development: One has to do with a change in the structure of the business system, another with changes in attitudes toward business. Both are particularly influential in the United States, but their influence is apparent in Europe as well.

The Changing Nature of the Firm

The view that corporate responsibility reflected the enlightened self-interest of business or its obligations to society rather than its contribution to profits was associated with a distinctive structure of industrial organization. Such a firm was typically large and professionally managed, and its shares were widely held. It enjoyed a reasonably secure or very secure market position—often an oligopolistic one—and faced little if any foreign competition, at least in its domestic market. Importantly, neither the compensation nor the tenure of its managers was directly linked to its earnings or share price.

The emergence of the modern doctrine of corporate responsibility in the United States is linked to the managerial revolution that occurred around the turn of the century. George Perkins of U.S. Steel, the professional manager of the world's first billion-dollar corporation, wrote in 1908:

> The larger the corporation becomes, the greater become its responsibilities to the entire community. The corporations of the future must be those that are semi-public servants, serving the public, with ownership widespread among the public, and with labor so fairly treated that it will look upon the corporation as its friend.[28]

In the view of many observers, it was the separation of ownership and control—first noted at the turn of the twentieth century and subsequently documented by Berle and Means in 1932—that made it both possible and necessary for business leaders to behave more responsibly. As Walter Lippmann put it in his 1914 book *Drift and Mastery*, "The cultural basis of property is radically altered. . . . The men connected with these essential properties cannot escape the fact that they are expected to act increasingly like public officials. . . . Big businessmen who are at all intelligent recognize this. They are talking more and more about their 'responsibilities,' their 'stewardship.'"[29]

This change in the pattern of corporate ownership meant that professional managers and owners had different priorities. Unlike owners, managers were in a position "to balance the claims of the firm's "stockholders, consumers and the public in general."[30] Freed from the pressure to earn as much money as possible for their shareholders, managers could use corporate resources to pursue a variety of goals—essentially making companies into "multipurpose social institutions."[31]

This firm, popularly depicted in Galbraith's *New Industrial State*, could "afford" to engage or support programs or policies that were unrelated or only tangentially linked to its business objectives since its market position was relatively stable, and equally important, its shareholders were relatively passive. Its managers might not always, or even often, have acted like "public officials," judiciously and responsibly balancing the claims of the firm's many stakeholders, only one of whom was its shareholders, but in principle they were in a position to do so. And in fact, many adopted highly paternalistic labor policies, provided job security for their white-collar employees and generous benefits for their blue-collar employees, and made substantial philanthropic contributions.

For better or worse, the world in which these corporations existed has disappeared in the United States and increasingly in Europe as well. Thanks to increased domestic and international competition, threats of hostile takeovers, the concentration of ownership in the hands of institutional investors, and changes in the basis of executive compensation, the creation of shareholder value has become a central objective of managers. Their personal wealth and continued employment as well as the survival of their firms now depend on their ability to shape and meet the expectations of financial markets. Accordingly, "the freedom of top executives to pursue corporate goals unrelated to the bottom line has been circumscribed. . . . Managerial capitalism tolerated a host of company objectives besides shareholder value. Investor capitalism does not."[32] In a sense, managers now have little choice but to follow Friedman's dictum: they *must* strive to maximize shareholder value.

Ironically, one might have thought that these changes in both management incentives and the competitive environment would have led to the conclusion that it has become much *more* difficult for firms to act responsibly. Instead it has led to a shift in the rationale for corporate responsibility. Now the main justification for corporate responsibility *is* its contribution to the bottom line. While criticizing Friedman's article remains de rigueur in virtually every book and article on corporate responsibility, many contemporary advocates of CSR have implicitly accepted Friedman's position that the primary responsibility of companies is to create wealth for their shareholders. But they have added a twist: in order for companies to do so, they must now act virtuously.

The New Embrace of Money and Morals

The contemporary importance of the business case for CSR is linked to a second development: the popular embrace of business and the values of moneymaking. The movement for corporate responsibility of the 1960s and 1970s took place during a period of considerable hostility to business. Indeed, companies began to talk more about their social responsibilities during the late 1960s and early 1970s in part as a response to the disenchantment expressed by many college students and graduates with business values. *Fortune* noted in 1966 that "the prejudice against business is undeniable, and permeates the country's highest-ranking colleges."[33] A student at the Harvard Business School admitted, "If people are really interested in tackling social problems, they will have nothing to do with business."[34] A 1967 survey of college students reported that 61 percent found "their fellow students to be indifferent or hostile toward working in industry."[35] During the second half of the 1960s, enrollment in business schools increased only one-third as fast as total college enrollment.[36]

The current revival of interest in corporate responsibility began in a somewhat different cultural and social context. While surveys continue to report widespread hostility to and suspicion of business, the 1990s were also a decade when many of America's and Europe's "best and brightest" became attracted to business careers. Successful entrepreneurs became admired and respected, and the growth of Silicon Valley became a focus of national pride in the United States and envy in other countries. "Making money" became more respectable, popular interest in business grew, and not coincidentally, business school enrollment soared in both the United States and Europe.

Still, some of the people who enrolled in business schools or began to work for or start companies also cared about social and environmental concerns. And many were highly critical of corporate social and environmental practices. How could their interest in business—and making money—and their social values be reconciled? The business case for corporate responsibility provided an answer. Like investors in socially responsible mutual funds, they did not have to abandon their values to become prosperous. On the contrary: they could simultaneously become financially secure *and* make the world a better place. Indeed, they could now become prosperous *by* making the world a better place.

One strain of the contemporary movement for corporate responsibility links the "counterculture" values of the 1960s with those of the "decade of greed," as the 1980s came to be known. This vision appeals not only to those who came of age during the 1990s, but also to those a decade or two older who were influenced by the values revolution of the 1960s and 1970s, in some cases belatedly. Many of the latter individuals now hold positions of leadership in corporations. They too want to believe that there is a business case for corporate responsibility since it enables them to link their personal values with their responsibilities as managers. And it is the baby-boomer generation, many of whose members have become relatively affluent but still hold liberal social values, who are the major individual investors in socially responsible mutual funds.[37] These investors care about social values, but they also want to protect the value of their savings.

The emergence of "companies with a conscience" represents a particularly vivid expression of the contemporary reconciliation of social values and the business system. These are companies whose vision of social responsibility was integral to their business strategies from the outset. They were formed by individuals with strong personal social commitments who regarded their businesses both as vehicles to make money and as a means to improve society. Among those that became widely known and celebrated are the Body Shop, Seventh Generation, Domini, Esprit, Celestial Seasonings, Stonyfield Farm, Tom's of Maine, Ben and Jerry's, and Patagonia. As Ben Cohen, one of the founders of Ben and Jerry's, put it: "We are in the process of creating . . . a business climate in which the right way to go about solving social problems is by founding and maintaining and sustaining a socially responsible business." Anita Roddick, the founder of the Body Shop, acknowledged, "I think a lot of us would have slit our wrists if we ever thought we'd be part of corporate America or England." Likewise, many of the individuals who established socially responsible funds and research services, such as Peter Kinder and Amy Domini, had political as well as financial motivations: they wanted to use SRI to bring about social change by improving business practices, as well as create successful businesses.[38]

In 2000 Goldman Sachs began funding a national—subsequently international—business competition in which business students and recent MBAs develop business plans that are judged on how well they meet *both* social and financial criteria. The most promising plans are often funded. Many business schools now offer courses in social entrepreneurship—in effect teaching MBA students how to form and secure funding for future Ben and Jerry's. One of the largest American MBA student organizations is Net Impact. Its well-attended annual conventions feature inspirational speeches by business leaders—entrepreneurs and professional managers—who personify both the financial benefits of corporate responsibility and the social contributions of successful firms. In Britain, First Tuesday, which formerly functioned as a "dating agency" for dot.com entrepreneurs and venture capitalists, now hosts meetings that bring together entrepreneurs with sustainable ideas and investors with environmental concerns, with the goal of building a "global sustainability business network."[39]

In short, the increasing influence of the business case for CSR reflects changes in the nature of business competition and changes in beliefs about the potential social role of business. It is both widely believed and influential. But what is the evidence that such a business case exists?

Putting the Business Case to the Test

An extensive body of academic research examines the relationship between corporate responsibility and profitability.[40] A detailed examination of this large and still growing literature is beyond the scope of this book. But its central conclusion can be easily summarized: at best, it is inconclusive.

What the Studies Show

While many studies report a positive relationship between ethics and profits, some find a negative relationship, and still others find the relationship to be either neutral or mixed. These results hold both for those studies that use financial performance to explain social performance and for those in which the causal relationship is reversed. Equivocal results also characterize those studies that assess a wide variety of measures of corporate social responsibility as well as those that focus on specific areas such as environmental performance, corporate philanthropy, and community relations.

In the area of environmental performance, one study found a moderate positive relationship between levels of emissions reduction between 1988 and 1989 and the financial performance for firms involved in manufacturing, mining, and production, though the direction of causality was not clear.[41] Another study reports a strong positive relationship between the financial performance of large manufacturing and mining firms and their adherence to relatively stringent uniform global environmental standards, though such firms may perform better just because they are better managed.[42] A third study reports a positive relationship between financial performance and various dimensions of environmental performance based on ratings by the Franklin Research and Development Corporation. This relationship was especially strong for firms in high-growth industries.[43] But reviews of a broader range of research suggest that environmentally responsible behavior does not raise firm performance:

Researchers have yet to demonstrate that environmental expenditures improve firm profitability in a structural way, and that it is not a matter of reverse causality, where profitable firms can afford to invest in environmental performance. A more likely explanation of the research to date [which demonstrates a positive relationship between environmental and financial performance] is that various omitted variables affecting both environmental and financial performance are responsible for the apparent statistical relationship.[44]

Research that relates measures of corporate environmental performance to measures of financial performance suffers from several shortcomings. Few studies attempt to explain how better environmental strategies have changed financial analysts' views of a firm's future earnings. Among those studies that compare the portfolios of environmental leaders and laggards, virtually none correct for differences in risk other than environmental performance. These studies also do not address the issue of causation. It is as likely that more profitable firms are able to devote more resources to environmental protection as it is that such firms are more profitable *because* they have adopted better environmental practices.[45] It is also possible that good environmental performance is a proxy for management quality.

It is hard to draw broad conclusions about the relationship between CSR and profits because the studies often measure different things. In the ninety-five studies summarized by Margolis and Walsh, financial performance is measured in seventy different ways: these studies employ forty-nine different accounting measures, twelve different market measures, five measures that mix accounting and market indicators, and four other measures of outcome performance.[46] Accounting measures are usually used as indications of prior financial performance for studies that seek to explain the impact of CSR on financial performance, while market measures are usually employed to assess future performance when financial performance is used to explain CSR.[47]

Measurements of corporate social performance also vary widely.[48] In ninety-five studies, twenty-seven different data sources were used. These range from multidimensional screening criteria, surveys, conduct in South Africa (which has since become irrelevant), organizational programs and practices, disclosure, money spent, environmental performance, and reputation. The most frequently used are environmental practices, followed by omnibus measures such as the *Fortune* reputation rankings and the indexes of Kinder Lyderberg Domini (KLD) Research & Analytics.

Not only does the diversity of these measures make drawing conclusions from this literature difficult, but there is considerable debate about the validity of some of them. For example, one of the most commonly employed measures of CSR is based on *Fortune's* annual reputational survey of America's most admired corporations. One of the attributes rated by *Fortune* is a "company's responsibility to the community and the environment." However its raw scores appear to be heavily influenced by a company's previous financial performance, which means that any relationship between it and corporate profitability is tautological. In addition, the surveys on which the rankings are based poll only industry executives and market analysts.[49]

The most exhaustive and widely used measure of CSR is KLD's extensive database of 400 mainly U.S. companies. KLD evaluates five different measures of corporate performance: community relations, diversity, employee relations, natural environment, and product safety and quality. The rankings rely on publicly available data such as information supplied to tax and regulatory agencies, newspapers, and magazines, and on company reports, supplemented by surveys of the 400 firms. Companies also have the opportunity to review KLD's assessments before they are released. However, KLD does not reveal its basis for weighing each screening category in determining a firm's overall CSR ranking. Many of its rankings are subjective; few are based on quantitative measures. In many instances the data on which ratings are based are incomplete, particularly with respect to the non-U.S. operations of the companies in its database.

Studies that employ a narrower range of criteria capture only some of the policies usually associated with corporate responsibility, while those that employ a broader range are unable to identify which policies might be affecting financial performance. And it is not uncommon for firms to exhibit more virtuous performance in some areas than in others. Even within a relatively narrow category such as environmental performance, measures can be inconsistent with one another. Thus how should a firm's environmental responsibilities be assessed if it has relatively low emissions, but a poor record of compliance and a weak environmental management system?[50] Virtually every measure employed has been subject to substantial criticism: no consensus has emerged as to how either environmental responsibility or corporate responsibility more generally can or should be measured.

Any effort to explain a firm's financial performance must also control for other antecedent factors. But not all studies adequately do so. For example, McWilliams and Siegel, in reexamining the conclusions of a study that strongly linked corporate social and financial performance, found that "when R&D intensity is included in the equation, CSP (corporate social performance) is shown to have a neutral effect on profitability," since firms that actively engage in CSR also tend to make strategic investments in R&D.[51] Some studies employ no control variables, which means that any relationship they find may be spurious. In all, nearly fifty different control variables have been used by different scholars. Industry, size, and risk are employed most frequently, but most control variables have been used only once. This also increases the difficulty of identifying the relative contribution of social performance to financial performance.[52]

Equally important, correlations drawn from surveys and other cross-sectional data cannot establish the direction of causality. It is just as likely that more successful firms are more responsible than others as it is that more responsible firms are more successful than others. For example, if firms identified as "good places to work" are more profitable, this may be because they can afford to treat their employees well, not because their labor policies increase shareholder value. Moreover, correlations between social and financial performance may reflect the fact that well-managed firms are also better at managing CSR, making it difficult to discern whether or to what extent they are more profitable *because* they are more responsible.

The dozen literature reviews published between 1979 and 1999 identify nearly fifty shortcomings of the broader body of research. They agree that the connection between CSR and financial performance has not been established and that neither academics nor practitioners should rely on the research results because they are noncomparable.[53] Summarizing both their own analysis and these studies, Margolis and Walsh concur:

> The clear signal that emerges from thirty years of academic research—indicating that a positive relationship exists between social performance and financial performance—must be treated with caution. Serious methodological concerns have been raised about many of the studies and about efforts to aggregate results. . . . Questions arise about the connection between the underlying CSP [corporate social performance] construct and efforts to measure it; the validity of the measures used to assess social performance; the diversity of measures used to assess financial performance; and the direc-

tion and mechanisms of causation; given the heavy reliance on correlation analyses and contemporaneous financial and social performance data.[54]

It is thus difficult to know what to make of the claim that "those hoping for a positive or neutral impact of social performance on financial performance can feel some satisfaction, because the vast majority of studies support the idea that, at the very least, good social performance does not lead to poor financial performance."[55] If this is true, it might reflect the fact that corporate responsibility is not sufficiently costly to affect earnings. Or it might be attributable to the fact that many corporate CSR expenditures are discretionary and therefore more likely to be made by more profitable firms. But although CSR may not make firms any less profitable, it is possible that some more responsible firms might be even more profitable if they were less responsible.

Putting CSR in Its Place

Studies of the links between social responsibility and profitability continue to be published and are becoming increasingly sophisticated. It is possible that future research will confirm the validity of the several studies that have posited positive causal relationships between the two. However, the effort to demonstrate through statistical analyses that corporate responsibility pays may be not only fruitless, but also pointless and unnecessary, because such studies purport to hold corporate responsibility to a standard to which no other business activity is subject. For example, it is highly unlikely that there is a positive correlation between advertising expenditures and corporate profitability; some profitable firms spend little on advertising, and many advertising expenditures produce disappointing results. Yet no one would dispute that there is a business case for advertising.

But just as firms that spend more on marketing are not necessarily more profitable than those that spend less, there is no reason to expect more responsible firms to outperform less responsible ones. In other words, the risks associated with CSR are no different than those associated with any other business strategy; sometimes investments in CSR make business sense and sometimes they do not. Why should we expect investments in CSR to consistently create shareholder value when virtually no other business investments or strategies do so?

It is not necessary to find a positive statistical relationship between CSR and profits to claim that some firms may benefit financially from being more responsible or suffer from being irresponsible. This is certainly true. Such a claim, however, does not satisfy CSR advocates. The reason they have placed so much importance on "proving" that CSR pays is because they want to demonstrate, first, that behaving more responsibly is in the self-interest of *all* firms, and second, that CSR *always* makes business sense. Were they able to satisfactorily do either or both, then presumably all firms would begin to behave more responsibly so that they too could become more profitable.[56]

But even if it were possible to convincingly demonstrate a positive causal link between CSR and business financial performance, it is unclear what this would prove. If some firms are actually more profitable *because* they are more responsible, it does not necessarily follow that their less responsible competitors would be more profitable if they were more responsible. It is equally possible that the market niche for relatively responsible firms is limited and that they would be better off continuing to pursue a less responsible strategy. And a link between responsibility and profitability does not necessarily mean that firms would be even more profitable if they were more responsible, since there may be declining returns for behaving more responsibly. In fact, if all firms behaved responsibly—which presumably is the goal of the CSR movement—then at least some of the advantages a firm receives from being *more* responsible than its competitors would disappear, and thus, ironically, future studies of the links between CSR and profits would find no statistically significant relationship.

Moreover, if CSR were actually a significant source of competitive advantage, then it might logically be in the interest of more responsible firms to discourage their competitors from following their example. After all, a firm that has developed a profitable new product does not want its competitors to imitate it, or even learn from its example. But in the case of CSR the opposite is true: rather than seek to protect their "first mover" advantages, these firms frequently encourage their less responsible competitors to emulate their behavior.[57] Hence the popularity of industry codes of conduct in business sectors that are under public pressure to improve their social performance. This suggests that more virtuous firms are frequently not able to capture the financial benefits of their more responsible behavior.

Instead of being defined as a necessary condition for business success, corporate responsibility is better understood as one dimension of corporate strategy. Corporations pursue a wide variety of strategies: some are highly diversified, others are specialized; some invest heavily in research and development, others focus on marketing; some pay relatively high wages, others pay close to the minimum wage; some are global, others focus on national or local markets. CSR is no different: firms have chosen and will continue to choose different levels of corporate responsibility, depending upon the risks and opportunities they face. There is no reason to expect a convergence of CSR strategies, any more than companies can be expected to converge on any other strategy. That said, it is of course possible that the baseline or benchmark for corporate behavior could steadily improve. But correlations of responsibility and profitability will not tell us whether this is occurring.

Taking a Second Look at CSR: Socially Responsible Investment

The validity of the business case for virtue can also be explored through the financial performance of socially responsible mutual funds. The results of this analysis reveal that socially responsible funds and indexes perform no better or worse than those of any other kind of fund or stock index. The three most widely used ethical fund indexes are the Domini 400 Social Index, which is based on the research of KLD discussed above; the Dow Jones Sustainability World Index (DJSI World); and the FTSE4Good Index. In addition to using positive screens, the Domini uses negative screens based on military contracting, the manufacture of alcohol or tobacco products, revenues from gaming products or services, and the ownership of nuclear power plants. DJSI World, which was established in 1999 by the Sustainability Asset Management Group, a Swiss company, in cooperation with Dow Jones Indexes, tracks the performance of the top 10 percent of leading sustainability firms in each industry group. The FTSE4Good Index includes firms that meet its criteria on social, environmental, and human rights issues and excludes tobacco, arms manufacturers, and firms that produce nuclear power or uranium.

The Performance of Socially Responsible Funds

Between May 1, 1990, and June 30, 2004, KLD's Domini 400 Social Index, which is used as the basis for selecting the Domini Social Equity Fund (the fourth largest social fund with $1.2 billion under management), returned $5.40 for each dollar invested, while the S&P 500 returned

$4.60. But this difference is largely attributable to the industries in which the fund invested; there was no evidence of a "social" factor.[58] For its part, the FTSE4Good has closely tracked the performance of the FTSE All Share Index since 2000.

The DJSI World has performed more poorly than the benchmark Dow Jones Global Index since its inception in 1999, but much of this difference can be traced to the relative size of the two indexes. The DJSI World consists of only 250 companies, while the DJ Global comprises 5,029, making the former much less diversified and therefore more susceptible to changes in the market valuation of any one firm. It is also overweighted in large-capitalization stocks and growth companies, and it adds and deletes companies more frequently than do most indexes: in 2002 it replaced more than seventy companies, nearly one-quarter of its portfolio. Although the performance of the DJSI World index is often taken as evidence for or against the financial case for SRI, the lack of comparability between it and the DJ Global Index renders any such assessment problematic. Alois Flatz, its former research director, cautions: "It is premature to draw definitive conclusions regarding the business case for sustainability. . . . A much longer time frame is needed to attribute index or fund performance to particular sustainability criteria or strategies.[59]

As in the case of the Domini Social 400 and DJSI World, much of the relative performance of SRI mutual funds and indexes is affected by the performance of the industries in which their investments are concentrated.[60] For this reason, in some years they have outperformed their mainstream counterparts and in other years have lagged behind them. For example, during the latter part of the 1990s, many social funds showed relatively strong returns due to their heavy exposure in financials, "clean" technology, health care, media, and communications. But their performance was then negatively affected when the value of many of these firms declined.

In addition, social investors are not free from the fads that affect all other investors.[61] In Britain during the late 1980s there was considerable excitement about the financial prospects of "green" companies, and a "green index" of thirty companies involved in environmental services increased in value from 100 to 147 in just five months. This green euphoria, however, could not be sustained, and over the next five years the index steadily underperformed the FTSE All Share Index. A similar development occurred in the United States, where the fifty worst mutual funds listed by the *Wall Street Journal* in 1993 contained a number of environmental funds, most of them involved in environmental remediation.

More recently, a study by researchers at Erasmus University found that firms selected by the New York investment firm Innovest on the basis of their "eco-efficiency" commanded an impressive 6 percent premium over their "worst-in-class" counterparts between 1995 and 2002; and State Street Global Advisors reported in 2004 that Innovest's eco-efficient companies had outperformed the S&P as a whole by roughly 7 percent compounded annually. State Street plans to launch a fund based on the Innovest strategy.[62] It remains to be seen how successful this investment strategy will prove.

The performance of specific ethical funds has varied as widely as that of any other kind of fund. For example, the well-managed Parnassus Fund outperformed the S&P 500 from 1998 through 2002; the Calvert Fund trailed the S&P by a substantial margin every year between 1993 and 1998, though its performance improved after it hired a new manager. [63] During the five years before July 31, 2004, the annual return of the ten largest socially responsible mutual funds reported in the Social Investment Forum ranged from 24.68 percent (Bridgeway Ultra Small Company Tax Advantage), 7.85 percent (Ariel Appreciation), and 7.58 (Parnassus Equity Income), on one hand, to 2.44 percent (Pax World Balanced), .05 percent (Calvert Social Investment Balanced A), and −7.30 percent (Dreyfus Premier Third Century), on the other.

While there continues to be debate over whether the use of negative screens by virtually all SRI funds increases risk or lowers returns (or both), or alternatively, whether socially screened investments are less volatile and result in higher returns, the consensus of the more than 100 studies of social investment funds and their strategies is that the risk-adjusted returns of a carefully constructed socially screened portfolio is zero.[64] In other words, share returns are neither harmed nor helped by including social criteria in stock selection. This explains why SRI investment vehicles have recently grown in popularity in both the United States and Europe: there appears to be little cost associated with making such investments. But it also undermines the frequent claim that more responsible firms, at least as assessed by SRI fund managers and researchers, perform better. It also explains why the funds that manage 98 percent of investments in mutual funds in the United States continue to pursue other investment strategies, none of which is necessarily any better or worse.

Ironically, if more socially responsible firms did systematically perform better, we would expect all fund managers to heavily weight their portfolios with those firms' securities. This would both erase all differences in financial performance between socially responsible and "normal" funds and raise the price of the shares of more responsible firms so as to reduce the return from future purchases of them. Still, if the financial markets undervalue corporate social performance, then more responsible investors might in principle be able to earn higher returns when the financial consequences of responsible or irresponsible behavior eventually affected earnings. But there is no persuasive evidence that the market does so.

Some advocates of SRI continue to claim that socially informed investment funds will perform better because their managers are more aware of the significance of corporate social and environmental policies on long-term financial performance.[65] As one environmental foundation writes: "We believe that we are once again on the cusp of redefining the responsibilities of a prudent fiduciary—this time to recognize that improving environmental performance is a primary pathway to increasing shareholder value."[66] Its claim is that, as an environmentally conscious investor, it possesses insights into the long-term financial benefits of corporate environmental efforts, which more conventional investors have overlooked.

That such claims have not yet been validated does not mean that they never will be. But there is reason to be skeptical. For this claim cannot rest on an investor's ability to accurately measure current corporate environmental practices. It must be based on an ability to predict future corporate environmental practices, or more precisely, the relationships between current and future corporate environmental practices and between those practices and current and future environmental pressures and opportunities. But how can anyone know which environmental issues will become politically salient or whether a firm that has successfully addressed environmental issues in the past will also manage them well in the future? Such uncertainties about future financial performance are no different from those that confront any investment strategy.

In this context it is worth recalling that the social investment community was no more able than any other investors to identify the failures of corporate governance that created such massive shareholder losses at the beginning of the twenty-first century. Enron, WorldCom, Adelphia, and Healthcare were all widely held by SRI funds. Enron was widely respected for its CSR: it was ranked one of the 100 best companies to work for; received several environmental awards; issued a triple-bottom-line report; established a social responsibility task force; developed codes of conduct covering security, corruption, and human rights; supported progressive climate change policies; and was known for its generous philanthropic contributions. These practices, which led a number of SRI funds to include Enron in their portfolios, did not make Enron a sound investment. And Shell, whose environmental and human rights initiatives led it to be included in many SRI portfolios, also did not turn out to be a prudent investment when in 2004 it was revealed to have falsified the amount of its oil reserves.

The Dubious Claims for Socially Responsible Investing

Implicit in the very existence of SRI is the claim that it is possible to identify which firms are more or less responsible. Not only is this claim questionable, but the selection criteria employed by SRI fund managers and researchers can be criticized on several grounds.

First, questions have been raised about both the information that fund managers rely on to make investment decisions and the consistency of the criteria they employ. According to a study of eight of the most prominent funds, "Sources of social information used varied widely from fund to fund with data provided by firms themselves being the most frequently used."[67] While all investors depend heavily on corporate self-reporting, the shortcomings of corporate financial reporting pale when compared with those of corporate voluntary disclosures of nonfinancial performance, in part because, with one rare exception (discussed in chapter 4), there have been no legal penalties for providing incomplete or misleading information. Another common source of data, articles in the business and popular press, may reflect the effectiveness of a firm's public relations, or that of its critics, rather than its actual behavior. Moreover, many SRI fund managers use screening methodologies that are proprietary and thus they cannot reveal why a particular firm is excluded or included.

A second criticism focuses on the criteria employed by SRI funds to determine corporate "irresponsibility."[68] Tobacco and alcohol are the two negative screens American funds use most often. The reasons for the former are relatively straightforward, but the latter is more problematic: why should a firm automatically be considered irresponsible because it produces or distributes wine, a product that shareholders in ethical mutual funds are as likely to enjoy as any other group of investors? More substantively, many funds restrict or prohibit investments in firms that produce military equipment or nuclear power. But should such firms be considered "irresponsible" in light of the fact that the former may contribute to legitimate national security needs and the latter may contribute to reducing carbon emissions? Despite all their claims to be on the cutting edge of changing public expectations of business, no fund has relaxed its exclusion of military contractors since September 11.

SRI has also been criticized for being *too* inclusive. According to a survey of more than 600 SRI funds, by Paul Hawken, more than 90 percent of Fortune 500 companies are included in at least one SRI portfolio. Hawken argues that the selection criteria employed by many social funds allows virtually any publicly held firm to be considered responsible. The most widely held firm by socially responsible investment funds is Microsoft, a firm that Hawken criticizes for "its ruthless, take-no-prisoners management tactics," as well as for antitrust violations in both the United States and Europe. (According to Calvert, "aside from its [Microsoft's] legal troubles, the company has a number of exemplary practices with respect to workplace issues, international operations and human rights.")[69] Hawken is also critical of the social and ethical practices of other firms that feature prominently in SRI portfolios, including Wal-Mart (held by thirty-three SRI funds), Halliburton (held by twenty-three funds), and ExxonMobil (held by forty funds).

Finally, the emphasis many funds place on competitive rates of return renders problematic a critical raison d'être of social investment, namely that social responsibility pays. These funds typically apply their social attributes or yardsticks only *after* firms have been screened by normal financial criteria. The result may be the exclusion of investments in firms whose social performance is outstanding or highly innovative, but whose financial prospects are uncertain or modest. An innovative or pioneering firm that has chosen to sacrifice short-term profits in the pursuit of social goals thus might not be owned by many socially responsible funds. This may be counterproductive from the perspective of promoting more responsible corporate behavior, and it also calls into question the popular claim that being more responsible can and should make a firm a better investment.

These criticisms suggest that even if SRI funds were to consistently outperform nonsocially screened portfolios (which there is little evidence that they do), it is unclear what this would prove about the relationship between corporate responsibility and profitability.

Are Virtuous Firms Built to Last?

CSR advocates assert that while CSR may not affect short-term earnings or share performance, *in the long run* the more responsible firms will perform better. One way of investigating this assertion is to examine the social performance of companies that have performed extremely well financially over an extended period of time.

Consider, for example, the U.S.-based firms included in the 1994 bestseller *Built to Last* on the basis of their having attained "extraordinary long-term performance." According to its authors, James Collins and Jerry Porras, these firms are "more than successful. They are more than enduring. In most cases, they are the best of the best in their industries, and have been that way for decades."[70] The firms that meet their criteria are 3M, American Express, Boeing, Citicorp, Ford, General Electric, Hewlett-Packard, IBM, Johnson & Johnson, Marriott, Merck, Motorola, Nordstrom, Philip Morris, Procter & Gamble, Sony, Wal-Mart, and Walt Disney. To this list of distinguished financial performers we can add the companies featured in the sequel *Good to Great* published in 2001, whose cumulative stock return was 6.9 times that of the market as a whole. These firms are Abbott, Circuit City, Fannie Mae, Gillette, Kimberly-Clark, Kroger, Nucor, Philip Morris, Pitney Bowes, Walgreens, and Wells Fargo.

Some of these twenty-eight firms do enjoy reputations for exhibiting above average levels of CSR on some dimensions, including American Express, 3M, Hewlett-Packard, IBM, Johnson & Johnson, Citicorp, and Merck. And it is possible that their social responsibility has contributed to their above average financial performance during the time frame considered in the two best-sellers, though it is unlikely to have been critical to it. But no one would confuse all or even most of these companies with firms that are also leaders on many dimensions of CSR. (Note that the only company featured in both studies is Philip Morris.) It is true that these firms have been built around values, visions, and goals other than profit maximization, and, according to Collins and Porras, these factors have contributed to their financial success. But only in a few instances do these values have anything to do with social responsibility.

Social responsibility and irresponsibility may well matter, but their impact on the long-term financial performance of companies is typically dwarfed by a host of other factors. Particular firms succeed or fail for many reasons, but exemplary or irresponsible social or environmental performance is rarely among them. And there is no evidence that the relative importance of CSR to financial success is increasing for most or even many companies. For all the claims that being responsible is a necessary condition for long-term business success, what is striking is how few responsible firms have been "built to last." There are certainly firms that have been both relatively profitable and responsible over more than one or two decades, but the list is not long. More important, it does not appear to be growing. It is of course possible that in ten years the number of financially successful "responsible" companies will be much larger. But the historical record to date gives few grounds for such optimism.

During the 1970s, lists of the most socially responsible firms would have included Atlantic Richfield, Control Data, Cummins Engine, Dayton-Hudson, Levi Strauss, and Polaroid.[71] Polaroid filed for bankruptcy in 2001. In 1992, Control Data, faced with losses that at one point totaled more than $1 billion, was divided into two companies; its CSR practices are no longer distinctive. Dayton-Hudson barely survived a hostile takeover in the 1980s, and Levi Strauss's sales have been declining since the mid-1990s, forcing it to abandon its prior commitment to source some of its products from domestic manufacturers. Cummins Engine has survived—and prospered—but competitive pressures have forced it to abandon many of its highly paternalistic employment policies and the community contributions that made it socially distinctive. In 1999, Atlantic Richfield was acquired by British Petroleum as part of a general consolidation of the oil industry.

Merck, a firm widely recognized for its decision in the 1980s to develop and distribute without charge a drug for river blindness and more recently for its work with the Gates Foundation to make AIDS drugs available in Botswana, began experiencing declining profits and an underperforming stock price after 2000, leading some analysts to question the continued validity of George Merck's celebrated 1950 credo: "Medicine is for the people. It is not for the profits. The profits follow."[72] (The firm's financial difficulties predated but were exacerbated by its withdrawal of the painkiller Vioxx from the market in late 2004.)

The retailer Marks & Spencer (M&S) has long enjoyed a reputation as one of Britain's most virtuous companies. It has been a highly benevolent employer and for many years had a policy of selling only British-made goods. In July 2004 Business in the Community, a prominent British NGO, named M&S company of the year for putting responsible business practices at the heart of its strategy and for producing "measurable, outstanding positive impacts on society."[73] The Dow Jones Sustainability World Index rated M&S "the most sustainable retailer in the world" in 2002 and 2003, and a survey of worldwide labor standards carried out by Insight Investments and Accountability gave the firm its top ranking.[74] But in the same month it received its CSR award, M&S attracted a hostile takeover bid made possible by the firm's recent poor earnings and poorly performing share price.[75] Although the investor attempting to take over M&S had promised to continue the firm's progressive policies, and the takeover bid was ultimately unsuccessful, the juxtaposition of these two events prompted a column in the *Financial Times*, which noted:

> The battle for CSR has to be won in an environment more hostile than many of its proponents appreciate. . . . CSR is best seen as the management of risk, as the avoidance of damages to the company's reputation. But it is no substitute for the avoidance of the larger risk: that consumers may go elsewhere because the company's offering is not good enough. As models we need companies whose risk management has made them commercially successful. CSR is only as sustainable as the companies that practice it.[76]

Another journalist concluded that M&S showed that "being a good corporate citizen has nothing to do with being profitable," an appraisal apparently confirmed by a contemporary survey of London financial analysts, which found "that they placed most corporate responsibility issues well down their list of company concerns."[77] Competitive pressures have also forced M&S to abandon its "buy British" policy.

During the late 1990s, Chiquita Brands International (an outgrowth of the United Fruit Company), which produces a quarter of the world's bananas and is the largest agricultural employer in Latin America, implemented a highly innovative program aimed at improving the environmental practices of its growers in Central America; more than 79 percent of its independent suppliers have been certified by the Rainforest Alliance. The funds spent by the company to bring its farms up to the Rainforest Alliance's environmental standards have resulted in considerable cost savings by reducing pesticide use and recycling the wooden pallets used to transport the fruit. Nonetheless the firm was forced to declare bankruptcy in November 2001.[78]

Some of the recent generation of ethical business "icons" have not fared any better. Both the Body Shop International and Ben & Jerry's had strong financial results for several years. Yet both began to experience financial difficulties in the late 1990s. Pressures from investors relegated founder Anita Roddick to an advisory nonexecutive role at the Body Shop, and in 2000, Ben and Jerry's, faced with a highly undervalued share price and declining profits due to a series of management failures, was taken over by Unilever. The carpet manufacturer Interface, whose chief executive, Ray Anderson, was called "the green CEO" and whose environmental practices have been described as "leading the way to the next frontier of industrial ecology," has been unprofitable since 2000.[79] In 2001 it consolidated its services operations, exited the broadloom market in Europe, and cut about 10 percent of its workforce, making further cuts the following two years. Notwithstanding Hewlett-Packard's widely applauded CSR initiatives under CEO Carly Fiorina, the firm's disappointing financial performance forced her resignation in 2004.

The more responsible firms, no less than the less responsible ones, must survive in highly competitive markets. Consumers can choose to purchase pharmaceutical products, household products, ice cream, herbal tea, clothes, jeans, computers, or body care products from many companies. Socially responsible firms, like all other firms, are subject to the vagaries of shifting consumer preferences and poor management. And when such firms find themselves in financial difficulty, many of their distinctive CSR practices can become more difficult to sustain.

The less-than-strong financial performance of many firms with strong CSR reputations hardly suggests that such firms represent the wave of the future. Rather it says that while the business system has a place for socially responsible firms, this place is at least as precarious and unstable as for any other kind of firm. The market for social responsibility is dynamic. Some companies with strong CSR reputations are prospering (for example, Patagonia, Seventh Generation, Starbucks, Stonyfield Farm, Ikea, BP), while others are not (Levi Strauss, Merck, M&S, HP, Interface, Shell); still others perform well financially but have become less socially distinctive (Cummins Engine). At the same time, new relatively responsible firms continue to emerge, some of which will be financially successful and some of which will not.

Proponents of CSR tend to view the dynamics of responsible business in evolutionary terms. Since they assume that only the most responsible firms can or will survive in the long run, they believe that over time there will be more responsible firms and fewer irresponsible ones—a kind of survival of the virtuous. However the dynamics of corporate responsibility are better understood in ecological terms. There *is* a market or ecological niche for the relatively responsible firms. But there is also a market or ecological niche for less virtuous ones. And the size of the former does not appear to be increasing relative to the latter.

Conclusion

The belief that corporate virtue pays is both attractive and influential. It appeals to those who wish to encourage firms to become more responsible as well as to those who want to manage, and work and invest in, virtuous enterprises. It is also an important component of the business model of the SRI industry and informs much popular and academic writing on CSR. And it reflects the business reality that firms are under pressure to satisfy the financial markets by producing strong earnings.

Unfortunately, a review of the evidence, including academic studies of the relationship between profitability and responsibility and the relative performance of SRI, finds little support for the claim that more responsible firms are more profitable. But this does not mean that there is no business case for virtue. It is rather to suggest that any such claim must be more nuanced. CSR does make business sense for some firms in specific circumstances. Exploring those circumstances in more detail is the focus of the next chapter.

CHAPTER 3

What Is the Demand
for Virtue?

What are the foundations of the business case for corporate social responsibility? The best way to answer this question is by analyzing what drives it—namely pressure from consumers, workers, and investors. These are not the only forces driving business virtue, but they are among the most important. In principle, if most individuals' decisions about what and where to buy, and where to work and to invest, were informed by how responsibly firms acted, then the market for virtue would work effectively: all companies would have a strong incentive to change their policies and practices in order to attract and retain customers, employees, and investors.

Unfortunately, while many people profess to care about CSR and claim that it informs their marketplace decisions, relatively few act on these beliefs. A company's degree of social responsibility or irresponsibility has rarely affected its sales, its attractiveness to potential employees, or its access to capital. Nonetheless, many companies have changed their social and environmental practices in response to "civil regulation"—that is, in response to pressures from social activists, socially oriented consumers, shareholders, and employers. Despite the lack of evidence indicating that "bad" behavior reduces profitability or harms other measures of corporate performance, many companies remain concerned about the potential for harm to their reputations and in some cases their brands. Some firms regard a reputation for virtue as an advantage in attracting employees. Most important, social investors, notwithstanding their lack of impact on capital allocation, have become an effective source of pressure on some companies. Thus many companies act as if civil regulation does or could affect their financial performance, even though it is rarely possible to document such a relationship.

Consumers: Purity versus the Pocketbook

To what extent do consumers favor the products of socially responsible firms or shun those produced irresponsibly? Many studies claim that consumers place a high value on corporate social or environmental performance in their purchasing decisions. A 1995 study by Cone Communications reported that "31 percent of respondents viewed a company's sense of social responsibility as a key factor in their purchasing decisions."[1] Nearly 90 percent of the consumers surveyed by the Walker Group stated that "when quality, service and price are equal . . . they're more likely to buy from the company that has the best reputation for social responsibility."[2] Even more important, significant numbers of consumers claim that they are willing to pay a premium to do business with more virtuous companies. More than 75 percent of American consumers report that they would avoid purchasing products made under poor working conditions, and a comparable number report they are willing to pay more for garments not produced in sweatshops.[3] Thirty percent of American consumers claim to have avoided purchasing products made by companies that pollute the environment, and 65 percent state they would pay more for products that protect the environment.[4]

Similar results emerge from European studies. A 1997 survey found that 71 percent of French consumers would choose a "child-labor-free" product even if it were more expensive than the alternatives.[5] In two separate studies, 67 percent of British consumers claimed to have bought environmentally friendly products even though they were more expensive, and 22 percent said that in the previous twelve months they had avoided using the services or products of a company they considered to have a poor environmental record.[6] In 1995 nearly 60 percent of British consumers said they would protest a company's policies by ceasing to buy its products, more than 30 percent claimed to have boycotted stores because of concerns about their ethical standards, and 60 percent said they would be prepared to participate in a boycott in the future.[7] Worldwide, according to a 1999 survey of 25,000 people, 40 percent of consumers had boycotted or considered boycotting companies they viewed as irresponsible.[8]

Many analysts have concluded on the basis of such evidence that a company's reputation for social responsibility can affect sales. Craig Smith observes that "boycotts may only be the most manifest example of a broader phenomenon of consumer behavior influenced by perceived CSR lapses," adding that "firms may be rewarded by increased patronage if they have a reputation for being socially responsible."[9] According to Frank Walker of Walker Information, "The consumer . . . want(s) to know what the company behind the product or service stands for in today's society, and to make certain that they are not contributing to any corporations that are harming society, its resources or its people."[10]

But there is little evidence to support these assertions. There is a major gap between what consumers say they would do and their actual behavior. After assessing several consumer studies done in the 1990s, one analyst concludes that the proportion of consumers who are willing to pay more for green products is about 10 percent. Surveys that yield higher estimates are attributed to the "halo effect" in human research, which can cause respondents to give what they consider the "right" answer in an attempt to please the researcher.[11] Other studies suggest that the true number of socially conscious consumers may be even lower. A 2004 European survey found that while 75 percent of consumers indicated that they are ready to modify their purchasing decisions because of social or environmental criteria, only 3 percent actually had done so.[12] And other studies in Britain have reported that approximately 5 percent of the public strictly follows ethical concerns in their purchasing, while "ethical boycotts" affect less than 2 percent of market transactions.[13] A notable exception is in northern Europe, where the Nordic Swan label attracts consumers who prefer to use household products, such as toilet paper and detergents, that don't harm the environment.[14]

Back in the United States, notwithstanding more than two decades of green marketing, only 10 to 12 percent of consumers actually make any effort to purchase more environmentally sound products.[15] "Green" consumption has actually been declining as measured by purchases of recycled products. According to a 2002 survey almost half of American consumers thought it was the responsibility of business and not themselves to do more to protect the environment.[16] In part, this is a problem of information. Even for eco-labeled products, many consumers remain uncertain about what the labels imply about the environmental attributes of particular products. But it also reflects a broader reluctance to alter well-established purchasing patterns. As one study concludes, consumers will only buy a greener product [if] it doesn't cost more, comes from a brand they know and trust, can be purchased at stores where they already shop, doesn't require a significant change in habits to use, and has at least the same level of quality, performance, and endurance as the less-green alternative.[17] Few products are likely to meet such a daunting list of conditions.

Marketing CSR: A Limited Opportunity

A few firms and organizations have sought—with varying degrees of success—to buck the odds by focusing their marketing messages on CSR. The Rugmark label, for example, certifies that rugs and carpets have been made without child labor. The Fair Trade (FT) label certifies that producers of coffee (and several other products) are paid above world market prices for their products. And the Forest Stewardship Council has developed a label for wood products harvested from sustainably managed forests. All three labels have modest market shares, though somewhat larger in Europe than in the United States. (Each is discussed in greater detail in chapters 4 and 5.)

Rugmark and Fair Trade products are prominently labeled and sold in retail outlets, including by some firms that specialize in such products. They often command a price premium. In this sense, they epitomize the market for virtue: consumers are willing to pay more for more responsibly made products based on their understanding that developing country producers will benefit. By contrast, there is little consumer awareness of or demand for Forest Stewardship Council products. These products are primarily marketed to companies, such as office products retailers and builders, not because consumers demand them but because of pressure from activists. They are also unable to command a price premium.

But these three labels are relatively unusual. Notwithstanding public concern about labor conditions in the factories that produce apparel, there have been few efforts to market garments based on the ethical practices of the firms that produce them, despite claims that consumers would pay an ethical premium of 15 to 25 percent.[18] Many consumer goods companies do not highlight their investments in CSR, restrained not by modesty but by the belief that such marketing efforts would not help sales. Levi Strauss, whose commitment to the welfare of both its domestic and overseas employees is long-standing, has never publicized its social reputation to help market its products because it did not believe doing so would increase sales.

The environmental practices of nearly four-fifths of the firms in Central America that produce bananas for Chiquita are independently certified by an environmental NGO, which is not the case for its major competitors.[19] Yet to date Chiquita has not marketed its products on this basis (though some bananas are sold in supermarkets in Europe under FT labels). Unilever has embarked on a number of important environmental initiatives, notably promoting sustainable fisheries. The company justifies its policies on the grounds that "we will only be able to maximize shareholder value . . . if we operate in a more sustainable way." But to date there is no evidence that its environment policies have affected consumer purchases of its products.[20]

There is a market for products made by firms with strong reputations for social or environmental responsibility or for products created in a socially responsible way, says Robert Frank: "Ben & Jerry's sells more ice cream because of its preservation efforts on behalf of Amazon rain forests . . . [and] the Body Shop sells more cosmetics because of its environmentally friendly packaging," as well as its commitment not to sell products tested on animals.[21] These claims may well be correct because those firms have linked their values and marketing strategies in a way that differentiates their brands from their competitors'. Other companies whose marketing is closely integrated with their social or environmental practices include Patagonia and Seventh Generation in the United States; Coop Italia, Italy's largest retail cooperative; VanCity Savings Credit, Canada's largest credit union; and the British food retailer Green and Black. Another British firm, the Co-operative Bank, reports that 31 percent of its individual customers say the Co-op Bank's ethical and ecological policies were the main reason they opened and maintain their accounts.[22]

However, most firms that have successfully marketed their "values" are small companies operating in niche markets. They make or sell relatively high-priced goods such as organic food, gourmet ice cream and chocolate, specialty coffees, herbal tea, footwear, outdoor or fashionable clothing, cosmetics, rugs, and household cleaning products. These products typically appeal to a subset of educated, upper-middle-class consumers who often place as much value on the products' attributes— for example, "natural" ingredients—as on the social or environmental practices of the companies that produce them. But no ethical brand has more than a small market share, and the products associated with them are hardly typical of the wide range of goods and services in the global marketplace. Indeed, it is striking how few products have been successfully marketed or command price premiums based on the CSR practices of the firms that produce them.

Consumer Boycotts: More Bark than Bite

To the extent that brands have been affected by corporate social practices, "bad" practices outweigh "good" ones. Consumers appear more willing to avoid a product produced in ways they regard as irresponsible than to purchase a responsibly produced product. Since the early 1990s, scores of firms have been the target of protests against their policies and products.[23] Nike's labor practices made the giant sporting goods company a target of boycotts, and its sales appear to have suffered owing to controversy over its labor polices, though it is unclear by how much. Some consumers boycotted Shell to protest its human rights policies in Nigeria and its plans to sink the Brent Spar oil platform in the Atlantic. Customers returned their Citigroup credit cards to protest the environmental impact of the firm's lending policies, and activists organized boycotts against PepsiCo and Union Oil because of their business ties in Burma. Ford has also been the target of a boycott due to the poor fuel economy of its vehicles. Boycotts have also been directed against product categories, such as sport utility vehicles (SUVs).

They have been particularly popular in Europe, where consumers have boycotted rugs and soccer balls because child labor was used to produce them, and many have refused to buy wood products made from tropical forests, environmentally harmful washing machine detergents, batteries made with mercury, paper produced with chlorine, and food products grown from genetically modified seeds. Some of these boycotts have had a measurable impact on sales: consumers forced manufacturers to eliminate mercury from batteries; soccer ball producers and rug importers were forced to restrict the use of child labor; tropical wood imports measurably declined in much of Europe; and consumer pressures have virtually eliminated sales of genetically modified foods in Europe, causing significant financial injury to Monsanto. The consumer boycott of Shell in Europe had a measurable impact on its sales.

But these are unusual. Typically, even high-profile protests have only negligible financial impact. Consider the experience of Dow Chemical during the U.S. war in Vietnam. In the late 1960s, Dow's Saran Wrap became the most politicized brand in the United States because of Dow's role in manufacturing napalm. Yet despite the controversy, Saran Wrap sales did not suffer. More recent protests have failed to hurt sales at the Gap, Disney, Ford, or Wal-Mart—or for that matter, sales of SUVs. And even when boycotts have an impact, it is usually short-lived.[24]

Explaining the Gap between Intentions and Actions

An important reason relatively few consumers either punish or reward companies for their social performance has to do with the lack of public awareness of CSR policies. Notwithstanding the wealth of information now available about corporate social and environmental practices, as well as the large number of consumers who profess to believe that companies should promote CSR, relatively few corporate practices or policies—either positive or negative—have attracted significant public attention. According to a 1993 Roper poll, the majority of respondents were unable to identify any company they considered to be socially responsible.[25] Consumers remain largely unaware of how the vast majority of products they purchase are produced, and most would be hard pressed to identify the social or environmental practices of almost any firm. Only a handful of firms whose social or environmental practices have become highly visible—companies such as Nike, Shell, and BP—are exceptions to this rule.

Even in Europe, where consumer awareness of corporate responsibility practices is greater, relatively few products have become politicized in the sense that there is widespread consumer awareness of the social and environmental practices underlying their production. Few consumers anywhere have given much thought to where or how products such as appliances, electronic equipment, and automobiles are made. The number of activists is limited, and they constitute only a small portion of consumers. Relatively few consumers appear to be willing to change their purchasing habits in response to corporate practices that do not affect them directly.

"Naming and Shaming"

Although protests rarely affect sales or share prices, the NGO strategy of "naming and shaming" has often been effective. Many companies now regard it as in their self-interest to be, or at least appear to be, responsive to NGO and media criticism, lest their reputations suffer significant damage. According to a 2002 survey of 1,000 chief executives from thirty-three countries, "CSR is . . . driven [primarily] by the negative consequences of ignoring reputation."[26]

The importance of reputation varies across companies and sectors. Firms that sell only intermediate goods or generic goods are less likely to feel threatened by challenges to their reputations. But companies with highly visible brands are much more vulnerable. A firm's brand can be a valuable asset, just as important as the products it produces. The brand distinguishes a firm from its competitors by the ideas, emotions, values, and beliefs that it conveys. Accordingly, as the *Financial Times* notes, "Chief executives . . . dare not risk damaging their brands by being seen as hostile to people or the planet."[27] Even the threat of a protest campaign often produces a company response. The Gap, Disney, Mattel, Ikea, Sainsbury (a British food retailer), Carrefour (a French global retailer), Starbucks, McDonald's, Shell, Unilever, Staples, Home Depot, Mars, Hershey, and C&A (a European clothing retailer) all have made policy changes in response to NGO and media criticisms of their social or environmental practices.

Yet relatively few corporate brands have been affected by the social or environmental practices of the firms that produce them. Consider, for example, *Business Week's* annual lists of the world's 100 most valuable brands, which include one or two sentences describing changes in each brand's performance during the previous year. In its 2003 report, only one of these admittedly brief accounts mentions social or environmental performance: one of the two sentences about BP—whose brand was ranked 69—notes that "John Browne was again front and center with his controversial 'Beyond Petroleum' campaign." A survey published in August 2004 includes only one such mention: "With allegations of sweatshop operations behind it and a growing soccer line, Nike rules the athletic market."[28] The most striking feature of the *BW* list is that the overwhelming majority of these brands have *no* public association with CSR, either positive or negative. This raises an important question. As a World Resources Institute report asks:

> If the threat to highly valued brands is such a powerful motivation for companies to pursue sustainable development priorities, then why are none of the owners of the ten top brands [based on the relative value of the top sixty global brands to a firm's market capitalization] typically identified with the corporate sustainability agenda?[29]

The Mixed Impact of Building a Good Reputation

CSR is only one component of a company's reputation and seldom the most critical. The reputations of the most admired companies are still based primarily on other attributes, such as customer satisfaction, technological innovation, or strong financial performance. When American consumers were asked in a 1996 survey cosponsored by the *Wall Street Journal* to evaluate forty-three activities that influence their opinions of corporations as good citizens, the two most often regarded as very important were "standing behind products/services and honoring warranties" and "producing high quality products and services."[30] From the other side of the cash register, a 2003 survey of CEOs reports that CSR has much less impact on corporate reputation than "bottom line issues such as increased sales and enhanced stock price." When CEOs were asked to identify the most important threats to their reputations, "interest group/ NGO criticism" was ranked eighth. When asked what factors affected their reputation other than financial performance, the "handling of social/environmental issues" received a similarly low ranking.[31]

Moreover, while corporate CSR initiatives or responses may provide some short-term public relations benefits, a positive reputation for CSR can be a mixed blessing. The more a company changes its policies in response to public pressures, the more likely it is to be continually targeted. Not only will there always be a gap between what a business is doing, or says it is doing, and what some CSR advocates want it to do, but prior responsiveness suggests future responsiveness. As the *Financial Times* noted, "Starbucks has become a target of environmental pressure groups partly because its socially responsible image makes it an easy target."[32] After Starbucks agreed to sell Fair Trade coffee, critics next attacked it for using milk from cows that have been treated with growth hormones. Ford has found itself targeted by activists because its CEO had promised to create a more environmentally responsible automobile company; its competitors, who made no such commitment, have been subject to much less scrutiny. As one British environmental activist admits, "the more accountable you are, the more vulnerable to being attacked."[33]

Similarly, Gap and Nike have been subject to more intensive scrutiny from the CSR community than Target and Sears, Shell and BP more than ExxonMobil and ChevronTexaco, Ford more than General Motors or Chrysler, Sainsbury more than Safeway, and Starbucks more than Procter & Gamble—precisely because the former have claimed to act more responsibly. The Body Shop's share price fell significantly when it was accused of misleading the public about its efforts to help community producers in developing countries and about the "naturalness" of its products—precisely because it had sought to distinguish itself from its competitors by making such claims in the first place.[34] An executive from ExxonMobil has concluded that since "BP and Shell actually attract counter-pressure for talking green but not doing enough," the firm sees little value in improving its environmental image. He added, "There is a Norwegian saying that 'the spouting whale gets harpooned.'"[35]

The evidence that CSR makes a positive long-term contribution to a firm's reputation is mixed. Johnson & Johnson's highly visible and responsible handling of the tampering with Tylenol in 1982 certainly had an enduring impact on its reputation, and the management of Marks & Spencer believes that the firm's positive social reputation has helped it through its financial difficulties. The impact of the explosion at Union Carbide's plant in India and the *Exxon Valdez* oil spill negatively affected both firms' reputations for several years. However, the length of the public's memory can be short. Merck's social contributions have been all but forgotten in the context of the controversy surrounding its handling of the Vioxx drug withdrawal; they provided the company with no moral "credit" on which it could draw. And who now remembers which firms stayed in or left South Africa?

Moreover, companies that wish to enjoy a public reputation for good citizenship have less demanding alternatives than changing their corporate policies. Becoming associated with good causes is another option. In 2004 CEOs and NGOs ranked Microsoft as the most responsible corporate citizen.[36] Yet this honor was unrelated to any of its corporate practices or policies. Rather it was recognized for the substantial contributions made by the Gates Foundation to improving public health in developing countries.

Companies without similarly deep-pocketed CEOs can burnish their reputations through corporate donations or cause-related marketing (as discussed in chapter 2). Wal-Mart has responded to criticism of its business practices by environmental groups by increasing its donations to conservation programs. As part of its response to allegations of sweatshop abuses in its overseas suppliers, Nike donated $1 million to the Lance Armstrong Foundation for cancer research and sold yellow bracelets to support the foundation through Nike's website. Avon, Revlon, Nivea, and Estée Lauder have each contributed substantial sums to breast cancer research and report positive consumer responses. In 1998, 26 million women purchased a product or service linked to breast cancer during October, which was designated National Breast Cancer Awareness Month.[37] There is substantial evidence that cause-related marketing, like corporate philanthropy, can enhance a company's reputation for CSR, even though it does not require any substantive changes in corporate policies. In addition, consumers are more likely to consider a company more socially responsible if it is a major advertiser.[38]

Employees: You Are Where You Work?

A company's workforce is also a source of demand for greater corporate virtue. CSR advocates frequently claim that more responsible firms enjoy a comparative advantage in attracting and retaining motivated employees. Some believe that a strong reputation for corporate responsibility can help firms lower their personnel costs because people who want to work in responsible companies will be willing to do so for lower wages than they could earn elsewhere.

Does the Labor Market Reward CSR?

Certainly many people are attracted to firms whose values and behavior are similar to theirs, and the leadership and employees of successful companies often share a common, compelling vision.[39] A few studies have attempted to measure the impact of a company's reputation for corporate responsibility on their attractiveness as employers.[40] These researchers employ a similar methodology: they measure a group of students' awareness of a company's social or environmental reputation and then correlate these assessments with the students' expressed employer preferences. All report a positive relationship, leading to the conclusion that firms may develop competitive advantages by being perceived as attractive places of employment because of their social and environmental policies. According to a 2004 survey of more than 800 MBAs from eleven leading North American and European business schools, nearly all—97 percent—would be willing to forgo an average of 14 percent of their expected income in order to "work with an organization with a better reputation for corporate social responsibility and ethics."[41]

But these results are hardly conclusive. Because there are no follow-up studies, it is unclear if the preferences students expressed actually affected their selection of an employer or whether they made any financial sacrifices to work for firms closely aligned with their values. Nor do we know what, if any, incentives firms with poorer social or environmental reputations may have offered to attract the employees they considered most desirable. And perhaps most important, we do not know what criteria prospective employees use to decide whether a prospective employer is "responsible" or "ethical." Arguably, the survey responses of these students are no more credible than those of consumers who tell interviewers about the frequency of their ethical purchasing decisions.

Skepticism about these survey responses also seems justified by *Fortune's* 2004 survey of employer preferences among MBAs. The ten most popular companies were McKinsey, Citigroup, Goldman Sachs, IBM, Johnson & Johnson, BMW, Bain, Coca-Cola, GE, and Booz Allen Hamilton.[42] The results of this survey suggest that while CSR may play a role in the employer preferences of some MBAs, it is typically overshadowed by other business trends and opportunities.

It is likely that firms whose business strategy is closely aligned with various social values, such as Patagonia, Shorebank, the UK's Co-operative Bank, Stonyfield Farm, Interface, Seventh Generation, the Body Shop, and Celestial Seasonings—enjoy strong employee commitment and lower turnover as a result of these companies' strong CSR reputations. Thanks to its decision to develop and then give away a drug to cure river blindness, Merck became an employer of choice for many scientists. According to Roy Vagelos, Merck's chairman and chief executive, "We could hire almost anybody we wanted to for ten years because of the feeling in the company."[43]

Timberland allows employees to take one week off with pay each year to help local charities and offers four paid sabbatical positions each year for workers who agree to work full time for up to six months at a nonprofit organization. It also closes for one day a year so that its 5,400 workers can take part in company-sponsored philanthropic projects involving the local community. These initiatives are expensive—the all-day event alone costs the company $2 million in lost sales, project expenses, and wages—but the company's management believes that "offering its employees a chance to be good Samaritans helps to attract and retain valuable talent." According to Jeffrey Swartz, Timberland's chief executive, "People like to feel good about where they work and what they do."[44] He reports that at least some employees have turned down more lucrative jobs at other firms as a result of Timberland's strong commitment to community responsibility.

There are other examples to suggest that having a strong social commitment can help attract, retain, and motivate employees. Shell reports that its commitment to sustainable development has enhanced its "ability to attract and retain high calibre talent and to maintain the loyalty and commitment of staff." Since Novo Nordisk aligned its business with sustainable development principles, the company reports it has experienced a turnover rate of half the industry average.[45] According to the consulting firm A. D. Little, "We find that attracting and retaining the best talent from Europe's top business schools and the UK's top universities requires us to demonstrate commitment to corporate citizenship in our consulting services." Accenture's experience with recruiting in Europe is similar. Its international chairman notes that "graduates especially, but also more experienced applicants are interested in the values and approach of the company to corporate citizenship/responsibility."[46] According to a survey of British Telecommunications employees, 17 percent valued the company's "reputation for social responsibility [which] influence[d] their decision to apply/accept a graduate placement." And 49 percent stated that the company's social responsibility reputation made them "more proud to work for BT."[47] A BP executive observes, "The strongest job candidates clearly place social responsibility high on their agendas and will naturally migrate to companies that share their values."[48]

But if some firms are more attractive to some employees because of their social reputation—and those firms believe they benefit as a result—this does not mean that the labor market provides incentives for *all* firms to behave more responsibly. There is no evidence that firms *without* strong reputations for social responsibility find it more difficult or must pay higher salaries to attract first-rate, highly committed employees. Nor is there any evidence that the morale or commitment of these employees is less than in firms with better CSR reputations. People choose to work for companies for a variety of reasons, among the most important being financial rewards and, during periods of high unemployment, because they have been offered a job. Philip Morris and ExxonMobil may well attract different kinds of individuals than those who work for Levi Strauss or BP, but there is no reason to assume that the former are less competent or less motivated than the latter—or that the latter firms are able to pay lower salaries.

When asked in 2004 if British American Tobacco had to pay more to attract and keep staff in a "much-reviled industry," Martin Broughton, the firm's chairman, replied: "No. One thing that quite surprises me is that we offer a job publicly and we are inundated." He did admit that recruiting newly minted MBAs might be more difficult: "There would be more people who wouldn't consider working for us than any of the other companies." But then he added, "But those who consider it come away saying that 'this was the best company that I spoke to.'"[49] In this context, it is worth recalling that Enron was highly attractive to MBAs, who were drawn to it not only by the potential financial rewards but also by its highly competitive, free-wheeling, and risk-oriented culture.[50] There are many ways of making a firm a desirable place to work; having a strong reputation for CSR is only one of them.

Employee Pressure for CSR

CSR may not have a measurable effect on labor markets, but in some companies employees have pressed for more responsible corporate behavior. Merck's decision to develop a cure for river blindness and then manufacture and distribute the drug for free (since no commercial market for it exists), was largely due to employee pressure, as was Levi Strauss's decision to (temporarily) cease expanding its supplier network in China. Many CEOs consider employees to be key drivers of their corporate citizenship efforts.

Sometimes internal pressures from employees reinforce external ones. Nike employees who were embarrassed to be working for a firm identified with sweatshops caused Nike to change its labor policies. As Maria Eitel, Nike's vice president for corporate responsibility, recalled, "They [employees] were going to barbecues and people would say: 'How can you work for Nike?' I don't know if we were losing employees but it sure as hell didn't help attracting them."[51] Citigroup's senior executives hated being "pilloried and heckled" by environmentalists critical of the bank's lending policies, and their uneasiness played a critical role in the bank's decision to meet the demands of the Rainforest Action Network that it establish policies to monitor the environmental impact of its lending policies in developing countries.[52] Similarly, protests against Dow Chemical's production of napalm took a toll on company morale. As one company executive remarked after Dow bid unsuccessfully to continue napalm production: "To deny that the protests [which included 183 major campus demonstrations in three years] had any impact on our bid would be to deny the fact. We were getting awfully tired of the protests and the people who prepared the bid were hoping that we wouldn't get it."[53] Dow Chemical's subsequent embrace of environmentalism was motivated in part by the desire to rebuild the company's reputation among both current and prospective employees.

The role of employees in shaping CSR is in many respects similar to that of consumers. In both instances there is little evidence that the market for virtue works by making it easier for responsible firms to attract or retain customers or employees, or to charge customers more or pay employees less. Still, there is a subset of firms and employees for whom CSR has become more important.

Investors: The Role of Informal Pressures

What about the role of investors? Do enough individuals or institutions invest enough money according to social criteria to make the financial markets an effective driver of social responsibility? According to a 1994 study, 26 percent of potential investors in the United States said social responsibility was extremely important in making investment decisions, and 25 percent of current investors said they always check on values and ethics before investing.[54] Two-thirds of respondents to a 2002 survey claimed that social responsibility affects which stocks they buy, and another reported that 83 percent of its respondents said they would refuse to invest in a company with negative social practices.[55] These responses strain credulity.

Since most investors, like most consumers, are unable to identify more or less virtuous firms, socially responsible investment (SRI) funds have provided an efficient mechanism for them to vote their values in the marketplace. In the United States there are 200 social funds: most are offered by firms that specialize in socially responsible investments, but others are offered by mainstream financial institutions. Many of these funds engage in extensive marketing, and in recent years the amount invested in them has grown substantially. In 2003 socially screened mutual funds had approximately $151 billion under management. But the total assets of all mutual funds in 2004 was $7.9 trillion, meaning that the combined market share of social funds is less than 2 percent.[56] The percentage of individuals who have invested in such funds may well be higher; a 2003 survey put it at about 16 percent, though it is unclear what portion of their investments are in SRI portfolios.[57]

The 2003 report of the SRI industry trade association, the Social Investment Forum, calculates that if one includes all professionally managed portfolios that engage in either social screening, shareholder advocacy, or community investing, then $2.16 trillion—or approximately one out of every nine dollars under professional management—is invested "responsibly."[58] However, these statistics seriously exaggerate the amount of socially oriented investment. For example, a fund or institution that uses only one negative screen, such as for tobacco firms, is still counted as engaged in socially responsible investing. The same is true for a fund or institution whose managers consider any social or environmental criteria in making any of their investment decisions or who file public interest proxy resolutions. Nonetheless, there is no question that the growth of socially oriented investments has been substantial on the part of both institutions and individuals.

It has also become a global phenomenon. There are approximately 800 SRI funds worldwide. Calculating the size of institutional SRI in Europe is difficult because some asset managers claim to engage in social screening—in part because they are under pressure, and in part because several European countries require them to do so—but it is unclear to what extent they actually do. According to the European Sustainable and Responsible Investment Forum, approximately €34 billion is invested using elaborate screening processes; asset managers for €218 billion employ one or more negative screens, most commonly for tobacco or activity in Burma; and funds that total €336 billion engaged companies on CSR issues, for a total of €588 billion.[59]

Ethical mutual funds in Europe have a considerably lower market share than in the United States—approximately .36 percent. Two-thirds of SRI in Europe takes place in Britain, where institutional investors and retail funds with about $25 billion in assets follow the SRI indexes compiled by the *Financial Times*. In France investments in social investment funds more than doubled between 1998 and 2003. In December 2003 there were 108 such funds with a total capitalization of €4.4 billion.[60]

The Impact of Social Investing

Social investors can affect corporate social behavior in three ways. First, if the demand of social investors for shares in responsible firms raised their share prices, thus lowering their costs of capital, those firms would have an advantage over their less responsible competitors. Second, the existence of a large pool of capital managed according to social criteria might encourage companies to change their policies in order to make their shares eligible for purchase by this pool of capital. Third, socially oriented investment funds can use informal mechanisms to press for changes in management policies, such as communicating with managers or submitting and supporting public interest proxy resolutions. Each of these is considered in turn.

SOCIAL INVESTING AND SHARE PRICES. The most obvious way for socially oriented investors to affect business is through the capital markets. According to a Conference Board report:

> Socially responsive investing has reached the scale where it has begun to make a difference in the shareholder relations of publicly trade companies. Investor concerns about corporate social performance can give a significant advantage . . . to companies that have a clear commitment to, and strategy for attaining, positive corporate social performance as part of their plan for increasing shareholder value.[61]

Similarly, Juan Somavia, the director general of the International Labor Organization, claims that the SRI movement is "making waves" on share prices.[62] This view is clearly shared by managers of socially responsible investment funds, 30 percent of whom believe that social and environmental risk management has a positive impact on the company's market value in the short term, while 86 percent claim that it provides long-term benefits.[63] Yet there is virtually no evidence that any of these claims are true.

Were a sufficiently large number of social investors to avoid purchasing a firm's shares because it ran afoul of their criteria, thus depressing its share price, other investors would presumably see the company as a buying opportunity, and its price would return to its "normal" level. The same dynamic would also occur if social investors increased their holdings in a company based on their assessments of its superior CSR performance: other investors would presumably then regard these securities as overvalued and sell them. But both these scenarios are far-fetched because social investors constitute only a small portion of global investors, and only a minority actively employ social screening. Moreover, various social funds employ different—indeed at times contradictory—criteria, thus further limiting their collective leverage. According to one model, changes in the purchases of at least 25 percent of a company's shares would be required to affect its share price, a figure far beyond the scope of global social investors even if they all purchased or avoided the same shares, which they clearly do not.[64]

CSR investors are price takers, not price makers: The demand for stocks is driven by many investors from many countries with many different preferences, so that the withdrawal of even a large number of investments in large firms or in entire sectors would make very little difference to stock values.[65] No industry has been more shunned by social investors than the tobacco industry. Yet tobacco firms seem to have had little difficulty securing the equity they need to grow. In fact, in the ten-year period between 1987 and 1996, a tobacco-free index slightly underperformed the S&P 500.[66] According to a Texas-based research and investment agency, "Unethical . . . (defense) stocks like Lockheed Martin or General Dynamics . . . [have] outperformed the S&P 500 Index by wide margins over the past 15 years."[67] Likewise, the performance of a no-load "vice fund" consisting of shares in alcohol, gaming, tobacco, and aerospace/defense firms, many of which are excluded from SRI portfolios, has sharply outperformed the S&P 500.[68]

During the 1970s and 1980s, many institutional investors sold their shareholdings in firms that did business in South Africa. The impact of this unusually widespread divestment has been extensively studied. Some studies report that it redistributed ownership from socially active investors to other investors without affecting their stock prices, while others conclude that firms that withdrew from South Africa experienced a reduction in shareholder value.[69]

CRITERIA FOR INCLUSION IN SOCIAL INVESTMENT FUNDS. Companies might still consider it beneficial to change their policies in order to qualify for investments by socially responsible institutions and funds, within reason. In October 2000 the California Public Employees Retirement System (Calpers), the largest pension fund in the United States, announced that it would sell its tobacco holdings. The FTSE4Good also excludes tobacco companies, as well as arms manufacturers and nuclear power and uranium producers.[70] But it would be unrealistic to expect a tobacco company to stop selling cigarettes or a major defense contractor to leave the weapons business in order to make their shares eligible for purchase by an ethical fund or inclusion in an ethical index. If, however, modest changes in their policies would make their shares eligible for inclusion in SRI funds, some firms might be willing to adopt them, if only because inclusion in the portfolios of such funds has come to represent a kind of public certification of their CSR performance. Following a series of meetings between the Calvert Group and Bristol-Myers Squibb, the pharmaceutical firm agreed to publicly disclose its bioethics policies, which resulted in Calvert's decision to include the firm in its influential Calvert Social Index.[71] Some South African mining firms adopted more active CSR policies after they were listed on the London Stock Exchange, which exposes their social practices to screening by social investors.[72]

According to Will Oulton, deputy chief of FTSE International, numerous companies have modified their SRI policies in order to be included in the FTSE4Good Index.[73] This index, which has significantly increased the visibility of social investment in Europe and serves as a benchmark for many European social investors, has been relatively inclusive, consisting of approximately 900 firms. In 2003 the FTSE Group, which manages the FTSE4Good, announced a more stringent set of human rights criteria designed to raise the standards for entry and thus put human rights more firmly on the corporate agenda.[74] According to a member of its advisory board, "The specific aim of FTSE4Good is to be demanding but achievable. As the average standard of good practice rises, so will the FTSE4Good bar rise."[75] For many firms, being included in the more highly selective Dow Jones Sustainability World Index has become an important public recognition of their corporate virtue. The index consists of only 250 firms, or 10 percent of the largest 2,500 firms included in the Dow Jones World Index. It is based on a "best-in-class" formula, meaning that every time a firm is added, another must be dropped. Hewlett-Packard credits its inclusion in the DJSI World with prompting changes in its internal management processes and increasing interest among investors.[76] While complaints about the arbitrary selection procedures of both indexes persist, an increasing number of companies are actively seeking to be included in them.[77]

SHAREHOLDER RESOLUTIONS AND OTHER FORMS OF PRESSURE. Social investors, including those that do not employ social screens, have filed public interest proxy resolutions seeking changes in corporate policies and practices. U.S. shareholders filed 236 such resolutions in 2001, 270 in 2002, and 282 in 2003. They have focused primarily on global labor standards, followed by equal employment, and environmental policy. Although such resolutions are rarely adopted, the average number of shares supporting them increased from 7.9 percent in 2001 to 10.5 percent in 2003, with twelve resolutions on global climate change receiving 20 percent of the shares voted. More significant, between 2001 and 2003, 256 socially inspired resolutions were withdrawn after the targeted firms made concessions.[78]

For example, following the repeated filing of public interest proxy proposals, Wal-Mart, Home Depot, and American Electric Power agreed to bar employment discrimination on the basis of sexual orientation. Staples announced a policy to increase the postconsumer recycled and alternative-fiber content in the paper it sells, while both Gillette and Reebok agreed to establish a baseline for greenhouse gas emissions. In 2003, after a prolonged campaign by labor unions, Unocal agreed to formally recognize the rights of workers to freedom of association and collective bargaining. In France pressures from ethical investment funds encouraged numerous firms listed on the French stock exchange to adopt social standards for suppliers: no firm wanted to be regarded as a social outcast.[79] Shareholder pressures have also contributed to improving the environmental and human rights policies of Shell, which in the mid-1990s was widely criticized for its plans to dispose of an oil rig in the North Atlantic and for not stopping the execution of Ken Saro-Wira, who protested Shell's social and environmental policies in his native Nigeria.

The successes of activist shareholder campaigns have sparked a debate within the SRI community about the value of negative screens, since their use precludes shareholder campaigns to pressure less responsible companies. Some social investors have purchased shares of companies precisely in order to be able to file and vote for public interest proxy resolutions. Many activist funds in both the United States and Europe have stepped up their pressure on companies in which they own shares.

Mainstreaming Socially Responsible Investment

The fact that a relatively small portion of investors choose their investments using social or environmental criteria clearly limits the financial impact of the SRI community on share prices and thus on corporate behavior. In order for CSR practices to affect share prices, mainstream investors must make greater use of CSR criteria in their investment decisions. Such a development would presumably improve the performance of SRI portfolios, at least in the short run. For the CSR community as a whole, the resulting impact on share values would both confirm their claims about the positive relationship between corporate financial and social performance and presumably encourage all firms to improve their CSR practices, which is their ultimate objective. In principle, the ultimate goal of SRI is to eliminate the distinction between it and mainstream investment strategies as all investors come to recognize the business risks of irresponsible behavior and the business benefits of corporate virtue.

There have been many efforts to persuade mainstream investors, asset managers, and securities brokers to improve the integration of environmental, social, and corporate governance (ESG) factors in their financial analyses. The Global Corporate Citizenship Initiative of the World

Economic Forum, in association with the NGO AccountAbility has brought investors together with corporate managers and nonbusiness constituencies to identify both opportunities and obstacles to "mainstreaming responsible investment." In September 2002 the Corporation of London launched the London Principles of Sustainable Finance. Working with more than fifty financial institutions, an organization called Forum for the Future proposed a set of principles "under which financial market mechanisms can best promote the financing of sustainable development."[80] The United Nations Environmental Program has established an asset management working group composed of twenty-one leading firms for the purpose of developing the ability of mainstream fund managers to identify and respond to relevant social and environmental issues. Other organizations, such as the Aspen Institute, the World Resources Institute, the World Business Council for Sustainable Development, and the UN Global Compact, are working with financial institutions to facilitate the ability of financial markets to recognize the value of good CSR practices and the risks of poor ones.

To further assist this process, between 1999 and 2004 Britain, Sweden, Belgium, Germany, and Italy enacted legislation requiring pension funds to declare how, if it all, social, environmental, and ethical factors influence their investment decisions. In 2001, France adopted a law requiring managers of employee savings funds to consider corporate social, environmental, or ethical impacts when buying and selling shares. However, there is no evidence to date that these requirements have actually affected investment strategies, let alone share prices.

Interest in the financial implications of CSR among mainstream investors has certainly increased. According to the president of Innovest Strategic Value Advisors, "Institutional investors are increasingly aware of the edge environmental overlays provide. Our clients include mainstream asset managers, banks and some of the largest pension funds in the world," including ABN-AMRO, Bank Sarisan, Cambridge Associates, Schroders, BP Pension, and Zurich Scudder. He adds, "Environmental overlays are becoming a key tool in financial analysis. . . . Sophisticated financial folks are asking about the potential of SRI."[81] Overall, Innovest's research is used to positively screen and manage approximately $2.5 billion in invested assets.[82] In 2002 both Dreyfus and Mellon Capital Management launched eco-enhanced index funds.

The Association of British Assurers, whose members control roughly one-quarter of British equities, states: "Companies that fail to meet basic social, environmental and ethical considerations run the risk of damaging their reputation and financial well-being. . . . Failure to take these risks into account can lead to a long-term loss, not just in a company's reputation, but also in its value."[83] Likewise, PricewaterhouseCoopers, after surveying the sustainability practices of 140 major American corporations, concluded that "companies that ignore the risks associated with ethics, governance and the 'triple bottom line' of economic, environmental and social issues—are courting disaster."[84] Similarly, the *Financial Times* observes, "Large investors want companies to explain what they are doing about social and environmental risks that could affect their value."[85]

But despite these beliefs, the impact of social and environmental criteria on mainstream investor analyses and stock selection remains limited. A 2003 survey by the World Economic Forum's Corporate Citizenship Initiative found that 79 percent of CEOs and CFOs "expect to see increased interest in ESG issues by mainstream investors in the future," but added that this had not yet occurred. The head of investor relations at one company reported that environmental or social issues "never come up unless there is a problem—no one cares unless there's a financial risk or short-term exposure"; a CFO observed, "With a few honorable exceptions, most mainstream investors ask little or nothing about social responsibility. That might change in the event of a serious environmental/community/political incident, which raised questions about the company's performance."[86] Another obstacle is the short-term outlook of many traditional investors. Many investors tend to focus on quarterly or annual results, but it can take much longer to demonstrate the benefits from corporate citizenship. According to one CEO: "Many mainstream investors are still not convinced by the business case and see corporate citizenship issues as a cost rather than an investment that can produce a return. One important reason is that mass markets seem unwilling to pay the required premium for corporate citizenship quality."[87]

Improving CSR Reporting

A critical obstacle to the inclusion of CSR in mainstream investment analyses and decisions is the lack of reliable information about corporate social and environmental practices. Since the early 1990s the amount of corporate nonfinancial reporting has steadily increased, moving from a marginal activity into a mainstream one. In 1993 fewer than 100 companies issued reports on their social or environmental performance. By 1999 more than 500 had done so. Approximately 2,000 companies worldwide now publish nonfinancial reports, most of them based in North America, Scandinavia, and western Europe. Equally significant, in 2003 nearly 49 percent of these reports were audited, as compared with only 17 percent three years previously. A survey of corporate sustainability reporting by KPMG shows a similar trend: between 1999 and 2002 the percentage of nonfinancial reports issued by the top 250 companies of the global Fortune 500 increased from 28 percent to 45 percent.[88] The percentage of Fortune Global 100 issuing sustainability reports grew from 48 percent in 2003 to 72 percent in 2004.[89] To promote corporate disclosure, six European countries now require companies to issue reports on their social or environmental practices.[90]

Although the quality and comprehensiveness of such reports has improved, it remains uneven: some include quantitative measures of nonfinancial performance, such as changes in carbon dioxide emissions. But not surprisingly, since the firms themselves choose what to report, they can tout their strengths and ignore the rest. Those who regard their reports primarily as a public relations document focus on "feel good" subjects such as community support and emphasize policies and processes rather than targets and outcomes.[91] Some firms may have a strong incentive to disclose as little as possible about their CSR practices or policies, since the more issues they cover, the more they may expose themselves to NGO and media scrutiny. Thus paradoxically, a more reticent firm may enjoy a more favorable social reputation.

Many companies prominently feature information about their codes of conduct, but then do not report the extent of compliance with them. Other firms describe their own practices, but ignore those of their supply chain. Most important, only half of nonfinancial reports are audited, even minimally. The growing length of these reports—the size of the average report increased from fifty-nine to eighty-six pages between 2000 and 2002—has also made them less useful. SustainAbility, which periodically reviews and ranks these reports, calls this "carpet-bombing . . . bombarding readers with an increasing amount of information without explaining its relevance."[92] According to a 2004 report published by AccountAbility (an institute for social and ethical accounting) and CSR-network (a corporate responsibility consulting firm), the world's 100 largest companies continue to have a poor record of accounting for their impact on society and the environment.[93]

The weaknesses of these reports is acknowledged by the companies themselves. According to a 2004 survey by the Economist Intelligence

Unit, almost three-quarters of the 247 executives and directors of large global firms said that their nonfinancial measures remained mediocre or poor. And only 9 percent believed that such measures helped the capital markets to make an "an appropriate evaluation" of their company.[94] To date, "social and environmental practices—intangible aspects of a company's value—are notoriously difficult to measure and thus to incorporate into security analyses."[95]

To standardize corporate nonfinancial reporting, in 1997 the Coalition for Environmentally Responsible Economies collaborated with the Tellus Institute and the United Nations Environment Program to establish the Global Reporting Initiative (GRI). The purpose of the nonprofit foundation, headquartered in Amsterdam, is to promote the international harmonization of corporate nonfinancial reporting. Its guidelines, which are revised periodically, include more than ninety indicators of environmental, social, and economic performance, which it requires companies to update annually.

While some firms have found collecting such data from hundreds of sites around the globe both time-consuming and expensive (estimated to be $500,000–600,000 for a large international firm), should the GRI become the international standard for nonfinancial reporting, companies would then be spared the increasingly burdensome task of filling out scores of different questionnaires about their social and environmental practices.[96] In January 2005 the GRI website reported that approximately 600 firms were either using or referring to its guidelines. This number had more than tripled since 2001 but still represents less than a third of the companies that voluntarily publish social reports, though pressure from socially oriented institutional investors may compel additional firms to participate.[97] The GRI encourages firms to verify their reports, but it neither assesses their conformity with the guidelines nor verifies their accuracy, both of which reduce their value to investors, as well as their credibility to NGOs. In addition, the steadily growing length of the GRI checklist may have made it more difficult for financial analysts to use these reports effectively.

Socially Responsible Investment: The Bottom Line

For the nonfinancial dimensions of corporate performance to affect share prices, at least two things must happen: firms must provide verifiable information about their social and environmental performance in a form that is comprehensible and relevant to mainstream investors, and those investors must take this information into account in making investment decisions. Substantial efforts are being made in both areas. The amount of corporate disclosure has increased, and at least some mainstream investors appear to have become more aware of the financial implications of corporate nonfinancial performance, most commonly with respect to environmental practices and human rights policies.

Yet there are still no standardized metrics for CSR. Whatever the considerable difficulties of measuring and auditing corporate financial performance, they are modest when compared with the challenges of measuring and auditing corporate social or environmental performance, and, more important, comparing firms' records on these dimensions. For example, how can the environmental practices of a chemical and a software company be compared? What metric would enable a comparison of one firm's philanthropic contributions with another's human rights practices? For all the extensive use of the term "triple bottom line" (52,400 web pages mention it and it is referred to in many company reports), the second two bottom lines, namely environmental and social impact, remain more akin to aspirations than actual standards of corporate performance. No one has developed a way to calculate either of them.[98]

But even if the quality of CSR reporting were much better, it is not yet obvious that investment analysts would regard it as material. There is a curious disconnect between discussions of companies and of CSR in the business press. Articles on CSR frequently emphasize both the financial benefits of responsible behavior and the business risks of irresponsible practices. But read the typical article in the *Wall Street Journal*, the *Financial Times, Investor's Daily*, the *Economist, Business Week*, or *Fortune* that describes a firm that is doing well or poorly. How often does it mention either the business threats or the opportunities associated with CSR? The answer is rarely. CSR can and does matter to investors under some circumstances, but its *relative* importance to the financial performance or prospects of most firms most of the time ranges from modest to nonexistent.

The financial impact of both positive and negative CSR-related policies and events is almost invariably overshadowed by other business developments. As *Fortune* noted in an article on the business importance of CSR: "Investors [do not] appear to care that McDonald's sells antibiotic-free chicken, or that HP wants to deliver technology to the world's poor."[99] They still care more about their sales of hamburgers and copiers. A comprehensive study of boycotts and boycott threats in the United States found that targeted firms suffered no decline in shareholder value.[100] According to an unpublished study by a major accounting firm, "Even the very high profile civil campaigns against the likes of Shell, Nestlé and Nike have had little or no demonstrable effect on share prices or dividends."[101] In fact, while Reebok's labor policies were generally regarded as better than Nike's, between 1997 and 2000 the former's share price fell more dramatically and remained low for a longer period of time than that of the latter.[102]

Whatever effect socially responsible investors have had on corporate behavior has taken place through mechanisms other than their impact on share prices. The filing of public interest proxy resolutions, the interest of some companies in being included in SRI portfolios, requests by investors for more information on corporate social and environmental performance—all have affected the behavior of some firms, even though they may have had no discernible impact on share prices. In a sense these pressures are analogous to the impact of corporate reputation on consumer sales. Neither impact can be quantified, yet many companies consider it prudent to respond to them.

The Financial Markets as a Constraint on CSR

But the financial markets represent more than a possible or potential source of pressure on companies to behave more virtuously—or at least to reduce their propensity to make "irresponsible" decisions. They also represent an important constraint on CSR. A 2004 survey of companies by AccountAbility reported that while a majority of respondents believed that "responsible business practices can be a significant competitive advantage for us," a nearly equal percentage cited "short-term financial targets" as the biggest constraint on implementing responsible business practices.[103]

In April 2000 the news that Ben and Jerry's Homemade had been acquired by the British/Dutch multinational Unilever "sent shudders and shivers through the socially responsible business community."[104] It also prompted considerable discussion of the impact of the capital markets on CSR. When Anita Roddick, the founder of the Body Shop, was asked what she might have done differently to avoid being removed from the management of the company, she replied, "I'd tell anyone *don't take the company public*. Stay private at any cost. Going public is, in my experience, total bloody disaster!" (italics in original).[105]

A former executive at Celestial Seasonings, the highly successful herbal tea company founded in the late 1960s, which went public in 1993, told *Business Ethics* magazine: "I think there's no question that being a public company has caused a major set of pressures that the company never faced before."[106] Jeffrey Hollender, who took his green cleaning products company, Seventh Generation, private in 1999, noted that "other companies that have cited—to us—the benefits of private ownership as a path to social responsibility are Patagonia, Eileen Fisher, and Working Assets"—to which list he might add Ikea, Levi Strauss, C&A, and Birkenstock.[107] These ownership patterns do not eliminate pressures for short-term financial performance, but they can reduce them.

Cantor Fitzgerald, the privately held bond trading firm that lost two-thirds of its New York employees in the terrorist attack on the World Trade Center on September 11, 2001, has pledged to pay the families of those killed 25 percent of the firm's profits for five years as well as to provide them with health insurance for a decade.[108] As of June 30, 2004, Cantor had paid $145 million to those families, including more than $85 million from its profits. How likely is it that the firm would have been able to make or honor such a commitment if it were publicly held?

A striking, if rare, confirmation of how financial markets can respond to firms that are "too" responsible was reported in the American financial press. In the spring of 2004, Costco reported earnings that substantially beat Wall Street's expectations. The market responded by reducing the value of its shares by 4 percent. Why? Apparently, Costco treats its employees too well. It pays substantially higher wages than its major competitor, Wal-Mart, and covers a higher portion of employees in its health care and retirement plans. But even though Costco's employees are more productive, the firm's employee turnover rate is more than one-third lower, and it experiences less employee theft than Wal-Mart, the financial markets are unimpressed. As one financial analyst put it, "From the perspective of investors, Costco's benefits are overly generous. *Public companies need to care for shareholders first*" (italics added).[109]

As long as financial markets are unable or unwilling to recognize the business significance of social or environmental performance, their role in promoting CSR remains limited. While some institutional investors and analysts place a high value on corporate responsibility, its impact on share prices continues to be overshadowed by the financial markets as a whole, which typically do not regard most corporate social or environmental practices as material.

Reevaluating the Business Case

We are now in a better position to explain why the numerous studies that seek to correlate corporate financial and social performance have produced such inconclusive results. One reason is that the social and environmental practices of the vast majority of companies have not had any demonstrated effects on their sales. Nor have their responses to civil regulation affected their ability to hire and retain motivated and competent employees. Most critically, remarkably few firms have been rewarded or punished by the financial markets for their social performance. And those few that have are not sufficiently numerous or important to affect the results of statistical studies that correlate corporate virtue with financial performance. Of the myriad factors that affect corporate earnings, CSR remains, for most firms most of the time, of marginal importance. Nonetheless it is clear that even if the bottom-line costs and benefits of CSR are difficult to measure and are rarely material to investors, *many firms act as if CSR matters*. How can we account for this?

For a subset of firms, CSR does appear to make business sense. These firms fall into two broad categories, though in a few instances they overlap. For a few firms, CSR is a part of their corporate strategy and business identity: it is a way for them to differentiate themselves from their competitors and is often linked to their strategies for attracting and retaining customers or employees. The so-called companies with a conscience, such as Ben and Jerry's, Seventh Generation, and Patagonia, fall into this category, as do some larger firms, such as Levi Strauss, Starbucks, C&A, Interface, the Gap, Marks & Spencer, HP, Timberland, Ikea, and Merck. Their embrace of corporate virtue frequently reflects the values of their owners or major shareholders, or the legacies of their founders. Some of these firms have been targeted by activists, but many of their social commitments are internally driven.

A second category of firms for whom CSR makes business sense are those that have been targeted by activists, who are concerned that they could be targeted, largely because of the visibility of their brands. For firms such as Shell, Nike, Home Depot, Dell, General Electric, Mars, McDonald's, Disney, Carrefour, and Hennes & Mauritz (a fashion company commonly known as H&M), displays of corporate virtue have been primarily defensive. These firms are highly risk-averse: they consider it in their interest to act more responsibly not so much to distinguish themselves from their competitors, but to *avoid* becoming distinguished. At least initially, their objective was not primarily to use CSR as a source of competitive advantage, but to prevent it from becoming a source of competitive disadvantage.

Both categories of companies regard their reputations for corporate virtue as important. Accordingly, they have decided that it is in their interest to devote additional resources to improving their social or environmental performance and in many cases to cooperate with NGOs. For many firms, as well as other companies that have decided to embrace the CSR agenda, CSR has become an important component of their management of community, public, employee, and shareholder relations. This of course raises an important question: what have these firms actually *done*? In what ways have they become more virtuous? This is the subject of the next three chapters.

CHAPTER 4

Corporate Responsibility for Working Conditions in Developing Countries

Improving the conditions of factory and agricultural workers in developing countries has emerged as a major focus of contemporary corporate social responsibility. Since the 1990s more and more Western firms that market clothing, footwear, athletic equipment, and toys, as well as some other industrial goods and agricultural products, have been under pressure to accept responsibility for the working conditions of their suppliers. More than 1,000 companies have adopted codes of conduct establishing standards for child labor, wages, compulsory overtime, working conditions, and freedom of association. Numerous industry-specific codes govern the production of various products. A complex array of private organizations and mechanisms monitor and enforce compliance with these codes. In addition, some social labels inform consumers about the conditions under which some products are produced.[1] These developments reflect a significant broadening of the scope of CSR. As recently as 1990 only a handful of global firms acknowledged any obligations to workers whom they did not employ directly. Now, recognizing such responsibility has become part of the norm of good corporate citizenship, at least among highly visible American and European firms.

The Market for Virtue: Gains and Limitations

Assessing the effectiveness of these efforts is a challenging task. Many firms and industries do not disclose the results of CSR audits, and only a few firms allow their auditing results to be independently verified. Nonetheless, it is possible to offer some assessment of the accomplishments and limitations of this highly visible dimension of contemporary CSR.

Perhaps most dramatically, several export sectors have significantly reduced their use of child labor. In other areas, some working conditions have improved, and more workers are now able to exercise freedom of association. Wages and payments to farmers have increased in at least a few cases. These achievements suggest that there is a market for virtue. Though consumer purchasing decisions are rarely affected by allegations of irresponsible labor practices, the reputation of many highly visible firms has been adversely affected by allegations of "sweatshop" conditions in their suppliers. And many other firms are concerned that they or their brands will be challenged in the future. Because firms that rely on their brands to market to consumers are highly risk-averse, they have a strong incentive to attempt to avoid or reduce negative publicity stemming from allegations of irresponsible labor practices.

But the scope of the market for virtue remains limited. Voluntary codes primarily govern the manufacturing of products for retailers and branded-goods companies that sell to consumers in the United States and Europe. They do not usually affect the production of generic merchandise or intermediate goods, household assembly, or products manufactured by companies whose primary markets are domestic or are exported to other regions, all of which usually remain below the radar screen of Western activists. They also rarely extend beyond primary contractors, many of whom subcontract to other firms or to households. In addition, while their scope has expanded, they still cover a relatively small number of manufactured products. Most important, relatively few codes cover agricultural workers, who constitute the majority of the labor force in developing countries.

Moreover, the market for virtue works imperfectly. The gap between company and industry codes and actual working conditions remains large. Monitoring is often ineffective, and its results are rarely independently verifiable. Compliance remains highly uneven and violations pervasive. In some instances the enforcement of Western norms through codes of conduct has even backfired, notably with respect to restrictions on child labor. The market for virtue works more effectively in the case of socially branded products, such as those associated with Rugmark and Fair Trade. There is a market for these products. While they sometimes cost more, some consumers are willing to pay these costs. Sales of socially labeled products have reduced child labor in the production of rugs and channeled some additional resources to agricultural workers, primarily in the coffee sector. Though it has grown, the market for socially labeled products remains small, as consumers continue to place a higher value on other product characteristics.

This chapter describes how labor conditions in developing countries emerged on the CSR agenda, focusing first on Nike, the U.S. firm whose highly visible brand and initial indifference to the conditions under which its athletic footwear were produced made it and its brand a symbol of labor exploitation. It then analyzes some of the more important company and industry labor codes that were subsequently developed. The next major section describes and evaluates social labeling as a market-based strategy for improving working conditions, notably in the carpet and specialty coffee industries. The chapter concludes by summarizing the conditions under which CSR has improved labor practices in developing countries.

Nike: From Pariah to Pacesetter

Nike is a highly successful manufacturer of athletic footwear and sportswear. Founded by Phil Knight in 1972, it went public in 1980. Its revenues grew at double-digit levels for the next fifteen years, reaching $9 billion by the middle of the 1990s. In 1998, Nike controlled over 40 percent of the $14.7 billion athletic footwear market in the United States and was a major global player in the sports apparel market.[2] Nike's successful strategy was based on two elements: celebrity endorsements to raise the company's public profile, and the outsourcing of all its production to developing countries to reduce costs. Although it first sourced from suppliers in Japan, and then from South Korea and Taiwan, it subsequently encouraged its suppliers to relocate to lower-cost regions. In 2004 the largest number of factories producing goods for Nike were based in China, and the firm is now the largest employer in Vietnam.[3]

In the late 1980s and early 1990s, the media began focusing on labor conditions in Nike contractors' factories, primarily in Indonesia. A story broadcast on CBS in July 1993 said workers were paid nineteen cents an hour and were only permitted to leave the company barracks on Sunday. Nike's initial response was that the company could not be held responsible for the actions of independent contractors. The company's general manager in Jakarta, when asked why he had not investigated claims about problems in factories producing Nike shoes, replied, "I don't know that I need to know. . . . They are our subcontractors. It's not within our scope to investigate [allegations of labor violations.]"[4] Although Nike did draft a code of conduct and memorandum of understanding that addressed working conditions at its suppliers' factories, critics continued to complain that there was little credible evidence that conditions had improved.

In 1996 foreign labor abuses became a major focus of media attention when human rights activists reported that a line of clothing endorsed by Kathie Lee Gifford, a popular daytime talk show host, had been manufactured by child labor in Honduras. Gifford appeared on television, tearful and apologetic, and promised to take responsibility for improving the factory's employment practices. Nike was not implicated in these accusations, but soon thereafter it "emerged as a symbol of worker exploitation and a high-profile media scapegoat."[5] In July 1996, *Life* magazine published a story about child labor in Pakistan, which featured a photo of a 12-year-old boy stitching a Nike soccer ball. *Business Week* editorialized, "Executives . . . have protested, disingenuously, that conditions at factories run by subcontractors are beyond their control. . . . Such attitudes won't wash anymore." It prophetically added, "As the industry gropes for solutions, Nike will be a key company to watch."[6]

Nike responded by being the first company to join the Apparel Industry Partnership, initiated by a Clinton administration task force to promote collaboration between the apparel and footwear industries and their critics. It also hired an accounting firm to audit its factories and established a Labor Practices Department. Yet public criticism of Nike continued to intensify. Reporters hounded Nike's celebrity endorsers Michael Jordan and Jerry Rice with questions about Nike's labor practices, and the openings of many Nike new retail stores were greeted by noisy protesters. In May 1997 the popular comic strip "Doonesbury" devoted a full week to attacking the company. In effect, Nike had reached a cultural milestone. One media critic noted, "It's sort of like getting in Jay Leno's monologue. It means your perceived flaws have reached a critical mass, and everyone feels free to pick on you."[7]

Nike then hired Andrew Young, a noted figure in the civil rights movement and former mayor of Atlanta, Georgia, to conduct an independent evaluation of the implementation of its code of conduct. His report said labor conditions had improved but that more needed to be done. The report backfired on Nike: it was widely attacked for both its methodology and its conclusions. A subsequent report by students at Dartmouth's Tuck

School of Business, commissioned by Nike to examine wages and benefits paid to its Vietnamese and Indonesian contract factories, had a similar effect. While the students found that factory workers had significant discretionary income—enough to purchase items such as bicycles and wedding gifts for family members—it was the contrast between the daily wages of $1.67 paid to factory workers in Vietnam and the retail price of $150 for a pair of Nike's basketball sneakers that caught the public's attention.[8]

Another report that became public in November 1997 proved even more damaging to Nike. In an inspection report prepared for internal use but subsequently leaked, Ernst & Young reported that workers in factories in Vietnam producing Nike products were routinely exposed to hazardous chemicals. The report "painted a dismal picture of thousands of young women, most under 25, laboring 10½ hours a day, six days a week, in excessive heat and noise and in foul air, for slightly more than $10 a week . . . . More than half of workers who deal with dangerous chemicals did not wear protective masks or gloves."[9]

Notwithstanding its increasingly unfavorable press coverage, through the spring of 1997, Nike's strong financial performance continued: its stock reached a high of $76 and it had a large backlog of orders. But in the third quarter of 1998 its earnings fell by 69 percent and the company experienced its first loss in thirteen years, forcing it to lay off 1,600 employees.[10] It remains unclear what role public criticisms of Nike's labor practices played in these financial reverses or in the decline in its stock price during the second half of 1997, when unfavorable press coverage intensified. At least some of the company's sales decline seems due to allegations that workers in the company's suppliers were mistreated.[11] In addition, Nike found its coveted position as a supplier to the nation's top university sports teams threatened when students on several college campuses demanded that their schools quit buying collegiate logo gear manufactured under poor labor conditions. However, competition from more fashionable brands had increased as well. Adidas, New Balance, and Airwalk saw their sales grow at Nike's expense, though their labor practices were arguably no better than Nike's. As *Business Week* reported in 1999, "European apparel makers such as Adidas have gotten away scot-free while Nike and other U.S. rivals have been hounded by sweatshop charges.[12]

According to a Harvard Business School case study, "Nike's fiscal woes did what hundreds of hard articles had failed to do: they took some of the bravado out of Phil Knight."[13] In a May 1998 speech to the National Press Club, Knight admitted that "the Nike product has become synonymous with slave wages, forced overtime, and arbitrary abuse. . . . I truly believe that the American consumer does not want to buy products made in abusive conditions." Knight announced a series of sweeping reforms, including raising the minimum age of sneaker workers to 18 and apparel workers to 16, requiring all of its suppliers to adopt U.S. clean air standards, expanding educational programs for workers, and making micro loans available to their families. Nike also agreed to a demand from activists that the company had long resisted, namely to permit labor and human rights groups to participate in the auditing of Nike's suppliers. According to Knight, "We believe that these are practices which the conscientious, good companies will follow in the 21st century. These moves do more than just set industry standards. They reflect who we are as a company."[14] However, Nike made no commitment to raise wages.

Nike's code of conduct governs labor and environmental practices for the 700 factories employing more than 600,000 workers who produce its products in nearly fifty countries. Compliance is first monitored by an internal staff of 100 people and then reviewed by accounting, health, safety, and environmental consulting firms with whom Nike has contracted. Its suppliers are rated and compared with other firms in the same country; high scorers often garner more lucrative orders, whereas low scorers risk losing contracts.[15] Nike has canceled some contracts with poorly performing suppliers. At the same time, Nike's performance incentives to its procurement teams, which are based on price, quality, and delivery, have led some of its buyers to ignore whether suppliers complied with the code in order to hit targets and earn bonuses. The firm's tight inventory management often creates urgent short-term needs to meet market demands, thus forcing its contractors to violate Nike's restrictions on overtime.[16]

Criticism of the treatment of workers in the factories that supply goods to Nike has continued. A BBC documentary aired in 2000 accused Nike of using child labor, and an NGO whose report Nike had commissioned reported in 2001 that it found widespread verbal abuse and sexual harassment in all nine factories in Indonesia that it visited.[17] Nike's monitoring is primarily confined to its suppliers, yet the typical Nike shoe has around fifty components manufactured in six to ten countries, and few of these smaller subcontractors are inspected.[18] However, even many of Nike's critics concede that it has made substantial improvements, notably in health and safety conditions, though they continue to criticize the low wages paid to factory workers.[19] Although in October 1998, Nike announced that it would raise wages for entry-level workers in Indonesia by 22 percent to offset that country's devalued currency,[20] Jeffrey Ballinger, one of Nike's most persistent critics, claimed that wages in its contractors remain "below what is considered necessary to meet the minimum needs of a single adult."[21]

Nike, like many other global firms, has also initiated community development programs.[22] In partnership with the Ministry of Education of Vietnam, Nike hires teachers, rents classroom space, and provides books and other supplies as well as a meal allowance to enable employees to further their education after hours. Nike pays 50 percent of the costs of this program, which has involved more than 10,000 employees and has expanded to thirty-seven footwear contractors in Indonesia, China, and Thailand. Nike has also established a micro-enterprise loan program to enable women in the communities surrounding its facilities to start their own businesses. It began in Vietnam and has expanded to Thailand and Indonesia. It has made more than 3,200 loans, averaging $65 each. The total cost to Nike has been modest: just under $250,000.[23]

Nike's ability to support these programs and initiatives has been facilitated by the improvement in its financial performance. Between 1999 and 2004 its sales increased from slightly under $9 billion to around $12 billion, and its net profits rose from $450 million to more than $900 million.[24] Its share price in November 2004 exceeded its previous high in 1997.[25] Its new financial stability is primarily attributable to Nike's expansion into sportswear as well as improvements in its management practices.[26] While it is possible that Nike's sales would not have increased as substantially had it not attempted to improve the labor conditions in its suppliers, much of the sales increase stems from Nike's expansion in Asian markets, where there has been less criticism of its labor policies. In any event, Nike appears to have effectively addressed both of the image problems that plagued it in 1997 and 1998: its identification as a sweatshop employer and as a brand that had become less fashionable.

However, Nike's labor policies have remained in the news.[27] In 2003 the firm was sued by a California citizen acting as a "private attorney-general," on the grounds that its public claims to have effectively addressed allegations of worker mistreatment at its suppliers' plants were misleading and thus constituted deceptive advertising. The company's position, which was supported by the American Civil Liberties Union and a number of activists, was that its statements constituted free speech rather than commercial speech and thus were protected by the First Amendment. After a California court ruled against Nike and the Supreme Court declined to review its decision, Nike agreed to pay $1.5 million in damages. However, it also decided to engage in self-censorship, waiting until 2005 to issue its next social responsibility report.

In 2004 Nike acquired the low-priced sneaker brand Starter, which is sold by discount retailers such as Wal-Mart, and now faces a new set of challenges. The firm has less leverage in the market for "value" items, whose consumers tend to be highly price sensitive and less interested in how the goods they purchase are made. It remains to be seen how its entry into this new market will affect Nike's ability to maintain its social commitments.

Nike was targeted not because its labor practices were any worse than those of similar firms, but because its unusually high visibility and status as a market leader made it appear vulnerable. But it has responded by adopting and implementing policies that on a number of dimensions have made it a CSR industry leader. Perhaps more important, the intense criticism to which it was subjected, and its belated though ultimately successful efforts to respond, became an example to other firms who feared becoming the focus of similar negative media attention. Nike was a catalyst in placing the issue of labor conditions in developing country suppliers on the corporate agenda in the products with which it was associated: apparel, footwear, and athletic equipment.

Voluntary Codes in the United States

The controversy surrounding Nike during the 1990s was not an isolated case. During this period, several U.S.-based organizations were established to monitor and enforce workplace standards in developing countries, primarily in the apparel and footwear sectors, as a response to growing public scrutiny of corporate labor practices. Among the most important are Social Accountability International (SAI), created by the Council on Economic Priorities, a prominent NGO; the Fair Labor Association (FLA), which developed out of a Clinton administration task force; and the Worker Rights Consortium (WRC), which was created by student activists. In addition, a number of toy manufacturers and retailers jointly developed a voluntary code governing working conditions among their suppliers. Each code and organization operates in a distinctive manner.

Social Accountability International

SA8000 is a voluntary code governing labor standards for contractors and was developed in 1996 by a group of nineteen companies and organizations, including Reebok, the Body Shop, Toys "R" Us, Timberland, Dole Food Products, Otto Versand (Germany), Franklin Research and Development (a family of SRI mutual funds), Amnesty International, and the International Textile Workers Association. It is governed by an advisory board of firms, international unions, and NGOs.[28] Its corporate members represent more than $100 billion in revenues. Though not formally associated with SAI, AVE, the foreign trade association of German retailers, conducts SA8000 diagnostic audits on 2,500 suppliers in developing countries and provides a list of SA8000-certified facilities to its members. Many of Chiquita's operations in Central America are also SA certified.[29]

SA8000 is based on International Labor Organization standards but goes beyond them in requiring a "living wage"—which it has defined— and the facilitation of "parallel means of association and bargaining."[30] The latter language was aimed at China, which legally restricts the formation of independent unions. SA8000 also mandates a minimum working age of 15 and school attendance for young workers, as well as a safe and healthy working environment. SAI conducts extensive training sessions on health, safety, and workers' rights for both factory owners and workers as part of its audit process. It also requires that accredited firms develop management systems to ensure ongoing compliance with SAI standards. While some multinational firms provide training and technical assistance to suppliers, the costs of an SA8000 audit and related improvements are borne by the firms seeking certification. However, once a firm is certified, it is then in a position to do business with any Western firm that places a value on this standard or its requirements. All certified factories are audited twice a year. By August 2004, 4,430 facilities in forty countries and forty-three industrial sectors had been certified, covering approximately 270,000 workers.

Fair Labor Association

The Fair Labor Association grew out of the Apparel Industry Partnership convened by the Clinton administration in 1996 as a response to allegations of sweatshop conditions both in the United States and overseas. It originally focused on the apparel and footwear industries, but has expanded to cover other sectors producing university-logo goods. By 2003 it had ten corporate participants, representing many of the most highly visible American brands, including Eddie Bauer, Liz Claiborne, Nike, Nordstrom, Patagonia, Phillips–Van Heusen, and Reebok. The FLA also has about 170 university affiliates.

The FLA was initially criticized by unions, students, and NGOs for being overly controlled by the firms that belonged to it. In April 2002 the FLA board responded to these criticisms by increasing its own control over external monitoring. The FLA staff now selects factories for evaluation, requires that visits be unannounced, and receives all audit reports directly. Once 30 percent of its contractors have been independently monitored by FLA-accredited monitors, a firm can use the FLA service mark in its advertising, in its stores, or on its products, though few have actually done so.

Companies associated with the FLA have been urged to make public the results of their audits in order to assure activists and consumers that they are making progress in improving labor conditions. Otherwise they are essentially asking their critics to trust them, which few are prepared to do. In 2003 some companies, including Adidas, Gap Inc., Levi Strauss, and Liz Claiborne, placed audits of the overseas factories that produce their products on the FLA website. This move has in turn put pressure on other firms that have not, such as Wal-Mart and Walt Disney. According to Michael Posner, an FLA founder, putting these reports in the public domain gives companies an incentive to remedy the problems and "is an important first step in improving the ability of workers, advocates and the public to hold global corporations to their legal and moral obligations to protect the rights of workers."[31] Making public the location of specific factories, as Nike did in 2005, also facilitates the ability of local and international NGOs to conduct their own inspections—in effect to audit the auditors.

The Worker Rights Consortium

The WRC was developed in 1999 by a campus-based organization, the United Students Against Sweatshops, in cooperation with the AFL-CIO and several human rights and religious NGOs, in part as a reaction to the FLA, which they regarded as too industry dominated. By November 2002, 108 colleges and university were members. WRC relies on its network of local NGOs and activists, as well as its affiliated universities and labor and human rights experts, to investigate complaints and attempt to remediate them. According to its executive director, its compliance strategy relies on the fear of negative publicity to "create a permanent incentive for multinationals to upgrade their working conditions." He adds, "Spot investigations force each licensee to recognize that any plants located around the world can bring negative exposure at any time."[32] Its scope however is limited to those factories producing university-brand clothing, which represent a small portion of total textile imports.[33]

Production Codes in the Other Industries

Additional codes have emerged to govern the production of particular products, such as soccer balls and toys. China is the largest toy exporter to the United States, accounting for 70 percent of American imports.[34] Faced with public pressures, a number of American companies, including Mattel, Hasbro (the world's second largest toy producer and maker of Playskool toys and Parker Brothers games), Wal-Mart Stores (the largest toy retailer in the world), Toys "R" Us, Walt Disney, and McDonald's, developed workplace standards covering child and prison labor, payroll accounting systems, maternity leave, working conditions, limits on over-time hours, freedom of association, and the right to organize. In 1997 the International Council of Toy Industries approved a Code of Business Prac-tices that prohibited underage, forced, or prison labor; required compli-ance with legal maximum working hours per week, wages, and overtime pay; and addressed health and safety issues. Five years later the Toy Indus-try Association of America and the Toy Industries of Europe established a worldwide auditing process to implement and monitor compliance, though at this writing it had not been fully implemented.[35]

Voluntary Codes in Europe

In Europe one important program is the Ethical Trading Initiative (ETI), which was developed at the initiative of the British government in 1998. It is an alliance of companies, NGOs, and trade unions that seek to iden-tify and disseminate information about how to improve labor conditions in factories and farms in developing countries. ETI has approximately thirty-five corporate members based in Britain, including Sainsbury, Marks & Spencer, Safeway Stores UK, Tesco, the Body Shop International, and WH Smith.[36] In contrast to the four principal American labor codes, ETI seeks to improve working conditions for agricultural as well as industrial workers.

ETI works with its corporate members to investigate, propose, and urge improvements in working conditions. It has undertaken pilot projects to determine how best to monitor and enforce its base code in specific sectors, including clothing in China, wine in South Africa, horticulture in Zimbabwe and Zambia, and bananas in Costa Rica.[37] While not formally an accreditation scheme, firms that participate in it can claim an "ethical mantle" for their entire company, even though only a portion of the goods they sell are produced according to ETI standards. Membership renewal is denied to firms that fail to demonstrate compliance.

Other European Industry Standards

The Clean Clothes Campaign began in the Netherlands in the early 1990s and now involves retailers and unions in ten European countries.[38] Its goal is to get retailers to use their purchasing power to improve labor conditions in their suppliers by raising public awareness of specific abuses and then urging the public to communicate with the companies responsible for them, often by sending postcards.[39] Swedish activists have targeted the labor practices of H&M, "their country's hippest—and therefore most vulnerable retailer," and in 1998 Clean Clothes organized a "people's court" that attacked the European clothing retailer C&A for allowing a Zimbabwe supplier to suppress unions.[40] Twelve major French retailers associated with the Fédération des Entreprises du Commerce et de la Distribution have established a process for sharing factory audit results through a database that all participating companies can access. In 1996 the Fédération International de Football Association established a system for certifying that manufacturers and their contractors adhered to a code of conduct based on the core ILO convention.[41]

European Company Codes

Some major European retailers have established their own codes, standards, and auditing systems. Eager to avoid the kind of public campaign conducted against Nike in 1999, Carrefour, a French firm that is the second largest retailer in the world and the largest in Europe, began auditing its suppliers.[42] By April 2003 it had conducted audits in seven countries, involving 214,000 employees, primarily in the textile, footwear, and food sectors, representing about 15 percent of its imported products.[43] Other major European retailers that have established programs for evaluating and auditing supplier social performance include Marks & Spencer, Ikea, Leclerc, Monoprix, C&A, Casino, H&M, and Galeries Lafayette. In 1999, Adidas-Solomon joined the FLA after a German television station reported widespread labor abuses at a factory producing its products in El Salvador.[44]

In 2000, Ikea, the large Swedish home-furnishings retailer, responded to child labor critics by launching its India carpet project.[45] The company pays between 20 and 50 rupees a month into "self-help" groups, which enable lower-caste women to purchase their own handlooms. This in turn enables the women to borrow at market rates, rather than from usurious moneylenders who often demand the labor of their children as collateral. The children are then able to attend schools that Ikea has helped establish. The project covers roughly 1.5 million people in 650 villages. While the company aspires not to sell rugs made by children, it makes no claim to be able to monitor all the roughly 175,000 looms in India's "carpet belt," which account for 85 percent of the country's carpet exports. Other rug importers, such as the Swiss company Veillon, have imposed restrictions on the use of child labor in their products.[46]

Voluntary Codes in Agriculture

Codes of conduct are most common in manufacturing, but the majority of the labor force in many developing countries is employed in agriculture. Agricultural workers are often among the most impoverished and constitute the sector of the economy in which the majority of children are employed. Coffee and cocoa production have become the focus of substantial CSR initiatives.

Codes in the Coffee Industry

With the breakdown of the international coffee cartel in 1989, global production grew and the inflation-adjusted price of coffee beans declined 75 percent after 1990, and reached its lowest level in a century in the early 2000s. For some beans, world market prices are lower than the cost of production.[47] This has led to substantial pressure on coffee importers to use their considerable market leverage—half the world's coffee exports go to the United States, France, and Japan—to directly intervene in world coffee markets in order to ameliorate some of the economic hardships experienced by coffee growers and those they employ. In response,

Starbucks, the world's largest coffee retailer, has established a set of guidelines for its coffee suppliers known as CAFE (Coffee and Farmer Equity). These cover product quality, financial transparency, social responsibility, and environmental leadership in coffee growing and processing. Starbucks is also collaborating with Conservation International to trace the flow of money to ensure that producers are fairly compensated and to encourage sustainable growing practices.

In September 2004, Nestlé, Sara Lee, Kraft Foods, and Tchibo, four of the world's largest coffee companies, announced a plan to improve working conditions and environmental standards throughout the industry. Their Common Code for the Coffee Community resulted from eighteen months of negotiations from a program funded by the German government and the German coffee industry and was motivated by pressures from Oxfam and European retailers. Producers and trading companies adopting the code agreed to pay minimum wages, stop using child labor, allow trade union membership, and adopt international standards for pesticides and water pollution. The agreement will apply to coffee producers from Brazil, Central America, and Africa. The code, which will be enforced by independent auditors and evaluated regularly, was also signed by several NGOs, including Oxfam International, Greenpeace, and the International Union of Foodworkers. Dieter Overath, head of Transfair, Germany's leading fair trade organization, welcomed the initiative, which could eventually affect a substantial number of the 25 million people who are involved in coffee production in seventy developing countries, but cautioned that its implementation would require the industry to substantially raise the prices paid to coffee producers.[48]

Codes in the Cocoa Industry

While coffee production takes place in scores of counties, cocoa production is more geographically concentrated, with one country, the Ivory Coast, supplying more than 40 percent of the global market. North America and western Europe purchase two-thirds of global cocoa production, with two firms, Mars and Hershey, accounting for two-thirds of the U.S. $13 billion chocolate market. Cocoa producers in the Ivory Coast use children extensively, many of whom come from Mali, Burkina Faso, and Togo and were sold as indentured servants to Ivory Coast plantations. According to UNICEF, an estimated 200,000 children are trafficked through West and Central Africa each year, many of whom work in slave-like conditions.[49] The International Institute of Tropical Agriculture reported that approximately 130,000 children were involved in hazardous labor on Ivorian farms. Although more than 625,000 children work in some capacity, the industry claims that many work with their parents on family farms.[50]

Reports of child slavery in the production of cocoa first surfaced in the British and America media in 1998. Initially, the major American brands denied any responsibility for conditions in the cocoa fields, arguing either that they were unaware of any problems or that the supply chain was too complex for them to monitor labor practices on cocoa farms, many of which are small and family owned. According to Robert Reese, senior vice president of Hershey Foods, "[No] one, repeat no one, had ever heard of this. Your instinct is that Hershey should have known. But the fact is that we didn't know." But following a threatened consumer chocolate boycott, as well as the possibility of trade sanctions from the United States, major chocolate companies, including Nestlé, Hershey, Mars, and Cadbury Schweppes, publicly condemned the practice of forced child labor. In 2002 each of the world's major cocoa brands and processors, along with the International Cocoa Organization and two European trade associations, endorsed a Cocoa Industry Protocol. The protocol requires that by July 2005 the industry develop "a credible, mutually acceptable system of industry-wide global standards, along with independent monitoring and reporting, to identify and eliminate any use of the worst forms of child labor in the growing and processing of cocoa beans."[51] However, its implementation has been impeded by the outbreak of civil war in the Ivory Coast.

The Challenges of Compliance

Setting up effective compliance monitoring is a key challenge. An OECD survey of the garment industry estimates that two-thirds of the corporate and industry codes make no mention of monitoring systems.[52] And even for those that do, enforcement presents a number of challenges. The most obvious problem is the large number of contractors, especially in the garment industry, "where sourcing networks may involve tens of thousands of factories spread across dozens of countries, and a range of buying agents, suppliers and subcontractors." For example, Disney sources its products from more than 30,000 factories and Wal-Mart from an estimated 50,000 to 100,000. Even the much smaller Gap has 3,000 contractors. A Hong Kong–based garment supplier to major European and American brands sources production in almost forty countries, with scores of factories participating in the production of a single product. When the European clothing retailer C&A began its monitoring system, it took the firm four years just to identify the factories that were producing its clothes.[53] And this inventory excluded the agricultural sector that supplies the raw materials to its products, a dimension of production that is beyond the scope of virtually every manufacturing code.

It is not uncommon for some of the most hazardous jobs to be shifted further down the supply chain or into the informal sector to avoid international scrutiny.[54] Auditing is an even more serious problem in agriculture, where again there are literally tens of thousands of producers. For example, Cadbury Schweppes, the British food-and-beverage company, has made a commitment to improve labor standards in its supply chain. But this includes roughly 40,000 producers. Many are small farmers whose products pass through multiple layers of middlemen before they reach Cadbury Schweppes.[55]

Factory audits are typically based on written policies, on-site interviews with managers or workers, and the appearance of the factory during inspections. Yet such visits provide only a snapshot of factory practices, which may be misleading, especially when factories are notified of upcoming inspections. At least one former-employee-turned-labor-organizer has called the inspection system ineffective because "the factories are usually notified in advance and they often prepare by cleaning up, creating fake time sheets and briefing workers on what to say."[56] Such efforts at deception often succeed because most companies and organizations have limited resources to devote to inspections. SAI's annual audits usually last only a day. FLA audits are more extensive. In 2003 they averaged 9.6 staff days per visit. But because of the large number of firms that manufacture products for its corporate members, this represented only 5 percent of each company's applicable factory base in high-risk regions.

Questions have also been raised about the quality of audits produced by large commercial firms such as Ernst & Young, KPMG, and PricewaterhouseCoopers. Research by Berkeley scholar Dara O'Rourke, who reexamined a number of commercial audits of factories, found that they often missed significant violations, in part because they relied on information supplied by managers rather than by the workers themselves.[57] In response to scandals over their audits of financial statements, some commercial firms have left the social auditing business, and auditing is now frequently conducted by nonprofit organizations. For example, Verité, a nonprofit group based in Massachusetts that employs a global network of auditors, has signed contracts with several firms, including Timberland, Reebok, and Eileen Fisher, to audit the factories supplying their products.

Activists push companies to allow independent audits, but only a few have done so, including Nike, Liz Claiborne, Mattel, and C&A. Some local activist organizations such as the Asia Monitor Resources Center (AMRC) conduct their own audits, interviewing workers or former employees on street corners outside factories in China. A 1998 AMRC audit led Disney to terminate its contract with the Guo Nian Garment factory after it was accused of widespread abuses. SA8000 decertified one shoe factory in China after investigations by the Christian Industrial Committee, and another after investigators from the National Labor Committee found dormitory rooms packed with up to twenty-eight people and employees working twelve-hour shifts. According to SAI's executive director, audits by public certification programs can be triggered by anyone with evidence of noncompliance.[58]

The Burdens of Monitoring

An equally serious problem has to do with long-term sustainability of the codes and monitoring systems established by Western firms. The costs of maintaining effective auditing systems and inspections are high, with thousands of inspectors employed directly or indirectly by branded companies. For example, Disney has carried out 10,000 inspections, while Mattel, which has established an independent monitoring system that is considered a model, employs sixty auditors directly and several times that number of independent auditors on contract.[59] In 1998 Pricewaterhouse-Coopers conducted 1,500 audits in only one province in China. Gap Inc. spends $10,000 a year for independent monitors at just one factory in El Salvador, in addition to management time for dispute resolution.[60] Presumably, in light of the risks to their reputations from credible accusations that their labor practices are irresponsible, these companies consider such expenditures to be worthwhile.

But it is unclear how many additional resources firms are prepared to commit to monitoring and inspection programs. For example, replicating Gap Inc.'s monitoring in El Salvador throughout its supply chain would cost 4.5 percent of the company's total profits in the year 2000, an expenditure that the firm is unable or unwilling to make.[61] One reason that many auditors who monitor compliance for the FLA do not talk to workers off-site, even though this is considered the best way to uncover abuses, is that it is too expensive.[62] According to a World Bank study, "buyers . . . generally acknowledged that the costs of monitoring are becoming increasingly high and in the long run are not sustainable. This is especially true as some buyers have started to look beyond the first tier of suppliers, opening up the possibility of monitoring many more suppliers."[63] It concluded that "while the present system of implementation has resulted in some improvements, some of them substantial, it possibly has reached its limits, and may not be in a position to bring about further real and sustainable improvements in social and environmental workplace standards in developing countries."[64]

The Challenge of Responding to Violations

Public relations and corporate responsibility can sometimes conflict when a company wants to respond to evidence that its standards are being violated. On one hand, a company that does not terminate its contracts with a firm found to be violating a standard may find itself attacked by NGOs and by the press at home. On the other hand, a termination decision may impose considerable hardship on the factory's employees. In each case, therefore, a company must weigh the seriousness of the violations, how long they have persisted, and how remediable they are—as well as the likely public reaction and business consequences.

On occasion, workers themselves have challenged contract termination decisions. In 2002, faced with accusations that a factory in Bangladesh producing Winnie the Pooh shirts paid its employees 14 cents an hour and provided no vacations, holidays, or sick days, a Walt Disney licensee terminated its contract. Some of those workers then came to the United States to plead with American firms to save their jobs by working to improve the plants.[65]

The Costs of Compliance

A more fundamental constraint is the monetary cost of compliance. It is not coincidental that most of the reported progress, namely on age restrictions and health and safety conditions, is the least expensive to ameliorate, while much less progress has been made in addressing the more costly problems of compensation and overtime limitations. Since companies are unable to charge higher prices for sweatshop-free clothes or toys, the costs of compliance would eat into their profits.[66] Surveys of American consumers report that they would be willing to pay, on average, 28 percent more on a $10 item and 15 percent more on a $100 item for products made under "good" working conditions. One detailed analysis of consumer prices and labor costs for several garments concludes that if these increased payments were passed on to the assembly workers in developing countries, it would then be possible to double their average wages.[67]

But evidently Western firms do not believe consumers would actually be willing to pay more for more responsibly manufactured products, especially if comparable goods are readily available. And their skepticism is well founded. In a few instances, consumers have reduced, or have made credible threats to reduce, their purchases of goods produced by companies with irresponsible labor practices. But with the notable exception of the U.S. college logo apparel market, which is relatively small, there is little evidence that consumers are willing to increase their purchases from firms with more responsible labor practices, let alone pay more for their products. This in turn limits the additional resources firms can devote to improving labor standards in their suppliers.

As discussed in the Nike case, activists attack firms that are vulnerable to public pressure, not solely because they are less responsible. As a result, the pressures firms face to improve their labor practices vary considerably, but to the extent that shaming strategies are effective, targeted firms are at a competitive disadvantage. They have to spend more resources on monitoring and compliance than their less visible competitors in order to avoid a consumer backlash. And they are then forced to compete with the less costly products made by their less vulnerable competitors.

Consumers may want companies to act responsibly—and may threaten their reputation and brands if they do not—but they also want to pay as little as possible for clothing, footwear, athletic equipment and toys, as the commercial success of Wal-Mart demonstrates. The markets for most of the products manufactured for or sold by the firms that activists target are highly competitive; companies that make premium brands may not compete on price, but prices certainly affect consumer purchasing decisions.

In fact, the prices of athletic footwear and apparel have been declining to meet consumer demand and pressure from sportswear retailers such as Foot Locker and Intersport. Between 1997 and 2002–03 the average price for a pair of athletic shoes in the United States declined about 12.5 percent, and between 1998 and 2003 the average price of a pair of sneakers declined 23 percent.[68] In this context, it is worth recalling that Nike's original decision to outsource all its production to developing countries was due to cost considerations, while an important reason for the decline in Levi Strauss's sales of jeans was its unwillingness to lower its prices to compete with generic brands.

As U.S. and European firms face pressures to behave more virtuously, they are simultaneously experiencing increasing competition from a growing number of Asian firms based in China, Korea, and Taiwan. At the same time, Western firms increasingly produce for a worldwide market, including many countries where public pressure to act more responsibly is typically low, as in Japan.[69] Yet Western firms are under public pressure to source their products sold worldwide from the same responsible suppliers that they use to produce goods for sale in the more socially conscious markets of the United States and Europe.

To keep their costs as low as possible, those firms have sought to place the financial burden for more responsible labor practices on developing country suppliers. Other than technical aid, Western firms provide little or no financial assistance to suppliers to meet their standards. Under one code, SA8000, the cost of certification is borne by the factory being audited. The conflicting signals Western buyers send their suppliers is an important reason for the limited effectiveness of many labor codes. On one hand, public pressure to act more responsibly has forced Western firms to demand that their suppliers treat their workers better. On the other hand, pressure from investors and consumers requires them to find suppliers who can produce as cheaply as possible. If suppliers are discovered to not be in compliance, they risk losing their contracts. But if they are in compliance, they are just as likely to lose their contract to a lower-cost producer. One supplier told Oxfam, "I spent three years getting up to compliance with the SA8000 standard, and then the customer who had asked for it in the first place left and went to China."[70]

While some Western firms have developed long-term relationships with suppliers, they are exceptional. More typically, purchasing agents play suppliers against one another, especially in the apparel sector, where switching suppliers is relatively costless. All suppliers must then cut their prices, which in turn makes it more difficult for them to treat their workers responsibly. Thus the price paid for T-shirts produced for a well-known sports brand declined from $3.70 per dozen in 2000 to $2.85 per dozen in 2003, and a factory in Sri Lanka that supplies to Nike reported a 35 percent reduction in unit prices paid during a more recent eighteen-month period.[71] In China average garment export prices declined 30 percent between 1997 and 2002.[72] In 1996 J. C. Penney paid its overseas supplier $5.00 for the same two-piece toddler's outfit it had purchased for $5.75 four years earlier. A worker in an Indonesian factory told Oxfam, "The manager in our division often uses [this fall in unit prices] as a reason why our standard monthly wages can't be increased."[73] These cost pressures are likely to increase with the relaxation of textile trade restrictions in 2005 under the Uruguay Round WTO agreement.

In the view of many contractors, compliance does not produce more committed buyers or any additional business, though certification is critical to the ability of a firm to secure a foreign contract in the first place.[74] There is some anecdotal evidence that meeting certification standards can improve efficiency and reduce worker turnover: according to a Nike official, "The factory managers are telling us that as they increase their work around social responsibility, they are seeing [financial] improvements."[75] But this remains a minority point of view. It seems inevitable that higher labor standards will increase production costs, and many suppliers believe that addressing CSR issues makes them less competitive.[76] According to one study, "The majority of apparel suppliers in Honduras and China rejected the idea that CSR implementation would produce any business benefits," though some Indian suppliers have taken a more balanced view, noting that "selected aspects of CSR practices, most notably health and safety practices, held the potential for business benefit."[77]

In short, for suppliers, the business case for CSR is problematic. Behaving more responsibly may help them maintain their contracts with Western firms, but it does not permit them to charge higher prices. While noncompliance may reduce their sales, compliance does not necessarily increase them. Adding to this tension is that while the costs of compliance are borne primarily by developing country producers, the benefits accrue primarily to Western firms. Not surprisingly, "Most suppliers . . . lack trust in the motives of buyers for implementing CSR standards in their supply chains," and numerous firms have simply quit seeking contracts with Western firms because the costs of meeting their standards are too high.[78]

These tensions between CSR and the dynamics of global market competition emerge with particular clarity on the issue of overtime. Changes in the nature of apparel and footwear marketing have significantly shortened production schedules. Whereas there were formerly two to four fashion "seasons" a year, now the norm is six to eight. Companies with faster and more flexible supply chains enjoy a competitive advantage because they are able to more rapidly respond to sales trends and customer feedback. Factory managers in developing countries report steadily shorter lead times. According to one factory owner in Sri Lanka, "Last year the deadlines were about 90 days. . . . [In 2004] the deadlines for delivery are about 60 days. Sometimes even 45." Another, in Morocco, notes, "Three years ago a standard order could take a month. These days there are some orders where the lorry arrives on a Tuesday, and on Saturday it's on its way back to Spain with the finished articles."[79]

Because factories that miss tight production deadlines may lose out on future contracts, they must work to boost output, which may affect working conditions, particularly overtime requirements. Workers often find themselves under substantial pressure to work harder, longer, and faster, often without additional pay. Many firms have tried to expedite delivery times by using more part-time workers, to whom they can pay lower wages and provide fewer benefits than regular employees receive. Because they are often paid on a piece basis, it is also more difficult to monitor their treatment.

How Effective Are Voluntary Codes?

What have the voluntary codes adopted by Western manufacturers and retailers accomplished? There has been little systematic analysis of most codes, but detailed information exists on current compliance with some, including those of the Fair Labor Association and Gap Inc.[80] In addition, some evidence is available on changes in the employment of children.

Progress on Child Labor

The most substantial improvements in labor practices have been made in reducing child labor, though this has primarily occurred in manufacturing plants rather than in agriculture, where 70 percent of children are employed. The effort to reduce child forced labor in the cocoa plantations and farms in West Africa has had little impact. Child labor in the production of cotton seeds in India has declined thanks to an initiative on the part of Syngenta, a Swiss agribusiness.[81] In the case of rug production, which is highly decentralized, programs such as those sponsored by

Rugmark (see below) and the codes issued by European retailers have had a discernible though modest impact.

The production of soccer balls by children (those under 14 years of age) has also been reduced in Pakistan and China. However, a University of Iowa report cautions that the soccer ball project may be atypical: "[The region's] position as the [principal] source of hand-stitched soccer balls made it easier for the international brands to commit to stay and address the issue rather than simply shift production to another market. Had there been more options for sourcing soccer balls in 1995, the industry's efforts to mobilize the entire industry . . . would have been much more difficult."[82] In addition, according to the ILO, 6,000 children were enrolled in village education and action centers funded by local and global firms.[83] These results were largely due to a combined effort on the part of the international sporting goods industry in response to a "Foul Ball" public campaign that had targeted Nike, Adidas, and Reebok.

The most change has taken place in textile and footwear manufacturing, where the employment of children younger than 14 or 15, once common, has now become relatively rare. In Honduras, for example, there are now few workers under 16. One Korean-owned factory in Honduras laid off fifty teenage girls in order to attract business from J. C. Penney.[84] According to Nike, of the more than 500,000 persons employed in its contract factory base, only 100 were found to be underage. However, restrictions on child labor are largely confined to the codes of major garment manufacturers; only thirteen of the largest Fortune Global 500 firms include child labor provisions in their codes. [85]

The employment of underage children in factories is often easy to monitor (though less so in countries where many children do not have birth certificates, such as Cambodia), and imposing age requirements often does not raise labor costs; adult workers are paid more, but are also more productive. In industries that pay by the piece, such as the soccer ball industry, substituting adults for children has no impact on costs. According to one comprehensive study, "Child labor offers very little economic benefit to multinational corporations or their global supply chains. With rare exceptions, the supply of unskilled labor is more than adequate to meet the private sector's demands.[86] By contrast, "according to ILO studies in the bangles and carpet industries, loom owners can double their small income if they use children."[87] In these sectors the employment of children remains widespread.

Eliminating Child Labor—A Double-Edged Sword

Child labor is an emotionally charged issue: consumers are clearly uncomfortable with purchasing products that may be produced by children. Media attention and public interest have given companies a powerful incentive to address this labor practice, and many have done so reasonably effectively. But the net social impact of this dimension of CSR is debatable. For many children employment in a factory supplying goods for a Western firm is often better than the alternatives, especially if schooling is unavailable. One critic of CSR writes, "If they truly wanted to be more socially responsible, corporations would complement [the elimination of child labor] by offering scholarships to vocational schools . . . or internships to provide poor kids with work experience."[88] But only a few firms, notably Ikea, Levi Strauss, H&M, and Nike, have provided schooling for underage former employees. More commonly, the enforcement of child labor restrictions in export sectors does not stop children from working. Instead it forces them into lower-paying and more dangerous occupations. Between 1993 and 1994 in Bangladesh employers who feared losing their businesses fired thousands of child workers, who had no choice but to turn to prostitution to feed themselves.[89]

In one highly publicized case, manufacturers of soccer balls in Pakistan responded to a possible loss of export markets by moving production from private homes to a manufacturing facility in order to facilitate monitoring. The result was to eliminate employment for women who were unable to work outside their homes: "Preventing women from working . . . compound(ed) the income-loss problem created by the elimination of child labor" and also "threatened to reverse recent gains in their social status."[90]

A ban on the use of child labor in agricultural production in Zambia imposed by British supermarkets affiliated with the ETI may only have reduced their access to education.[91] Moreover, some company codes, such as Nike's, stipulate a minimum age for employees higher than that established by local governments, which leaves these firms vulnerable to the accusation that they are imposing Western standards and disrespecting host-country traditions and conditions. In many low-income households, the earnings contributed by children can make the difference between destitution and "poverty" for a struggling family.[92] As the father of a Pakistani family whose children worked stitching soccer balls put it, "It is not good for children to work, but if they don't, how shall we live?"[93]

It is also worth noting that only a very small percentage of all child workers, probably less than 5 percent, were employed in export industries in the first place.[94]

Improvements in Working Conditions

Public concern has also led to some improvements in working conditions. Nike and Reebok, for example, have required many Asian factories to stop using petroleum-based adhesives in favor of water-based adhesives. Nike has pledged that all of its supplier factories worldwide will meet U.S. Occupational Health and Safety Administration standards, has reduced organic solvent content in its shoes by 95 percent, and is phasing out the use of the toxic plastic polyvinyl chloride (PVC).[95] Some improvements are expensive, such as providing industrial-quality exhaust systems or equipment for handling chemicals. Mattel has spent substantial sums to upgrade its own production facilities and those of its contract manufacturers. But improvements in health and safety conditions can often be made inexpensively. For example, in one Nike factory, illiterate workers were protected from misusing dangerous chemicals by the adoption of a color-coded labeling system.[96]

Some working conditions are relatively easy to monitor, but others are harder. In many factories "managers have stopped hitting workers, have improved ventilation and have stopped requiring workers to obtain permission before going to the toilet."[97] But abusive treatment of workers clearly continues. According to a Honduran apparel worker, at a factory supplying the Sean John fashion company that produces garments for the hip-hop artist Sean Combs, "Employees were ordered not to talk during work hours, needed passes to go to the bathroom. . . . Managers often ordered female workers to take pregnancy tests . . . and if they were pregnant, they were immediately fired to help the company save on medical expenses and maternity leave."[98] At a factory producing for Levi Strauss in Thailand, inspectors found "dirty toilets, improperly stored chemical tanks, no drinking water in the dining facility," and at a plant producing goods for Liz Claiborne, workers are fined for talking on the job.[99]

Little Change in Compensation and Overtime

The issue of compensation lies at the heart of the moral case against Western companies. Critics of Nike, for example, frequently contrast the dollar or two a day paid to workers producing its sneakers with the multi-million-dollar endorsement fees paid to Michael Jordan. (One magazine article speculated that it would take an Indonesian worker 44,492 years to make the equivalent of Jordan's endorsement contract.)[100] Activists have repeatedly demanded that workers be paid a "living wage." However, only the SAI industry code requires payment of a "basic wage." Industry and company codes typically require that wages be paid at either the local industry prevailing wage or the local government-required minimum wage.[101] Many firms argue that higher compensation would distort local labor markets and create a "labor aristocracy" of employees lucky enough to work for companies that export branded goods to the United States and Europe. There is also debate about the extent to which these workers are actually exploited, as the wages paid in these factories are higher than those offered by alternative sources of employment.[102] The concept of a living wage is also ambiguous since not all factory workers are primary breadwinners for their families. In any event, only a few firms have committed themselves to paying a living wage, or even wages based on productivity gains and local living costs, though some, such as Levi Strauss, provide nonwage benefits such as medical services.

Arguably a more important problem is that many workers do not receive the wages to which they are contractually entitled. Many suppliers keep two sets of books and "coach" employees how to respond to the questions of inspectors. Some suppliers have lost contracts when evidence revealed that they cheated their workers or falsified pay stubs. However, not only are wages hard to monitor, but unlike banning child labor and improving working conditions, increasing workers' wages increases costs. Compliance with working hours is also hard to monitor because records can easily be falsified. And restrictions on working hours may interfere with contractors' ability to meet delivery deadlines. The social impact of overtime restrictions is also problematic. Some workers want to work longer hours than allowed by worker-protection codes, especially single women who are working to save money for a dowry or to send to their families.

Challenges in Promoting Freedom of Association

Freedom of association is included in some but not most corporate and industry codes. The paucity of independent unions is clearly critical:

if workers were able to effectively organize, the implementation of work-place standards would be self-enforcing and pressures for improvements by Western firms and activists would become less necessary. But in some countries, such as China, independent unions are illegal, and in others workers' efforts to organize have encountered domestic political and social opposition. However, thanks to pressure from Western firms and changes in local government policies, the number of workers covered by unions has increased in both Honduras and Indonesia.

In April 2004, Gap Inc. signed a contract with the first clothing export plant in El Salvador to operate with a fully independent union, an arrangement that has been hailed as a "breakthrough in the controversy over garment-factory conditions," with important ramifications for other workers.[103] Using their leverage over university purchases of apparel and sporting goods with university logos, the Worker Rights Consortium has had some notable accomplishments in this area. One of the first involved a garment factory in Puebla, Mexico, including "improvements in factory conditions and pay, . . . the formation of an independent union, and the signing of a collective bargaining agreement," one of the first in a Mexican maquiladora.[104] Another WRC investigation led to an agreement to recognize multiple unions in a factory in Indonesia.

In 2003 the WRC played a critical role in compelling a factory employing 1,600 people in the Dominican Republic to negotiate a labor contract. The result is the largest unionized plant in the region, with a contract that provides for increased wages, scholarships, and other benefits "that are unheard of among the country's 500 foreign-owned plants." According to a local labor official, "I never thought a group of students, thousands of them, could put so much pressure on these brands. We were determined to win, but without them it would have taken five more years. And it would have been more traumatic without them because all we would have had was the pressure to strike."[105]

But such campaigns require substantial resources, and such achievements are unfortunately atypical. Some unionized plants have not been able to retain their contracts with Western firms. Reports of workers being fired or disciplined for seeking to form or join unions remain common. On balance, progress in this area has been extremely limited. It is also an area in which there has been relatively less public focus in the United States and which many Western firms, such as Wal-Mart, do not support because their domestic employees are not unionized.

Social Labeling: An Alternative Approach to Improving Labor Conditions

Voluntary codes suffer from the lack of a strong connection in most consumers' minds between a company's labor standards and the products it sells. Most consumers are unaware of most corporate labor practices, except those that have attracted negative publicity. And they have little basis on which to judge firms who claim that their labor practices have improved. Social labels seek to address both problems by creating a new brand that explicitly associates progressive practices with certain products. Social labels often, though not always, rely on consumers' willingness to pay more for what they see as more ethically produced products. Therefore, although they may have a greater impact on individual producers, their reach—the number of workers they affect—is relatively limited.

Rugmark

One of the most successful social labels is in the carpet industry, where child labor has become a highly salient issue in Europe. Approximately 300,000 children work on looms making carpets in India, often with little or no pay and in hazardous physical environments. In 1990, German activists organized a public campaign against the use of child labor to make carpets. The campaign was highly effective: sales of hand-knotted carpets in Germany declined from $229 million in 1983 to $152 million a decade later. Pakistan lost $10 million in canceled orders from big European carpet importers of hand-knotted rugs.[106] In 1994 a group of German rug importers and Indian labor activists launched Rugmark, a "human rights" label.[107] The primary purpose of the Rugmark Foundation is to replace child labor with adult labor and provide educational opportunities for child workers. Signatories pay a licensing fee to the foundation, in exchange for which they are allowed to affix the Rugmark label, which signals that no children were involved in the making of rugs.

The fees collected from both certified local producers and importers pay for inspections and for schooling the children who formerly worked the looms making rugs, many of whom had been "sold" in debt-bondage to local manufacturers by their impoverished parents. More than 3,000 children in India, Nepal, and Pakistan have benefited from Rugmark's education and rehabilitation programs, and its inspection system is regarded as relatively effective, with inspectors traveling on motorbikes to make surprise visits to production sites.

Eager to avoid future consumer boycotts, 452 manufacturers representing two-thirds of Nepal's carpet exports are now certified by Rugmark, as are 15 percent of registered carpet exporters in India. Since 1995 more than 3 million carpets carrying the Rugmark label have been exported from Nepal, India, and Pakistan to Europe and North America. Rugmark-labeled rugs are distributed by major German retailers, including Karstadt and Hertie, as well as by Otto Versand, the country's second largest mail-order company.[108] Rugmark's market penetration has been significantly greater in Germany than in the United States. While approximately 20 percent of the carpets imported to Germany from India bear the Rugmark label, only 1 percent of the carpets shipped from India to the United States are so labeled, though 9 percent of the carpets exported to the United States from Nepal have been certified. Rugmark-labeled rugs are currently sold in approximately 300 stores in the United States.[109]

Fair Trade Coffee

Fair Trade is probably the best-known social label.[110] Among the products marketed under this umbrella are bananas, cocoa, tea, toys, flowers, oranges, nuts, chocolate, sugar, crafts, and jewelry. But Fair Trade labeling has focused primarily on coffee, an $80 billion industry and the second most widely internationally traded commodity. In 1988 a Fair Trade Seal was offered to mainstream coffee companies in the Netherlands that were willing to purchase some of their coffee on Fair Trade terms. Within a relatively short period of time, Fair Trade labeling had become a viable marketing concept in a number of countries. In 1997 seventeen Fair Trade certification programs in Europe, North America, and Japan established an international consortium, the Fairtrade Labeling Organization International.

For coffee to be certified as Fair Trade it must be purchased directly from farm co-operatives, the co-operatives must be guaranteed a floor price, and farmers must be offered credit by importers. While the primary purpose of Fair Trade is to increase the income of small coffee farmers, it also encourages them to adopt better environmental practices. Fair Trade has been more successful in Europe than in the United States. In 2002, Fair Trade certified beans accounted for 3 percent of coffee sales in the Netherlands, Luxembourg, and Switzerland, and 12 percent of the British roast and ground coffee market, but only 0.2 percent of the total American market.[111] Cafedirect, a leading FT brand in which Oxfam has an equity stake, now ranks sixth in the U.K. coffee market. Sourcing from seven countries, it sold 162 million cups of coffee in its first two years, affecting 460,000 growers to whom it paid a guaranteed price of 10 percent over the market rate. All told, 35,000 firms in Europe sell FT coffee. The relative success of FT in Europe is due to several factors, including a richer history of political mobilization around food purchasing, Fair Trade's links to social democratic, green, and labor political parties, and the financial support provided by Belgium, Denmark, France, the Netherlands, Switzerland, and more recently the EU. The employee cafes at the European Parliament and most national European parliaments sell only Fair Trade coffee.

In the United States, Fair Trade has encouraged religious organizations, colleges and universities, and local governments to sell its products, and several have agreed to do so. In 1999, Global Exchange asked Starbucks, which buys about 1 percent of the world's coffee, to buy FT beans, hoping to take advantage of both Starbucks's visibility and its reputation for social responsibility stemming from its relatively progressive domestic employee policies. The company initially refused, citing concerns about quality, which was critical to its brand and competitive position. It was also uncomfortable with the idea of labeling some of its coffee Fair Trade, because that would imply that the rest of its coffee was irresponsibly sourced. Company executives also deeply resented accusations that they did not care about the welfare of their growers. In fact, because Starbucks purchases only premium coffee, it was already paying its suppliers an average of only 6 cents a pound less than the minimum price set by Fair Trade, as well as a price premium for shade-grown coffee.[112]

Nonetheless, following a series of protests and demonstrations in front of the company's stores, in 2000 Starbucks agreed to sell Fair Trade coffee in its retail outlets as well as to feature it once a month as its brewed coffee. Starbucks is now the largest roaster and retailer of certified Fair Trade coffee in the United States, having increased its purchases from 653,000 pounds in 2001 and to more than 2 million pounds in 2004. Many Starbucks stores feature information about Fair Trade coffee, and the company sells FT-certified coffee in twenty-three countries, representing about 1.6 percent of the company's purchases. However, many Fair Trade–certified co-operatives do not have the volume or consistency of coffee quality that Starbucks requires, and Starbucks's large suppliers are precluded from FT certification because they are not co-operatives.

In September 2003 Procter & Gamble announced that it would sell FT coffee through its Millstone label, a move that could increase FT sales in the United States by between 2 and 3 million pounds annually. At Wild Oats, a health food chain, all coffee sold is FT, and in 2004 Dunkin' Donuts announced that the coffee used in its new line of espresso drinks would be FT. Sara Lee also now sells some FT coffee. In the United States, 140 companies now sell FT coffee through an estimated 10,000 retail outlets. This has increased the market share of FT coffee. In 2004 between 4 and 6 percent of premium coffee was FT certified. This represents slightly less than 1 percent of total American coffee consumption.[113]

The Impact of Fair Trade

Fair Trade coffee exhibits both the strengths and weaknesses of the market for virtue. It empowers consumers to put "their money where their values are."[114] By developing its own brand, Fair Trade enables consumers of premium coffee to directly contribute to the economic and social welfare of coffee growers by paying them more for their products. In 2003 nearly 200 coffee co-operatives representing 675,000 farmers were producing FT coffee; the FT minimum price for coffee was $1.26 a pound, while raw Arabica beans sold for about 82 cents a pound on the world market.[115] At the Oromiya Coffee Farmers Co-operative Union in Ethiopia, farmers receive 70 percent of the export price for coffee that sells as FT, while Ethiopian producers selling coffee in the open market receive only 30 percent.[116] According to Transfair, 5.6 million dollars in additional revenues to farmers were generated by Fair Trade sales in the United States in 2001, and certification has increased the income of more than half a million coffee farmers.[117] In 2004 a British retailer, Cafedirect, paid a £2.4 million premium over the world market price to its suppliers. While the increase in per capita income to coffee producers is modest, the price premium paid by FT can represent the difference between destitution and survival. It has also given some farmers the resources to upgrade production. FT-produced coffee also has a less damaging environmental impact as the majority of it is shade grown, which promotes biodiversity.

FT certification represents an important advantage over corporate and industry labor codes in that the ties between Western consumers and developing country producers are more direct and presumably more credible to consumers. According to Pablo Dubois, head of operations for the

International Coffee Organization, "In coffee, the Fair Trade movement has clearly shown that producers can be paid double today's disastrously low prices without affecting the consumer's willingness to purchase a good-quality product."[118] However, while industry and corporate codes can use the considerable leverage of major Western manufacturers to impose their standards of social responsibility on developing country suppliers, the impact of FT's "business model" is limited by its sales, which while growing, remain modest, especially in the United States. Although FT coffee sales have doubled each year since 2001, they still represent only .4 percent of global coffee purchases.

The primary challenge FT faces in expanding its share of the specialty coffee market is not price, but taste. FT coffee is more expensive than non-premium coffee, but is roughly comparable in price to other specialty coffees. FT coffee struggles for market share because consumers choose premium coffee primarily on the basis of taste, quality, and freshness. Some consumers prefer Fair Trade coffee; many more prefer other kinds. For most consumers, "quality" trumps "doing the right thing."[119] In fact, the makers of Cafedirect changed the product's name after market research showed that consumers were "more concerned with taste than helping Third World producers."[120] FT also does not address the poor wages and working conditions of workers on coffee plantations, because co-operatives usually do not employ workers. Perhaps most important, FT cannot effectively address the root problem of coffee production, which is oversupply.

Conclusion

The scope of voluntary standards is limited primarily to the manufacture of products that are sold in Europe and the United States. Among those products, CSR codes have most affected goods made or sold by firms with well-known consumer brands in a small number of industries, notably apparel, footwear, athletic equipment, rugs, and toys. The production of some other manufactured products has been affected by codes adopted by general retailers such as Wal-Mart and Carrefour. But "voluntary codes and monitoring primarily influence 'enclaves' in the global economy. They focus on workers in first-tier suppliers and often large-scale factories. They rarely affect informal-sector or home-based workers, where most developing country workers are employed."[121] Most CSR policies and programs also do not extend to generic and intermediate products or to a wide range of manufactured goods. And branded products constitute only a small portion of developing country apparel, footwear, toy, and sporting goods exports. In agriculture, CSR programs have focused on the production of coffee, and to a lesser degree on bananas and cocoa, though some other agricultural products have been affected by the voluntary standards of British and French supermarkets.[122]

In both manufacturing and agriculture, the impact of voluntary codes on labor practices has been largely affected by three factors: a firm's vulnerability, the structure of production, and the pattern of compliance monitoring. First, firms whose CSR efforts have been most extensive are those whose reputation, and thus possibly their sales, have been subject to public criticism of their labor practices. Nike, Liz Claiborne, Gap Inc., Disney, Starbucks, and Ikea were targeted by NGOs and in the media; others, such as Mattel, considered themselves vulnerable. As a consultant who helped organize Mattel's independent auditing program noted, "Even a modest boycott around Christmas would probably cost the company more than its compliance programs."[123] But this in turn means that "invisible brands, secondary goods producers, smaller multinationals, companies that are not brand-dependent, are able to slip under the radar screen. . . . [A] whole host of corporations are able to dodge censure quite easily."[124]

Second, in some sectors the larger and more diverse the base of contractors and subcontractors, the less likely monitoring is to be effective. Thus firms that source goods from factories that they own, such as Mattel, or that produce goods exclusively for them, such as sneaker manufacturers for Nike, are more likely to have effective monitoring than those that source from factories that produce goods for multiple companies. The latter is typical in apparel production, where suppliers often produce goods for several firms. Likewise, enforcing standards for the production of rugs, soccer balls, and agricultural products entails monitoring a vast number of small producers whose products pass through multiple layers of middlemen before they reach Western retailers.

Third, there is systematic variation in the pattern of compliance with specific standards. Compliance appears to have been greatest with respect to child labor and health and safety conditions, and least strong in the areas of wages, overtime restrictions, and freedom of association. Child labor and health and safety conditions are often easier to monitor, and compliance often does not significantly raise costs. By contrast, wages, overtime restrictions, and freedom of association are more difficult to monitor, and compliance usually increases production costs. It is therefore not surprising that progress in these areas has been much slower. According to one American labor official, "There are two areas where progress seems to grind to a halt: the effort to form unions and the effort to have wage increases."[125]

At the same time, more companies in more sectors are accepting responsibility for working conditions in their suppliers' facilities. In 2004, Hewlett-Packard trained forty-five auditors to carry out twenty-five audits in factories in Mexico, Thailand, Malaysia, and China and plans to conduct an additional twenty-five to fifty; it now includes social and environmental responsibility among the criteria it uses to assess supplier performance. For its part, IBM has identified five high-risk sites where it will assess working conditions, and it planned to conduct 100 site assessments by the end of 2004. Both Dupont and General Electric now monitor labor, health, environmental, and safety conditions in their suppliers' factories. Between 2002 (when its program began) and 2004, GE performed 3,100 audits.[126]

In November 2004, in response to a report entitled "Clean Up Your Computer" that criticized labor conditions in factories making computers for big-brand manufacturers, Cisco Systems, Hewlett-Packard, Microsoft, Dell, IBM, and Intel announced the formation of a supply-chain working group to implement a recently established Electronics Industry Code of Conduct. Compliance with the code, which addresses health, safety, labor, and human rights practices, will be audited.[127] Twenty European corporations, including Statoil (Norway), Danone (France), Norske-Skog (Norway), Volkswagen, and Ikea, have signed framework agreements with the international trade unions or global union federations that represent their employees in Europe. These agreements cover both a firm's own employees and those of its contractors; they are intended to "create a framework within which all workers are guaranteed established international minimum standards for work," throughout the world.[128]

These developments suggest that more firms now consider this dimension of CSR to be a business norm; even some whose labor practices have not attracted media attention now consider it appropriate to assume some responsibility for the labor conditions in the factories they own or that fabricate goods for them. However, to the extent that more responsibly made merchandise is more expensive to produce, these additional costs must be absorbed by Western firms or their foreign suppliers. To be sure, the ability of any firm to absorb additional costs depends on both the magnitude of these costs and the firm's profit margins. But in the long run, for the market for virtue to work effectively, more responsibly produced goods must enjoy some advantage in the marketplace. If they are more expensive to produce, they must be able to command higher prices or attract larger market shares. But this has rarely occurred. Accordingly, more responsible producers must compete in a highly competitive global marketplace with firms who face lower costs because they have not been targeted by activists—either because they are less visible or face fewer NGO pressures and media exposure in their home markets. And this global marketplace is becoming more rather than less competitive.

Media attention and NGO pressure on corporations to take responsibility for the labor practices of their suppliers has influenced changes in many corporate practices and policies. Without external pressures, few of the improvements described in this chapter would have occurred. From this perspective, "civil regulation" has been effective: many companies *have* become more virtuous. But as media attention to sweatshop abuses declines (as it has since 2000), companies have fewer incentives to devote additional resources to monitoring and improving labor conditions in their suppliers, especially since many have already effectively addressed what is clearly the most politically salient dimension of working conditions, namely child labor. In a sense, the "low-hanging fruit"—reducing child labor in primary suppliers—has largely been picked. The business case for continued improvements, especially if they prove costly, may be less compelling.

From the perspective of business, the adoption of codes of conduct has been effective. Reports of abuses continue to surface periodically, but the improvements companies have made or have assumed responsibility for making appear to have been sufficient to defuse or reduce most public criticism. Seen from this rather narrow perspective, the market for virtue appears to be working. The welfare of workers, consumers, and shareholders has been enhanced across the board: the working conditions of some employees have been improved on some dimensions in some sectors in some countries, Western consumers can feel more assured they are not complicit in labor abuses, and shareholders can worry less about threats to their companies' brands. This does represent an accomplishment. Unfortunately, it is far from the goal of increasingly responsible business performance driven by social market pressures that some CSR advocates envision.

CHAPTER 5

Corporate Responsibility
for the Environment

Environmental management and practices are important and highly visible components of CSR. But in contrast to labor standards, where a rough consensus has emerged about how firms in developing countries that supply Western companies should treat their employees, the standards for corporate environmental responsibility are much less clear. Notwithstanding all that has been written about "environmental sustainability," no one has been able to define or measure it satisfactorily.[1]

Environmental responsibility is complex and multidimensional. It encompasses corporate practices ranging from natural resource management and use to waste generation and disposal, recycling, the marketing of environmentally friendly products, and pollution prevention and control. The diversity of corporate environmental impacts—and of firms' efforts to ameliorate them—means that any discussion of corporate environmental responsibility must be highly selective. Moreover, whereas private labor policies primarily address business practices in developing countries, corporate environmental responsibility primarily affects business practices in developed countries, where there is either extensive government regulation or the prospect of additional state controls. This can make it difficult to distinguish between the role of corporate virtue and public policy in effecting improvements in corporate environmental performance.

Many improvements in corporate environmental practices involve the more efficient use of resources, particularly energy, or the creation of new products. Such improvements are relatively common because they may also reduce costs or create new markets. This distinguishes them from changes in working conditions in suppliers in developing countries, which usually increase costs and rarely create additional markets. And while often labeled CSR, these business decisions may represent normal business practices rather new initiatives in corporate responsibility. In any event, the line between the two is often difficult to draw.

Because some improvements in corporate environmental performance have raised costs only modestly, as in the case of forestry practices, or have proven cost-effective or even profitable, as in the case of carbon emissions reductions, many companies have embraced "beyond compliance" environmental strategies. In this sense, the market for virtue does work: many corporations have accepted greater responsibility for the environmental impact of what they produce, purchase, and sell. Nonetheless, the environmental impact of voluntary improvements in corporate environmental practices is limited by uneven corporate commitments to improving environmental performance, the small demand for greener products, and in some cases higher costs.

However, the most important shortcoming of corporate environmental responsibility is its narrow geographic scope. Although environmental problems are more serious in developing countries—with the notable exception of carbon emissions—a disproportionate amount of both NGO pressures and voluntary corporate programs have focused on improving environmental practices in developed ones. Far fewer industry or company codes govern environmental practices than labor standards in developing countries, and they tend to have fuzzier performance standards and weaker disclosure provisions. They are also harder for independent bodies to monitor.

This chapter begins by discussing one of the most prominent changes in corporate environmental practice in response to public criticism, namely Shell's decision to change its original plans to dispose of the Brent Spar oil platform. It then turns to two of the most visible contemporary environmental issues, forestry practices and global climate change. Both are the subject of considerable pressures from civil society to improve corporate performance and have led to the emergence of voluntary standards and agreements. Finally, the chapter looks at corporate environmental management and voluntary environmental standards in broader terms, seeking to assess both their accomplishments and limitations.

Shell: Facing a Storm at Sea

If public attacks on Nike's labor practices were the catalyst that broadened the scope of corporate responsibility for global labor policies, then Greenpeace's 1995 media campaign against Shell's plans to sink an obsolete oil storage platform in the North Sea played an analogous role in placing environmental responsibility on the global CSR agenda.[2] Shell had commissioned more than thirty studies to assess the technical, safety, and environmental implications of various disposal options for the 14,500 ton platform. They all recommended deep-sea disposal as the safest and most environmentally responsible alternative. Not only was sinking the platform in the ocean not expected to cause any environmental damage, but the second most feasible option, disposal on land, posed a sixfold higher risk for workers as well as the risk of onshore water pollution should the platform break up during transit.[3] In addition, land disposal would require Shell to find a deep-harbor port whose local authorities would agree to accept the environmental hazards of dismantling and recycling it. Deep-sea disposal was also more than four times less expensive than disposal on land: £11 million pounds ($17.2 million), compared to £46 million pounds ($72.2 million) thus presenting Shell with a win-win situation: the most responsible course of action was also the least costly. In February 1995, Shell received approval from the British Department of Energy to tow the platform out to sea and dispose of it 2,000 meters deep in the Atlantic Ocean.

However, Greenpeace, an international environmental NGO, decided to publicly challenge Shell's disposal decision, claiming that it was both irresponsible and dangerous to use the deep sea as a "rubbish bin." It placed ads predicting, "If you let Shell have its way, it'll soon be the only Shell left in the North Sea."[4] Since the Brent Spar was the first of ninety deep-sea platforms in the northeast Atlantic scheduled to be decommissioned, Greenpeace wanted not only to prevent this platform from being dumped in the ocean but also to prevent the other eighty-nine from being disposed of in a similar manner. Greenpeace allocated £600,000 ($942,000) for its campaign against Shell. To dramatize their protest, a group of activists along with nine journalists scaled the Brent Spar platform. The protesters had satellite telephones linked to a computer that downloaded photographs and video footage to a media base in Frankfurt. They employed their own photographer and cameraman to facilitate dramatic media coverage. After the protesters were removed, two activists used a helicopter to successfully remount the platform. Television stations throughout Europe broadcast footage of security boats firing water cannons at the helicopter: "Shell came away from the episode portrayed as a corporate Goliath, and Greenpeace was likened to David."[5]

The campaign against Shell gathered momentum. A consumer boycott of Shell stations began in Germany and quickly spread to other countries in northern Europe and eventually to the United Kingdom. Highly organized, and endorsed by a coalition of politicians, businesses, unions, and environmental and religious organizations, it was unusually effective. Some station owners reported up to a 50 percent decline in sales, though the average drop in Germany was estimated at 20 percent.[6] At one point consumer protests were costing Shell an estimated £5 million a day, and nearly fifty Shell service stations in Europe were vandalized. While Shell continued to insist that sea disposal was the soundest environmental option, the unexpected depth and scope of negative publicity proved too damaging to Shell's image and reputation. On June 20, 1995, Shell announced that it had decided to abandon plans to sink the rig in the deep sea. The platform was dismantled on land and subsequently became part of a ferry terminal in Norway at a cost of $40 million, a process that took five years. Greenpeace also succeeded in its larger objective: thanks in part to a rule passed by the Oslo-Paris Commission in 1998, all similar platforms would be disposed of on land.

The additional costs of land disposal for the ninety platforms are substantial, estimated to be at least $5 billion. However, as with the restrictions on child labor, the net social benefit of this example of corporate responsiveness to consumer and NGO pressures is debatable. It turned out that the quantity of oil sludge still in the tanks of the platform was only 100 tons, rather than the more than 5,000 tons Greenpeace had claimed. This error, for which Greenpeace subsequently apologized, did not affect the outcome of the campaign.

But Greenpeace's mistake does raise broader questions about the strength of the environmental case against ocean dumping. In fact, there is no scientific evidence that deep-sea disposal is environmentally hazardous. An article in the journal *Nature* concluded that Shell's original studies were sound and had been conducted using "rigorous scientific standards."[7] The guidelines of the International Maritime Organization also permit deep-sea disposal. The United States disposes of its obsolete offshore oil platforms in the Gulf of Mexico, under a scheme by which half of the cost savings of sea disposal are committed to environmental projects. No environmental damage has been found, and this method of disposal has created no opposition from American environmentalists. In any event, it is unlikely that the land disposal of the platforms represents a cost-effective expenditure of $5 billion.

In short, the outcome of this case of civil regulation may have done little to improve environmental quality, suggesting that voluntary environmental regulation is not necessarily any more welfare-enhancing than some government regulation, much of which is also driven by public pressures and unfounded fears. One Shell executive suggested that the controversy illustrated how easily pressure groups could use "mischievous methods" to challenge a decision that had been made on a "factual and scientific basis."[8] But another Shell executive was more open to a dialogue between activists and business: "Just relying on the scientific results does not cut it. At the end of the day, the feeling of the public was, Shell should not . . . dump the Brent Spar."[9]

The intensity of the public hostility to Shell's disposal plans, in addition to changing public policy toward the disposal of future platforms, also forced Shell and other multinational firms to recognize how the public's expectations of a company's social responsibilities had changed. Shell had created a "genuine CSR risk because it had insufficiently evaluated the breadth of the stakeholders who felt that they were entitled to an opinion about Shell's decision." Company after company encountered similar obstacles in the rest of the 1990s and into the early twenty-first century.[10]

Greening Forestry

Forestry practices have emerged as a highly salient dimension of corporate environmental responsibility. NGOs have pressed wood product retailers to stop selling lumber products from tropical and old-growth forests and to increase their purchases of wood and wood products from forests that are managed responsibly. As in the case of Fair Trade, a private certification mechanism has been established by NGOs to create a market for responsibly produced products.

Tropical Deforestation and Old-Growth Timber

The issue of tropical deforestation took root in Europe during the late 1980s. British, Dutch, and German activists launched boycotts of tropical timber imports from Malaysia to protest logging policies in Sarawak, a semiautonomous state located in the northeast corner of Borneo. In 1992, 240 timber companies, accounting for 95 percent of the Dutch market, agreed to import tropical timber only from sustainable managed forests. Tropical timber imports into the Netherlands fell by 50 percent between 1990 and 1995, mainly as a result of an NGO boycott campaign, and some European countries markedly reduced their tropical timber consumption.[11]

Activists in Britain mounted a series of demonstrations at do-it-yourself home improvement and furniture stores. These protests garnered considerable media and public attention and prompted a number of changes in business practices.[12] B&Q, Britain's largest home improvement store, along with Texas Homecare and Home Base, subsequently agreed to stop selling tropical rainforest timber from environmentally threatened areas.[13]

In the United States the Rainforest Action Network (RAN) has been particularly active in attempting to change forestry practices among retailers. Initially focused on protecting tropical rainforests, its scope has expanded to cover both temperate rainforests and old-growth forests, most of which are located in North America. Like the civic groups that challenged corporate labor policies, RAN's strategy has been to target large, brand-oriented corporations that were dominant in their industries and then to use those corporations' market leverage to change the policies of their subcontractors and to influence the policies of their competitors. RAN reasoned that boycotts would be ineffective because relatively few consumer purchasing decisions are influenced by forest management practices, and instead targeted companies with a high-profile public image and a strong brand. But at the same time RAN averred that its aim was not to hurt corporations: "If the playing field is leveled across an industry, then corporations can still thrive and be successful."[14]

One of RAN's first targets was Home Depot, the world's largest lumber retailer. After two years of protests in and around its stores, which included using the store's public address systems to sarcastically announce to consumers where they could purchase wood "ripped from the heart of the Amazon basin," Home Depot agreed to stop selling wood from endangered forests and to quit buying wood from endangered regions.[15] The company yielded out of fear that the protests might lead to a consumer backlash. Home Depot subsequently reduced the company's purchases of wood from Indonesia by 90 percent, restricting its purchases to suppliers who did not use slash-and-burn techniques. It also ended all wood purchases from Gabon after the company's suppliers there refused to change harvesting practices that threatened the habitat of the endangered lowland gorilla. However, since 95 percent of the company's wood comes from the United States, the cost of switching some of their foreign suppliers was small.[16] The purchaser of almost 10 percent of Chile's annual wood exports, Home Depot also negotiated an agreement with Chile's major lumber companies that established standards for forest protection and conservation among its suppliers.

Subsequently, Home Depot, along with eight of the ten top retailers of wood products in the United States, agreed to stop selling wood from old-growth forests, and shortly afterward, three of the top five home-builders in the United States also agreed not to build with old-growth wood. By mid-2004 the list of companies that had agreed to stop using old-growth pulp, paper, and lumber included Lowe's, Staples, Office Depot, Kinko's, 3M, IBM, Hallmark, and Hewlett-Packard, as well as hundreds of other firms. Some of these companies denied that pressure from RAN and its allies had moved them to change their policies; but undoubtedly all of them were reluctant to wage continual battles with the activist group, especially when the costs of changing their procurement practices were modest. As one public relations consultant put it, "When the bear of controversy enters the forest, no one clambers up a tree faster than the fabled beasts of commerce."[17]

Staples was selected to be the "leading campaign target" by a coalition of NGOs, including Forest Ethics, Dogwood Alliance, and EcoPledge, for the same reason that RAN had initially targeted Home Depot: it was the largest firm in its industry. With more than 1,000 retail outlets, Staples provided convenient physical targets in almost every major American city. The campaign had two primary demands: it wanted Staples to end sales of paper products made from endangered forests and to increase its sales of recycled paper. In the course of the two-year campaign, more than 600 protests, small and large, were held in front of Staples stores. EcoPledge cited evidence from consumer surveys that indicated substantial public opposition to logging in old-growth forests and threatened that its 10,000 members would not work for, invest in, or buy from a company that sold old-growth products. However, it did not attempt to organize a boycott of the store's products.

The campaign also targeted Staples' suppliers and buyers and worked with alternative paper suppliers to persuade Staples that sources of post-consumer recycled products existed and that these products could meet customer expectations. In November 2002 Staples announced new paper procurement policies: it would reduce its demand for virgin wood fiber, phase out paper sourced from endangered forests, and increase to 30 percent the average of postconsumer waste and alternative-fiber products available in its stores. In contrast to Home Depot, Staples has attempted to gain a competitive advantage by embracing environmental concerns. It has sought to position itself as a green office supplier, meeting the increasing demands of nonprofit organizations and governments, as well as some Fortune 500 companies, for recycled paper products. According to a company executive, "We think there is a huge opportunity to differentiate ourselves in this area."[18] However, the success of this strategy was undermined when the firm's largest competitor, Office Depot, adopted similar policies.

Voluntary Codes in Forestry

Following several years of negotiations among foresters, scientists, and industry, the Forest Stewardship Council (FSC) was established in 1993 and began operations three years later. Arguably the most ambitious example of the "privatization of environmental governance" on a global level, the FSC is an international private standard-setting body headquartered in Mexico that attempts to govern international forestry trade and consumption.[19] Its goal is to create a market for wood harvested in a socially and environmentally sound manner by providing "sound business incentives to support certification."[20] By bringing transparency to the supply chain of forest products, FSC attempts to prevent "bad" companies from hiding behind the excuse that they are unable to identify their supply sources and enables "good" companies to receive credit for using more responsible suppliers.

The FSC neither monitors forest management practices nor certifies forests, companies, or products. Rather it establishes forest management standards and then accredits and monitors other organizations that carry out assessments of wood production practices. In the United States, nine regional standard-setting groups, based on different forest types and different regionally specific conditions, have been approved by the FSC. Each has agreed to accept the FSC's principles and criteria for forest management. FSC also provides chain-of-custody guidelines for end-product certification and labeling. Essentially, FSC establishes a framework for collaboration and negotiations among retailers, civic organizations, and forestry operations.

Many large forestry companies have refused to join the FSC and instead have established their own certification systems. There are approximately fifty different forest certification systems in the world, many of which compete directly with the FSC and one of which, the Sustainable Forestry Initiative, was established by the American Forest & Paper Association as a response to it. Many of their performance-based standards for social and environmental practices are less rigorous and consistent than the FSC's, and they typically have weaker provisions for the engagement of civic groups in the certification process.[21] The FSC is also more transparent, making summary reports of its certifications public. Although the proliferation of standards and labels has created considerable confusion and has limited the FSC's impact, FSC does appear to be functioning as a kind of global benchmark for forest management policies and has influenced industry codes to incorporate stronger environmental provisions.

In the United States, both Home Depot and Lowe's Home Centers, respectively the world's second largest home improvement store and the second largest U.S. retailer of timber, have agreed to give preference to FSC-certified forestry products, as has Turner Construction, the largest construction company in the United States. Kinko's has also made a public commitment to give preference to FSC-certified suppliers. Approximately 400 U.S. companies and retailers are affiliated in some way with the FSC. The companies that have promised to give preference to FSC products represent 20 percent of the wood sold in the U.S. home-remodeling market.[22] However, the actual share of FSC-certified products sold or stocked in this country is much smaller, largely because so few forests have received the FSC label. The amount of FSC-certified wood is not even enough to supply Home Depot. In the United States, 7 percent of total forested area under management is FSC certified, and FSC-certified wood accounts for 1 percent of total sales of wood and wood products.[23]

The impact of the FSC has been much greater in Europe, where approximately 30 percent of all forests are certified.[24] FSC-certified wood and wood products have a 5 percent market share in much of western Europe. FSC has been particularly influential in Great Britain, where, by 1995, thanks to the efforts of the World Wildlife Fund, firms accounting for one-quarter of British consumption of wood products had agreed to sell only FSC-certified wood. Ikea, whose retail catalogue distribution is the largest in the world, now only sells FSC-certified wood products, and 60 percent of the raw wood used by SCAM, a Swedish paper company, comes from FSC-certified forests. Environmentalists have also persuaded major retailers in both Sweden and Germany to sell FSC-certified wood.

The FSC has issued more than 700 certificates guaranteeing a "chain of custody" for timber products and producers in more than forty countries. Worldwide, approximately 4 percent of all forests are certified, and 7 percent of the global commercial forest-product market is now linked to FSC, typically through forest and trade networks (FTNs), which include forest owners, timber processors, retailers of timber and paper products, and construction companies. Retailers and construction companies have various reasons for joining FTNs, but for the most part they seek to take advantage of a green image, and in some cases to gain a competitive advantage in the marketplace for eco-friendly products.[25] Approximately 600 firms (virtually all of them in the United States and Europe) have joined global and forest trade networks that commit them to buying FSC wood.[26]

The business logic behind the participation of forestry companies in FTNs is straightforward: notwithstanding the additional costs of certification, and the failure of retailers or builders to pay more for certified wood, FSC certification provides forestry companies with privileged access to the business customers who also participate in the networks. For companies such as Home Depot, Lowe's, Kinko's, and Staples, selling FSC products does not provide any competitive advantage because consumers are unwilling to pay more for certified wood products (though there is a market for recycled paper). Nor are consumers more or less likely to patronize stores that stock FSC-certified wood; few American consumers are even aware of FSC, though a few more specialized building supply firms have successfully bundled FSC lumber with other eco-friendly services to market to green builders.[27] Nonetheless, FSC certification, along with other environmental commitments they have made, has helped wood product retailers avoid or reduce negative publicity. Equally important, it does not appear to have significantly raised their costs.

THE IMPACT OF VOLUNTARY CODES ON FORESTRY PRACTICES. Although data on the impact of the FSC, as well as other company commitments and industry standards are scarce,[28] it does appear that tropical deforestation continues apace. In fact, the rate of tropical forest degradation and the concomitant loss of biodiversity seems to have accelerated.[29] Much of the demand for wood from tropical forests comes from countries where public pressure to improve tropical forest management policies is much less salient, notably Japan, which is the world's largest tropical timber importer.[30] Companies from Malaysia, Thailand, and Indonesia have begun logging in the tropical rain forests of Latin America, the South Pacific, and the Congo basin, and there appears little prospect for influencing these concessions through market or social pressures.[31] Significantly, only 2.4 percent of tropical forests are certified by either the FSC or any other certification scheme.[32] Accordingly, northern NGO activism may primarily have shifted international trade patterns, with certified timber from developing countries being exported to North America and Europe and noncertified wood to the rest of the world.

Changes in corporate purchasing practices have played a measurable role in reducing the rate of destruction of old-growth forests in the United States. But the broader impact of FSC forestry practices in North America and Europe, where 84 percent of FSC-certified forests are located, is less clear.[33] While certification has strengthened companies' environmental management systems, many certified companies were already following many of the FSC-mandated practices. Destructive logging practices continue in many developing countries, where FSC has had relatively little impact, and the gap between "good" and "bad" forest companies is not narrowing.[34] The costs of certification (like those of voluntary labor standards) impose a considerable burden on many developing country producers and typically privilege large producers over small ones.

QUESTIONING EFFECTIVENESS. The Rainforest Foundation has published a highly critical report on the FSC certification practices in several developing countries, including Thailand, Brazil, Indonesia and Malaysia, as well as some of those in British Columbia, Ontario, and Ireland.[35] It claims that, faced with pressures from retailers to increase the supply of timber carrying the FSC logo, as well as competition from other certification schemes, the FSC has compromised its standards, often giving its logo to wood harvested from forests with destructive ecological and social practices. It also criticized the FSC for poorly monitoring chain-of-custody (CoC) certifications, especially in "contexts where false paperwork and corruption is rampant, and the incentives for laundering of wood are strong." These practices, it says, make the "FSC logo . . . little more than another unverified and potentially false claim in the market." The report added: "While the incentives are strong for CoC certified companies to abuse the system by laundering illegal and non-certified wood into certified chains to see profits, the incentives are also strong for the certification codes to ignore false claims and fraud even when detected . . . . as to do so would potentially jeopardize their position in a competitive market for certification services.[36]

The FSC denies that it has weakened its requirements, though it has acknowledged the need to improve "all aspects of accreditation, standards and policy development."[37] There have also been differences between the FSC and the Sierra Club, which opposes the idea of certification for U.S. National Forest land on the grounds that this will undermine its long-standing efforts to reduce harvesting in public forests.[38]

As in the case of Fair Trade coffee, an important factor restraining the impact of FSC is its relatively small market share. However in the case of FSC, this is not due to the lack of consumer demand, because the buyers of FSC products are large companies who have responded to NGO campaigns by agreeing to give preference to its products. In this sense, FSC is more similar to a voluntary labor standard in that the primary consumers of more responsibly produced products are other firms. Rather, FSC's impact has been limited because there is not enough FSC-certified lumber to meet the needs of the firms that are willing to buy it. Many forestry companies prefer to be governed by other certification agencies, in part because their rules are less stringent and often less costly.

In sum, voluntary standards appear to have had a measurable impact on preserving old-growth forests in North America, a modest impact on improving forestry practices in North America and Europe, a limited impact on temperate forest practices outside North America and Europe, and no impact on curbing the rate of tropical forest destruction. At the same time, the cost of these improvements has also been relatively modest.

Action on Global Climate Change

The problem of global climate change and the responsibility of business to ameliorate it by reducing emissions of carbon and other greenhouse gases represents another important dimension of CSR. Two companies whose practices have attracted considerable attention are Ford and British Petroleum. Their responses to public pressures in this policy area illustrate both the potential and the limits of corporate environmental responsibility, as does an analysis of the impact of voluntary agreements to reduce carbon emissions in the United States and Europe.

Ford and the Limits of Good Intentions

When William Clay Ford Jr. became chairman of Ford in 1999, he publicly identified himself as an environmentalist. In a company report issued in 2001, he broke with the automobile industry by declaring, "Global warming stands out from other environmental issues because of its potentially serious consequences and its direct relationship to our industry."[39] Ford publicly promised to improve the fuel efficiency of the company's SUVs by 25 percent by the middle of the decade. This decision was also a response to pressure from NGOs, who had targeted Ford in their campaign to improve fuel economy. As part of its media campaign against Ford, the Sierra Club had sponsored a contest to name Ford's new sport-utility vehicle the Excursion, which used one gallon of gasoline for every twelve miles it traveled: the winning name and "advertising slogan" were "The Ford Valdez—Have You Driven a Tanker Lately?"[40]

In 2002, faced with declining profits—the company lost $5.5 billion in 2001—Ford admitted that "difficult business conditions made it harder to achieve the goals we set for ourselves in many areas, including corporate citizenship."[41] The overall fuel efficiency of the company's products has improved only marginally, and Ford's vehicles continue to be the most carbon intensive of any automotive manufacturer, largely because the company relies on sales of light trucks and SUVs. It is the largest producer of SUVs, and sales of light trucks account for 80 percent of Ford's profits from its North American operations.[42] The company further outraged environmentalists in 2002 when it backed an intense lobbying and advertising effort that successfully defeated a Senate proposal to raise fuel economy standards.

The Sierra Club has continued to target Ford. In June 2003 it ran ads in the *New York Times* and *Business Week* to coincide with Ford's 100th anniversary. They pointed out that "nearly a century ago, Ford's Model T got 25 miles to the gallon. Today, Ford's cars and trucks average 22.6 miles per gallon . . . that's not progress."[43] But according to one industry analyst: "You might irritate the environmentalists, but you have three other key constituencies. The consumers, who are not particularly interested in fuel economy; the U.A.W., who are not particularly interested in fuel economy; and the shareholders, who are not particularly interested in fuel economy. . . . Bill Ford is going to have to give up on his ambitions to create an environmentally friendly company."[44]

However, Ford did "green" its manufacturing processes. In 2002, notwithstanding the firm's financial difficulties, it announced plans to spend $2 billion to redesign one of the firm's oldest factories, the River Rouge plant in Michigan, to make it a model of sustainable manufacturing.[45] The project, which has now been completed, features the world's largest "living roof." It is composed of sedum, a low-maintenance succulent plant, which helps capture storm-water runoff, thus reducing the company's water treatment costs.

In 2004 Ford began the production of the first hybrid SUV, a gas-electric version of the Escape. Priced about $3,400 higher than the V-6 version, but getting twice the gas mileage, the vehicle was aimed at buyers who want space, power, and rough-weather capacity, as well as substantially better fuel economy than other SUVs. As one industry expert observed, "People don't want to sacrifice to drive a hybrid. People are willing to do the right thing for the environment—as long as it's easy."[46] Ford is marketing its new product to both technology enthusiasts and the "green crowd," to whom they are promoting it as a sustainable-lifestyle vehicle. However, even if Ford meets its sales goal of 20,000 vehicles, this will scarcely make a dent in the average fuel economy of its fleet, which (though it has improved by 5.6 percent since 1990) remains the lowest of any major automaker.[47] Moreover, Ford is planning to produce ten times as many gasoline-powered versions of the Escape as it does of its hybrid version.

British Petroleum: Beyond Petroleum?

BP, like Ford, has made claims to leadership in environmental responsibility. During the mid-1990s company executives felt increasing pressure to address the issue of global climate change. Their thinking was strongly influenced by memories of the public relations fiasco surrounding Shell's effort to dispose of the Brent Spar. In 1996 the company took the dramatic step of becoming the first major firm to withdraw from the Global Climate Coalition, a group formed by energy firms to challenge scientific claims about global climate change. The following year Lord John Browne, BP Amoco's chief executive, delivered a major speech on this subject at Stanford University. While noting that "there remain large elements of [scientific] uncertainty," Browne stated that "it would be unwise and potentially dangerous to ignore the mounting concern" over global warming. With the production and consumption of BP's output contributing about 1 percent of global carbon emissions from human activity, he stated that the company had a responsibility to take action. Browne then went on to outline a number of steps the company planned to take, including the development of alternative fuels and a reduction of its own carbon emissions.[48]

Press coverage of Browne's speech was widespread and favorable. The *Los Angeles Times* wrote that, from the perspective of the environmental community, Browne had made "a break as stunning as that which shook the tobacco industry . . . when the Liggett Group acknowledged that smoking causes cancer and heart disease," while the *Wall Street Journal* called BP's stance, a "maverick position in the oil industry."[49] The response of employees to the company's initiative was mixed. While the initial reaction was largely positive, many managers worried it would raise costs and increase business risk. However, as time passed BP's stance became more popular.

In December 1998 Browne pledged that by 2010 BP would reduce its own emissions of greenhouse gases by 10 percent from their 1990 level, a target roughly twice that specified in the Kyoto agreement on climate change being negotiated at the same time. Given the firm's anticipated growth, this meant an effective cutback of up to 50 percent from the emission levels that would have otherwise prevailed. Company managers initially estimated that about two-thirds of its committed reduction could be made at no cost. The company subsequently entered into an agreement with the Environmental Defense Fund to design an internal system for trading greenhouse gas emissions. Compliance with the emissions caps allocated to each business unit was also made part of each manager's performance contract, and a $50 million fund taken from the firm's environmental budget was made available for investments in projects that reduced emissions.

In addition to seeking to capture the moral high ground in the energy industry, the company's commitment also reflected political considerations. BP regarded the in-house trading scheme as a way to gain experience with a policy instrument that appeared likely to be adopted by Britain and the European Union. It also hoped that a successful demonstration of emission trading would help forestall the imposition of a carbon or energy tax, which was being explored by European policymakers and would be much more costly for the company than a regulatory system based on emission trading. Nonetheless, BP was the first energy company to acknowledge global warming as an environmental problem, and among the first firms to commit to reducing its own emissions.

BP met its target nine years ahead of schedule. Its emissions in 2002 were 10.6 percent lower than its 1990 baseline, a reduction of 9.6 million tons of CO_2 (carbon dioxide) equivalent.[50] Part of its success was attributed to the process of measuring emissions, which made managers aware of relatively simple, inexpensive, and cost-effective ways of reducing them. In addition, some capital projects to reduce emissions from natural gas were already being implemented as part of a broader corporate program to cut wasteful venting and flaring of natural gas, which produces methane and CO_2. Ironically, meeting their public target was made easier by the fact that BP's business grew less than it had projected. Finally, both the company's external and internal commitments to the project served as an important motivation for managers. In the words of Lee Edwards, a company engineer, "It transformed the company."[51]

The company estimated that, on a net present value basis, the emissions reduction project cost $20 million, but saved $650 million. The savings were achieved through such measures as increased energy efficiency and sales of the natural gas that was no longer being vented and flared. Numerous emissions reduction projects with high returns were not pursued until its Environmental Trading System began operations.[52] However, in 2002 the company discontinued its internal trading system just when the objective of emissions reductions threatened to cause distortions in the company's overall capital allocation and investment strategies, suggesting that BP may have exhausted the "low-hanging fruit." While the company also pledged to maintain emissions levels through 2012, future reductions are likely to prove more difficult.

Moreover, the $650 million cost savings does not take into account opportunity costs. The time and effort of its managers and the capital the company devoted to reducing greenhouse gas emissions may well have prevented BP's mangers from taking advantage of other, more profitable investment opportunities. In fact, while the company has touted the positive impact of the program on the morale of its employees, many of BP's managers resented the emissions trading scheme, viewing it as a distraction from more pressing business opportunities, and were relieved when it was discontinued.

BP also significantly increased its investments in solar electric equipment manufacturing, making it the largest solar power company, and announced that it would install its solar power technology in 200 gasoline stations in Europe. And in 2002 the company withdrew from a Washington lobbying group that was attempting to open up the Arctic National Wildlife Refuge to oil drilling.[53] These policy initiatives were accompanied by a high-profile $200 million public relations campaign. The world's second largest oil company shortened its name from British Petroleum to BP, coined the slogan "Beyond Petroleum," and changed its corporate insignia from its familiar shield to a more environmentally friendly green, yellow, and white sunburst. Billboards proudly announced that BP was "the first oil company to recognize the risks of global climate change" and that BP "believes in alternative energy. Like solar and cappuccino." Newspaper ads informed consumers of the company's various environmental commitments, concluding with the sentence, "It's a start."[54]

This campaign, however, also highlighted the contradictions inherent in being a green oil company, and skeptics were abundant. An article in the *New York Times* asked: "How can an oil company be 'Beyond Petroleum' without actively distancing itself from its core product, and how can a company that digs big holes in the ground possibly advertise itself as a sensitive steward of the environment?"[55] *Fortune* commented: "If the world's second largest oil company is beyond petroleum, *Fortune* is beyond words." The business magazine observed that while during the previous six years the company had invested more than $200 million in solar power, building an 18 percent market share, in 2001 alone it had invested $8.5 billion in the exploration and production of fossil fuels: "If BP put its advertising mouth where its money was, its ads would be featuring oil rigs in the Gulf of Mexico, where it will invest $15 billion over the next ten years."[56]

Another critic noted that the company's annual solar investment equals 0.4 percent of its annual expenditure on petroleum development and 0.02 percent of its 2002 net worth.[57] According to the *Washington Times*, "If BP executives were completely honest about it, they'd have to admit the company spends far more in a single year burnishing its environmental image than it has invested in solar power in the last six years."[58] A shareholder activist group, SANE BP, claims that the company spent more on its new eco-friendly logo than it did on renewable energy during all of 2000. For activists who have accused the company of "greenwashing," a more accurate company slogan would be "Burning Planet." Others, however, still give BP relatively high marks for its environmental commitments, particularly when they compare its commitments with those made by other oil companies. The public relations message also created confusion within the company itself.[59] And conservative critics of the company's CSR commitments claimed that BP stood for "Beyond Profit," although there is no evidence that the firm's environmental initiatives harmed its shareholders.

Lessons Learned

The experiences of Ford and BP provide a useful snapshot of the potential and limits of corporate environmental responsibility. The most promising area for cost-effective environmental programs for these companies was in the production process, where there appear to be multiple opportunities to both prevent pollution and reduce costs—as well as to create new markets. In reducing its carbon emissions, BP both increased efficiency and discovered a market for its "wastes," while Ford's rebuilding of its River Rouge production facility reduced the costs of wastewater treatment. BP's experience clearly demonstrates that a serious company commitment to reduce emissions can uncover cost-effective, even profitable, means of doing so. In this sense, there are "free lunches" if companies make an effort to discover them, and many have.

But even large gains in internal efficiency are likely to have a small global impact. BP's reductions in greenhouse gas emissions, for example, represent a minor, even trivial, portion of the emissions for which its business is responsible. The company's contribution to the production of greenhouse gases stems primarily from the consumption of the fossil fuels it markets and whose sales continue to form the basis of its business. It has no choice but to continue investing heavily in meeting the inexhaustible demand for oil and natural gas. It is also far from clear that BP's substantial investment in alternative fuels has paid off. As ExxonMobil, one of the company's main competitors, pointed out in a 2004 report, in the third quarter of 2003, BP took a $45 million charge for the consolidation of manufacturing operations and staff reductions in its solar business, while Shell took a $127 million impairment charge to Shell Solar.[60] A newsletter critical of CSR noted that in February 2003, ExxonMobil's price-earnings ratio was a third higher than both Shell's and BP's, suggesting that investors were more optimistic about ExxonMobil's growth prospects than about those of its greener competitors.[61] It also had a higher profit margin and a higher return on equity. Indeed, ExxonMobil had the highest return on equity in the entire petroleum sector.

Consequently, it is misleading to conclude, as did Glenn Pricketter, executive director of the Center for Environmental Leadership, that "the notion that environment is just an expensive cost is way out of date."[62] This argument may have some validity in the area of pollution control because the business case for such measures does not rest on consumers' willingness to patronize green companies. But when green strategies do rely on market demand for environmentally sensitive products, the limits of corporate environmental responsibility come into stark relief.

William Clay Ford Jr. was unable to deliver on his commitment to make Ford into an environmentally responsible automobile company for one simple reason: the consumers of Ford's products continued to prefer relatively inefficient vehicles. Other automobile firms face similar constraints. Notwithstanding the recent commercial success of Toyota's Prius and Honda's Civic hybrids, the continued popularity of gas-guzzling SUVs, minivans, and light trucks, which make up nearly half of all new vehicles sold in the United States, indicates that American consumers place a much higher value on vehicle product characteristics than on their impact on global climate change. As *Newsweek* observed, the extraordinary popularity of SUVs, "says much about the conflicted psyches of baby-boom consumers. They created Earth Day and then went to make a status symbol of gas-guzzling four-wheel drive trucks."[63] Although American consumers are buying more hybrid vehicles—Toyota plans to double its exports of Prius sedans and Ford plans to offer five hybrid vehicles by 2008—they continue to prefer vehicles with big engines. GM vice chairman Bob Lutz observed in January 2005, "Right now the drive for more and more power in cars is way larger than the drive for more hybrids."[64]

Voluntary Carbon Reduction Programs

Voluntary efforts to reduce greenhouse gas emissions provide further evidence of both the potential and the limits of corporate environmental responsibility. More than one hundred American corporations have achieved or set voluntary targets in this area, though their goals vary. These firms include Procter & Gamble, which reduced carbon emissions per ton of production by two-thirds; Interface, which has reduced its greenhouse gases by 46 percent; Coca-Cola, which is phasing out the use of hydrofluorocarbons as a refrigerant in vending machines; and Dupont, which has reduced overall greenhouse gas emissions 65 percent since 1990 and is aiming for a two-thirds cut below its 1990 levels by around 2100. Alcoa is committed to reducing its greenhouse gas emissions by 25 percent below its 1990 level by 2010, while Intel has promised to reduce them two-thirds by 2013. In 2004 Federal Express announced plans to convert its entire fleet of 30,000 vehicles to hybrid electric-diesel engines, and the truck fleet of the United Parcel Service (UPS) now includes 18,000 alternative-fuel vehicles. Motorola, Alcoa, and Waste Management have adopted internal trading systems similar to BP's.[65]

In addition, there have been several collective initiatives. In 2000 the Environmental Defense Fund formed Partnerships for Climate Action with several large global corporations, including BP, Shell, Dupont,

Suncor Energy, Ontario Power Generation, Alcan, and Pechiney.[66] These firms have agreed to reduce their aggregate emissions of greenhouse gases by 14 percent from their 1990 levels by 2010, using market-based mechanisms such as emissions trading. Their progress will be independently audited. The World Wildlife Fund has recruited six major firms, including Johnson & Johnson, IBM, Polaroid, and Nike, to join its Climate Savers program. Its members must commit to an audited program of greenhouse gas reductions, in return for which the WWF will publicize their efforts. According to Jim Goddard, Nike's director of environmental initiatives, Nike, having learned some lessons from being held in the spotlight, wanted to participate in a "completely audited, credible program." Johnson & Johnson hoped the partnership would provide expertise and innovative ideas for conserving energy.[67] Firms that have joined the program agreed to utilize an organization affiliated with Climate Savers to establish their baseline performance and to verify their emissions every two years.

Established in 2003, the Chicago Climate Exchange is pursuing a different strategy to institutionalize and improve the efficiency of greenhouse gas reductions.[68] It operates a private, nongovernmental emissions trading scheme. To participate, companies must agree to annual reductions in their total of six greenhouse gases or arrange for eligible offsets such as carbon sequestration in U.S. forestry or agriculture projects. Using baselines established between 1998 and 2001, members agreed to reduce their emissions of CO_2 equivalents by 1 percent in 2003, 2 percent in 2004, 3 percent in 2005, and 4 percent in 2006. Each emission baseline and annual report is independently reviewed.

Companies can "exchange" their emissions reductions with other firms, and prices of each CO_2 unit fluctuate. The exchange's corporate members include Ford, Dow Corning, Dow Chemical, Bayer, American Electric Power, Interface, International Paper, Motorola, IBM, and Roanoke Electric Steel Corporation, along with several nongovernmental organizations. During its first year of operations in 2003, the total emissions of participant firms were 8 percent below their initial commitments.

Part of the motivation driving many of these commitments is political: while the United States has not ratified the Kyoto climate change treaty, state and international pressure is building for the United States to adopt regulations restricting carbon emissions. If and when that happens, firms that have already begun to do so may find themselves in an advantageous position. On this issue, as the *Washington Post* observed, much of "business is far ahead of Congress and the White House."[69]

In addition, a number of companies have saved considerable sums by reducing emissions of greenhouse gases, often as part of their broader efforts to improve production efficiency. IBM reportedly saved $791 million between 1990 and 2002 through increased energy efficiency, Alcoa estimates annual savings of about $100 million from reduced energy use and related environmental improvements, Dupont has saved $10–15 million by using renewable energy sources and $2 billion by increasing energy efficiency, and ST Microelectronics reports savings of $100 to $120 million a year, in part by using renewable energy.[70] There are also markets for some products that use less energy, and some investments in alternative energy sources have proven profitable.[71] Clearly, many of these business decisions blur the line between virtue and "normal" business activities.

Forces for Change

While the issue of climate change has not attracted as many grass-roots campaigns against firms as forestry or labor practices—Ford is a notable exception—there has been considerable pressure from activist investors and shareholders. In April 2002 the Coalition for Environmentally Responsible Economies (CERES), seeking to make the case for a "direct link among climate change, fiduciary responsibility, and shareholder value," wrote: "Since climate change is arguably the world's most pressing environmental issue, it follows logically that companies' response to the threats and opportunity of climate change—or their lack of response— could have a material bearing on their financial performance and therefore on shareholder value."[72] In 2002 the Rockefeller Philanthropy Advisors mobilized $4 trillion from institutional investors to pressure 500 large corporations to quantify their greenhouse gas emissions on the grounds that their share prices could substantially decline unless they adopted adequate carbon risk management strategies.[73]

Shareholders have also asked firms to develop and disclose their policies toward global climate change.[74] Between 2000 and 2003, half of the socially oriented proxy resolutions received by ExxonMobil focused on environmental issues, including five on global climate change. None passed, but several attracted considerable support. A shareholder resolution filed in 2003 at ChevronTexaco that asked the firm to develop a plan for developing renewable energy resources was supported by 25 percent of the shares voted; climate change resolutions submitted to ExxonMobil received 20 percent of the shares voted in 2002, and two separate resolutions submitted the following year received just over 20 percent of the shares voted.

The U.S. government has also encouraged companies to behave more virtuously as an alternative to government regulation. At the heart of the Bush administration's strategy is a program called Climate Leaders, which has asked the nation's industrial polluters to commit to reducing their greenhouse gas emissions by at least 10 percent within a decade. The firms that have made this commitment include General Motors, Caterpillar, U.S. Steel, Xerox, and Raytheon. Jack Azar, vice president for environment, health, and safety at Xerox, has noted that energy conservation is both good business and good PR.[75] By January 2004, however, only fifty of the thousands of American firms with significant greenhouse gas emissions had adopted the Climate Leaders commitments, and of these only fourteen announced numerical goals. Of the fifty firms, only six are utility companies, notwithstanding the energy industry's major contribution to greenhouse gas emissions: Many of the companies with the worst pollution records have shunned the voluntary programs because even a voluntary commitment would necessitate costly expenditures.

Assessing Voluntary Compliance

Voluntary programs have had a measurable impact. One study of the effectiveness of all sixteen voluntary programs to reduce greenhouse gas emissions sponsored by the U.S. Environmental Protection Agency, including Green Lights, Energy Star, and the 1993 Climate Change Action Plan, found that they had reduced annual emissions by 24.7 million metric tons of carbon dioxide, representing 1.9 per cent of total annual emissions in the United States over roughly a decade. A more recent study reports that in 2002, 228 American firms claimed that they had achieved reductions totaling 265 million metric tons of CO_2 equivalents, or about 4 percent of actual gross emissions in the United States that year.[76]

At the same time, a large number of American firms have made modest or no commitments to reduce their greenhouse gas emissions either independently or through voluntary government programs. Some may be unable to do so in ways that they consider cost-effective—even the simple act of measuring carbon emissions is not costless. Others may not have acted because they felt little public pressure to do so. Many of the returns from improved energy efficiency may be too small to justify or too distant to justify on conventional grounds. Failure to invest in energy efficiency can also be caused by inflexible budgeting procedures or a lack of management time. Business leadership and corporate values also matter: CEOs clearly differ in the priority they attach to global climate change as well as in their commitment to environmental concerns more generally.

The unevenness of voluntary corporate efforts helps explain the results of an assessment of the General Accounting Office in 2003. It reported that although voluntary agreements in the United States are projected to reduce overall emissions of greenhouse gases over the next ten years, this represents "only 2 percentage points below what the nation would achieve with no federal program whatsoever."[77] This suggests that firms are unwilling or unable to make substantial reductions in their greenhouse gas emissions in the absence of legally binding requirements that they do so.

Corporate policies and priorities vary internationally as well.[78] In other countries there is a long-standing gulf in attitudes between the vast majority of firms and the relatively small group of companies taking an active stance on climate change. Some multinational firms based in Europe and North America belong to the Climate Group, a coalition of firms and governments formed to share best practices on climate change; they include BP, Shell International, IBM, Swiss Re, Dupont, Lafarge (an international building materials company), Alcoa, HP, Ontario Power Generation, the Canadian aluminum company Alcan, and the French aluminum company Pechiney. But even their commitments are restrained. As Steve Howard, executive director of the Climate Group, put it, "Most companies want to be one step ahead of the competition, not two steps." An April 2004 report by the World Economic Forum, while applauding the efforts of some forward-looking multinationals, concluded that voluntary actions would be inadequate to counter the effects of climate change.

The Climate Group argues that "tackling climate change is a strategic issue. As climate change becomes more disruptive and constraints on carbon emission tighten, companies will benefit from having planned ahead. Developing low-carbon technologies and products will give them a competitive advantage."[79] This claim may well be valid. However, it does not appear that a significant number of firms have found it sufficiently persuasive to change their business strategies. According to a study commissioned by CERES in 2003, a coalition of investor, environmental, and public interest groups that examined the twenty largest carbon dioxide–emitting companies in the United States, most are virtually ignoring the financial or environmental risk posed by climate change.[80]

The Shortcomings of Corporate Environmental Responsibility

No dimension of CSR has attracted as much attention from the business community as environmental protection. Since the mid-1990s, literally hundreds of corporations, both large and small, have initiated or expanded programs and policies to reduce their environmental impact and made "sustainability" part of their professed business mission. For firms that want to burnish their public reputation, environmental management offers a wide array of means to do so. And the fact that many improvements can take place at modest cost, or have even proven profitable, provides companies with an additional reason to profess their green credentials, even if some of these improvements would have occurred anyway in the course of their normal business operations. Still, to the extent that civic pressures have encouraged some firms to more aggressively explore ways of reducing their environmental "footprint," CSR has made a difference.

Government regulation and the threat of litigation, along with the cost savings associated with many environmental programs, make it difficult to assess the *net* impact of corporate virtue on environmental quality in the United States or Europe. From this perspective, the reductions of carbon emissions in the United States are somewhat anomalous: because there are no current federal requirements, it is possible to evaluate the relative impact of voluntary corporate efforts. Even so, some companies may be acting in anticipation of future federal controls, and some states have established or are considering imposing their own regulations. The same logic affects companies in Europe, where until recently, there were no government requirements for greenhouse gas reductions, though many national governments have promoted voluntary agreements.[81]

The more critical question is: to what extent and on what dimensions have the myriad examples of corporate environmental virtue in the United States and Europe actually improved environmental quality? The examples examined in this chapter appear to have had a measurable impact: some forestry practices have improved, primarily in Europe and the Americas; and BP and many other firms have reduced emissions of greenhouse gases more than they would have in the absence of civic pressures. But by any conceivable measure, in both the United States and Europe, government regulation has been a far greater influence on corporate environmental performance over the past three and one-half decades than has business self-regulation. Indeed, in the absence of extensive government regulation, far fewer corporations in the United States and Europe would have undertaken voluntary environmental initiatives.[82]

Constraints on the Market for Environmental Virtue

A shortcoming of the numerous books on corporate environmental responsibility is that they almost uniformly describe successes, whether measured by financial or environmental performance or by both.[83] And although there have been many win-win scenarios, not all corporate "greening" falls into this category. In the critical area of green marketing, for example, success has been mixed. Some consumers are willing to purchase greener products if they believe the products also benefit them. One example is organic food, which U.S. and European consumers are willing to pay more for because they believe it is healthier and tastes better.

Likewise, in Britain one noteworthy success of the ethical shopping movement is the growth in sales of free-range eggs, which consumers are willing to pay 25 percent more for because they fear salmonella in conventionally produced eggs. And the marketing of more energy-efficient appliances has succeeded because they reduce consumers' energy costs. Seventh Generation has successfully marketed a wide range of environmentally friendly household products, ranging from cleaning suppliers to diapers, appealing to consumers' desire to use nontoxic products. The Body Shop's market niche is similar: it markets toiletries made from natural ingredients. All of these products offer both individual and collective benefits.

However, for products whose benefits are exclusively public, the record is more mixed. Northern Europeans readily purchase phosphate-free detergents, paper produced without chlorine, batteries produced without mercury.[84] And U.S. consumers constitute a substantial market for recycled paper. But many corporate efforts to market greener products have been unsuccessful. For example, although the carpet manufacturer Interface has been widely praised for its CEO's commitment to make Interface "a completely sustainable company, producing no dangerous waste, no harmful emissions, and using not a drop of oil," it has not been able to persuade its corporate customers to lease replaceable and recyclable carpet tiles instead of purchasing the entire carpet.[85]

In the once-hyped market for electric cars, Ford and GM have spent $1.1 billion on research and development without producing a commercially viable product, and Ford discontinued production of its electric vehicle in 2002. When the Swiss chemical firm Ciba tried to market a low-salt dye that would reduce wastewater, it met with considerable resistance; its business customers focused on the apparent price—that is, the higher price per pound—rather than the lower overall costs of adopting a more environmentally friendly manufacturing process.[86] Starkist, after voluntarily adopting a dolphin-safe standard for harvesting its tuna, ran an advertising campaign that emphasized the firm's environmental leadership. The campaign raised customer approval of its brand and reinforced its already dominant position: in just three years, its market share increased from 36 to 42 percent. But it turned out that canned tuna was poorly suited to a green marketing strategy: the firm was unable to raise prices to compensate for its higher costs. On the contrary, competitive pressures forced it to lower them. J. W. Connolly, president of Heinz, USA, Starkist's parent company, observed: "Consumers wanted a dolphin-safe product, but they were not willing to pay more for it. If there was a dolphin safe can of tuna next to a regular can, people chose the cheaper product. Even if the difference was one penny."[87]

As the experiences of Ford, Starkist, and Interface illustrate, an important constraint on voluntary improvements in corporate environmental performance is consumer behavior. If environmentally sound products also provide consumers with what they perceive as tangible benefits, some consumers are willing to pay a premium for them. But if the benefits are exclusively or primarily public, consumer interest diminishes considerably, especially if the product is more expensive. In short, few consumers are willing to internalize the environmental externalities of what they consume:

> Green marketing has not lived up to the hopes and dreams of many managers and activists. Although public opinion polls show that consumers would prefer to choose a green product over one than is less friendly to the environment when all other things are equal, those "other things" are rarely equal. . . . When consumers are forced to make trade-offs between product attributes or helping the environment, the environmental almost never wins. Most consumers simply will not sacrifice their needs or desires just to be green.[88]

This may well be why only a handful of companies, outside niche markets, advertise the environmental attributes of their products or seek to create or maintain consumer loyalty by emphasizing their green virtues.

Moreover, many companies that tout their environmental commitments are really expressing the philosophy of the CEO, as in the cases of BP,

Ford, Interface, Ikea, Dupont, and Patagonia.[89] When these executives are replaced, the environmental commitments of the firms they manage may change. Furthermore, many of the highly publicized examples of improved corporate environmental and financial performance to date, like that of BP, have already done the easy things. Accordingly, the rate of future improvements in corporate environmental performance may decline unless additional regulation is imposed. The *Financial Times*, while noting that firms continue to address a wide range of environmental issues, does not expect the environment to benefit substantially in the near future: "The number of businesses that are integrating social and environmental factors into business decisions is still relatively small. In addition, environmental improvements are being overtaken by economic growth and increased demands for goods and services."[90]

Another serious shortcoming of corporate environmental responsibility is its limited geographic scope. The lion's share of improvement in corporate environmental practices has taken place in or around developed countries: the conflict over the Brent Spar oil rig focused on environmental quality in northern Europe; virtually all the forests whose management has been affected by FSC are in either North America or Europe; most hybrid cars are sold in the United States and Japan; and most of the production facilities of the firms that have reduced or committed to reduce their greenhouse gas emissions are in developed countries, though obviously the impact of these reductions is global. And virtually all of the examples of corporate environmental virtue featured in books touting corporate sustainable development initiatives focus on changes in corporate environmental practices in the United States and Europe.

Toward Global Standards?

The kind of multi-stakeholder reporting and monitoring of supply chains that has emerged with respect to labor conditions is generally lacking in the environmental area, with the notable exception of forestry. Two of the most visible international environmental codes, the Business Charter for Sustainable Development and the Coalition for Environmentally Responsible Economies, have neither performance standards nor reporting requirements.

Compared to labor standards, relatively few voluntary codes govern corporate global environmental practices.[91] One of the few, and among the most sophisticated, is Responsible Care (RC), established by the chemical industry in 1985 to improve its health, safety, and environmental performance and public reputation following a major chemical accident in Bhopal, India, in 1984.[92] It has national affiliates in forty-six countries, including fifteen developing countries. Responsible Care has specified nearly 100 management practices within and around manufacturing facilities, as well as product stewardship. Although the program is reputed to have improved environmental practices in affiliate firms in developing countries, its reliance on self-reporting makes it difficult to assess the extent or impact of these improvements. Outsiders give it mixed reviews.[93] Yet notwithstanding the shortcomings of Responsible Care, the chemical industry's effort to define and improve global environmental standards for its industry remains unique.

Arguably the most important international environmental voluntary standard is ISO 14001, an international process-based standard established in 1996 by the International Organization for Standardization based in Geneva. It specifies an elaborate series of requirements involving the development and periodic self-assessment of corporate environmental management systems, based on industry best practices. This standard, whose adoption grew rapidly in the late 1990s, is particularly influential in Europe. Nearly half of all certified firms are located there, and many European firms insist that the companies with which they do business are ISO 14001 certified; the latter policy has also encouraged developing country firms to become certified in order to be able to export their products to Europe. An American firm, Hewlett-Packard, gives preference to ISO 14001–certified suppliers, and the major American automotive firms require their suppliers to be ISO 14001–certified. In 2002, 39,390 firms were certified in developed countries and 6,218 in developing countries.[94]

The auditing of firms seeking certification addresses the implementation of ISO 14001 process standards rather than environmental performance: ISO 14001 has no environmental performance standards. In surveys, ISO adopters self-report that they have increased recycling, reduced waste, and adopted alternative technologies. But there is little independent evidence that certified firms have better or improved environmental performance, and a few studies have found that they do not.[95] For their part, environmental NGOs have been highly critical of ISO 14001. The World Wildlife Fund argues that there are "insufficient safeguards in place to prevent unscrupulous companies from using certification of ISO 14001 as a 'quasi label'" to certify their responsible economic practices, while others have expressed concern that the standard amounts to little more than "greenwashing," enabling its adopters to claim superior environmental management practices without actually improving their performance or investing in pollution abatement technologies. According to the U.S. Environmental Protection Agency, ISO 14001's "priority schemes for inspections are very unsophisticated."[96]

In some capital-intensive manufacturing sectors, including chemicals, oil refining, aluminum production, chip making, and pulp and paper, many multinational firms based in the United States and Europe apply similar environmental standards for all their plants throughout the world, which means that the environmental performance of Western firms with global operations is usually better than that of domestic firms.[97] These global firms have done so both for business reasons, as it is often more efficient to employ similar production technologies, and to avoid accidents that might damage their global reputations. But because few firms disclose their global environmental practices, it is difficult to assess their actual performance. Relatively few manufacturing firms systematically monitor the environmental performance of their suppliers in developing countries, and the inspections of those that do are rarely publicly disclosed. Corporate programs that provide for end-of-life product management are also largely confined to developed countries, though computer firms are under pressure to monitor and restrict exports of electronic wastes.

The relative underdevelopment of private governance mechanisms with respect to environmental supply chain management in developing countries reveals an important limitation of CSR: its agenda is shaped by the priorities of NGOs in developed countries and their ability to shine a public spotlight on specific corporate practices. In addition to the chemical and forestry sectors, others under scrutiny include oil and mineral developers whose practices have human rights as well as environmental impacts, a topic that is addressed in chapter 6. But environmental practices for the vast majority of manufacturing activity linked to Western firms in developing countries have largely escaped the scrutiny of the CSR movement. Issues such as child labor in developing countries have attracted more public and consumer outrage in the West than air and water pollution in these same countries, although the latter's negative social effects are probably more substantial. This is in turn represents another important limitation of the market for virtue.

6

Corporate Responsibility for Human Rights and Global Corporate Citizenship

Improving the welfare of citizens in the developing countries where international firms do business is a critical dimension of CSR. Often associated with human rights, this dimension of corporate responsibility has gone beyond working conditions to encompass community development policies, relationships with repressive or corrupt regimes and their security forces, decisions about where firms should invest, the social and environmental impact of bank lending policies, and the establishment of norms of global corporate citizenship.

As the salience of these issues has grown, a number of corporations, primarily in extractive industries, have found themselves targeted by activists because of their human rights policies—or lack thereof. Civic pressures have led to a number of changes in company policies. Some firms in extractive industries have attempted to improve their relationships with the communities in which their investments are located, some have divested from Burma, some firms have developed human rights standards for investment and sourcing decisions, and several international banks have agreed to voluntary standards for assessing and monitoring the social and environmental impact of their lending decisions. In addition, the UN Global Compact has established a set of global norms for corporate citizenship that have been endorsed by more than 1,300 firms, including several from developing countries.

However, the overall social impact of these developments remains limited by several factors. First, the standards for corporate human rights policies contained in the few voluntary codes that exist in this area are vague and poorly defined. Second, the "enforcement" of corporate commitments to human rights policies remains largely a function of NGO pressures and media attention, which means that many corporate practices are subject to little international scrutiny. Third, because the willingness of global corporations to factor the impact of human rights into their investment decisions varies widely, the impact of those firms that have attempted to do so has often been limited.[1] Finally, even the efforts of corporations that have tried to be responsible citizens have often been undermined or overwhelmed by the politics and policies of host-country governments.

This chapter evaluates the impact of several of the more salient dimensions of CSR for human rights. It begins by discussing one of the most visible disputes surrounding the role, behavior, and responsibilities of a Western company in a developing country, namely Shell in Nigeria. The conflicts Shell faced were instrumental in placing human rights issues on the agenda of firms involved in natural resource development. The chapter then turns to some of the human rights controversies surrounding the investments of extractive industries. Firms in these industries have experienced the major share of NGO and public scrutiny of their human rights policies, in large measure because they are often caught in the midst of violent conflicts between community residents and both government and private security forces responsible for protecting their investments. In addition, many natural resources are located in countries with corrupt and undemocratic governments, and with repressive security forces. As a result foreign firms have often found themselves accused of complicity in human rights abuses.

The next section examines the issues and controversies surrounding where companies should do business, describing the mixed successes of NGOs to force disinvestment from Burma as well as the broader debate over how firms should make investment decisions in countries where human rights abuses are well known. The final section of this chapter explores a broad policy initiative, namely the role of the UN Global Compact in promoting norms of global corporate citizenship.

Shell in Nigeria

Shell began its operations in Nigeria in 1937, while it was still a British colony. Large oil reserves were discovered in the late 1950s. After Nigeria became independent in 1960, a succession of governments, some civilian, though mostly military, squandered the country's oil wealth. Beginning around 1987, Shell became the target of a series of protests by various tribal groups, notably the Ogoni, an ethnic group of 500,000 people living in eighty-two communities in the Niger Delta region in southeast Nigeria. Shell, which accounted for half the country's oil production, was blamed for the harmful environmental impact produced by decades of energy investments as well for the continued poverty of the region, notwithstanding the substantial royalties paid to the Nigerian central government. According to two Nigerian environmental activists, Shell had exhibited "negligence and cynical indifference" to the welfare of the community in which its oil production was located. They added: "The general complaint is one of broken promises, developmental assistance programs that are abandoned halfway and poor quality facilities that break down and simply rust away as soon as they are installed."[2] Greenpeace reported that between 1982 and 1992 more than a third of Shell's oil spills worldwide, amounting to 1.6 million gallons, occurred in the Niger Delta region.[3] There were also frequent allegations of heavy-handed tactics by the police and army officers protecting the company's installations. Nigerian law required Shell to pay the salaries of many of these security forces, which further implicated the company in their activities.

A number of protests turned violent: at one demonstration in Ogoniland in 1990, eighty villagers were killed and 494 homes destroyed after Shell reportedly asked the commissioner of police for security protection. In 1993, as violence between Nigerian security forces and the Ogoni intensified, Shell withdrew its personnel from the region, stating that it would not return until it had "the local community on our side." It also asked the government to protect the installations it had left behind. The Nigerian government responded to continued attacks on Shell's installations by youth groups from the Ogoni tribe by expanding its military presence in the region, hoping that making the region more secure would persuade Shell to return. The commander of an internal security task force issued a memo calling for aggressive military action against activists and suggested putting "pressure on the oil companies" to help pay the costs of the operations.[4] Local groups estimated that the government attacks destroyed thirty villages and killed about 2,000 people, though this claim has not been independently verified.

In 1994, following the killing of four traditional Ogoni leaders by a mob, Ken Saro-Wira, an Ogoni activist who had been a prominent critic of Shell, along with a number of his associates, was arrested and charged with inciting his supporters to commit murder. Saro-Wira's arrest focused international attention on Shell's behavior in Nigeria. From his prison cell he called for an international boycott of oil from Nigeria. In Britain, Shell was strongly criticized by a coalition of unions, environmental groups, human rights organizations, and churches for its tacit approval of Nigeria's military regime, and several Internet sites called for a boycott of the company to protest its unwillingness to seek Saro-Wira's release from prison. Shell responded by averring that "politics is the business of government and politicians," adding that "the company does not and should not have [political] influence in Nigeria."[5]

After Saro-Wiwa was found guilty by a military tribunal, the company stated that it would be inappropriate for it to interfere with Nigeria's legal processes, though at the last minute it did lend its support to the international campaign for clemency for Saro-Wira.[6] On November 1, 1995, Saro-Wira and eight other Ogoni activists were hanged. The extensive global media coverage of the execution substantially increased public and media attacks on Shell and its role in Nigeria. Senior Shell officials conceded that the company's "image had been dealt a serious blow by the events in Nigeria." According to Shell's West African coordinator, "Saro-Wiwa's execution was a disaster for us."[7]

Shell, however, challenged the claims of widespread environmental degradation caused by its operations. In fact, Shell's facilities covered less than 1 percent of the land in the Niger Delta, and many oil spills were due to the sabotage of Shell's 6,000 kilometers of pipelines by local residents. Moreover, oil development was only one of several factors driving land degradation. While acknowledging that it should have acted earlier to address some of the local community's environmental concerns, a company official explained that the Nigerian government was its majority partner and that as a poor country it had been reluctant to sacrifice profits for environmental protection.[8] Shell did admit that the environmental standards at its oilfields in the Niger Delta were lower than in Europe or America and that it was responsible for oil spills that had contaminated a number of locations. Furthermore, its practice of burning off natural gas as a by-product of oil production created large and polluting flares.

Shell rejected the argument that it should withdraw from Nigeria, the source of 10 percent of the firm's total exploration and production profits. Shortly after the trial and execution, it announced that it was proceeding with plans to build a $4 billion natural gas pipeline in partnership with the government. But in what was widely regarded as a breakthrough, Shell revised its business principles in 1997, explicitly mentioning its "support for fundamental human rights in line with the legitimate role of business."[9] The following year, Shell published its first public report on community and environmental issues in Nigeria, promised to end the practice of gas flaring within ten years, and pledged to establish a youth training scheme in Ogoniland. The company also agreed to return 13 percent of federal oil and gas revenues it paid to the Nigeria government to the Niger Delta region—a fourfold increase from 1995. Shell also substantially increased its own funding to the area; to date it has sponsored more than 280 community development projects, primarily in health care and education, spending $84 million in 2003.[10] Shell has also offered to clean up all spills in the Ogoniland that occurred after its departure.

At the same time, in an internal report that was subsequently leaked, Shell admitted that its operations in the Niger Delta had exacerbated conflict in the region: "The cumulative effect of [its] practices is a perception among communities that they cannot engage with [Shell] other than through forceful or obstructive action."[11] Moreover, Shell has little to show for its community development expenditures. Most of the company's development expenditures wind up in the pockets of local officials. In other cases, Shell has paid for the construction of community facilities, but not provided funding for operating them.[12] But even if its community development efforts were more effective, they would only go a small way toward meeting the demands and needs of the delta's 7 million inhabitants, whose poverty will persist as long as state institutions remain ineffective. Shell cannot fill the vacuum created by the shortcomings of Nigeria's government. Moreover, government corruption has also reduced the effectiveness of the federal government's promises to increase revenue sharing.

Shell's new environmental policies and expanded community development efforts also have not succeeded in reducing local hostility to the company. In 2004, in order to protect the 185,000 barrels a day that go through its pipeline that crisscross the Niger Delta region, Shell requested the assistance of Nigeria's paramilitary police. Nicknamed by community residents "kill and go," the police have been accused of brutality. Furthermore, the efforts of a U.K. company hired by Shell to clean up an oil spill in the Ogoni region disappointed local residents. According to a report in the *Financial Times*, "The earth and reeds in the area are still blackened and a large pool glints with the iridescence of petroleum. A local farmer complained, 'When the spill occurred, it destroyed all the crops I had planted.'"[13] Not surprisingly, Shell's future plans for energy development in Nigeria emphasize offshore investments, to minimize both local grievances and the sabotage of its facilities.

In a 2004 annual report on CSR, the British NGO Christian Aid wrote that notwithstanding Shell's claims to have changed its ways, its oil spills are still ruining villages and its community development projects are still largely ineffective and divisive.[14] Yet in large measure because no local leader has been able to capture the international media attention accorded Saro-Wiwa, Western media attention and NGO criticisms of Shell's role in Nigeria have noticeably diminished. And despite Shell's wide-ranging efforts to behave more responsibly in the Niger Delta, the underlying social and environmental problems that led to protests against Shell clearly persist—graphically revealing some of the limitations of the exercise of corporate virtue in poorly governed countries.

Extractive Industries and Human Rights

The uproar over Shell's role in Nigeria, following on the heels of the international outcry over Shell's plans to jettison the Brent Spar platform in the deep ocean, proved a watershed for the company and for the human rights movement.[15] It also influenced other companies' policies. British Petroleum, faced with similar accusations about its handling of security problems in Colombia, acknowledged that the defense of human rights was part of its direct legitimate responsibilities.[16] Similarly, several European natural resource companies, including Rio Tinto, Norsk Hydro, Premier Oil, and Statoil, responded to the controversy over Shell's role in Nigeria by incorporating references to human rights into their business principles or codes of conduct.[17] These statements, which typically refer to the 1948 UN Universal Declaration of Human Rights (UDHR), include commitments to promote transparency and to work cooperatively with local community groups.[18] But many firms remain reluctant to include human rights in their corporate principles on the grounds that doing so would undermine their commitment to political neutrality.

In addition to expressing a stronger commitment to human rights more generally, a number of companies in extractive industries have also undertaken efforts, both individual and collective, to improve their record in the specific areas of security, sustainable development, and corruption. The most important of these initiatives are discussed in the following sections.

Balancing Security and Human Rights

In response to the increase in violence involving security forces responsible for protecting Western investments in developing countries, in December 2000 several extractive companies, along with NGOs and the British and U.S. governments, issued a set of "Voluntary Principles on Security and Human Rights."[19] The purpose of these principles was to guide companies in maintaining the safety and security of their operations within an operating framework that ensures respect for human rights. The principles focus on three issues: possible human rights abuses in corporate security arrangements, company relations with state security forces, and company relationships with private security forces. They were initially signed by seven American and British based firms—Chevron and Texaco (who signed separately before their merger), Conoco, BP, Shell, Rio Tinto, and Freeport McMoRan—along with a number of prominent NGOs. Subsequently, three other American firms, Newmont Mining, Occidental Petroleum, and ExxonMobil, formally endorsed the principles, as did two Norwegian firms, Statoil and Norsk Hydro, as well as the governments of Norway and the Netherlands.

The Voluntary Principles impose few real obligations, though they do potentially expose their signatories to more intense NGO scrutiny. There are no formal reporting requirements or monitoring mechanisms. Nor are firms obligated to follow any predetermined set of requirements. Among the challenges of implementing the principles is the difficulty of communicating new policies to managers in the field, many of whom have little experience balancing human rights concerns with the need to maintain the security of company operations. A more serious problem is the risk of conflict with host country governments, which may be interested only in maximizing revenues and are hostile to community concerns that would interfere with this objective, especially if they are linked to separatist pressures. Moreover, many of the disputes between central government authority and local interests are long-standing, often stemming from deep-rooted ethnic conflicts. Finally, it is often difficult for Western firms to balance the need to protect company operations and personnel with a commitment to avoid human rights abuses, especially since firms have little leverage over the behavior of local security forces.

Consequently, the impact of these principles on actual corporate practices is uneven. In Indonesia, BP has annexed the Voluntary Principles to its contract for a planned liquefied natural gas facility in Papua New

Guinea, and has developed security guidelines for private security contractors based on them.[20] But violent clashes between residents and security personnel protecting foreign natural resource projects continue.[21] In West Papua, Indonesia, where Freeport McMoRan operates one of the world's largest gold mines, the company has to use thousands of policemen and soldiers to pacify locals who have lost tribal lands.[22] A local conflict turned fatal in August 2002, when two Americans and an Indonesian were killed near Freeport McMoRan's Gassberg mine in West Papua, Indonesia. The Indonesian military blamed the killings on separatist forces, but there is speculation that they were arranged by government security forces in order to persuade Freeport to maintain funding levels for state-provided security arrangements. American military advisers arrived in Colombia to train two army brigades to help protect a 500-mile pipeline operated by Occidental Petroleum that has been the frequent target of attacks by guerillas. And in March 2003 a violent pre-election uprising by ethnic Ijaw militants in Nigeria resulted in fatalities and military intervention that forced ChevronTexaco and Shell to shut down their facilities temporarily.

Promoting Sustainable Development

In 2000 rising public concern over the environmental and social abuses associated with extractive industry projects in developing countries led a group of natural resources firms, led by Rio Tinto, Western Mining Corporation, and Phelps Dodge, to establish the Mining, Minerals, and Sustainable Development Project. The project is governed by its fifteen corporate members, which include Anglo-American, BHP Billiton, Alcoa, Noranda, Sumitomo, Mitsubishi, Newport Mining, Freeport McMoRan, and Placer Dome, as well as twenty-seven commodity and regional trade and industry associations. In 2003, after extensive consultations, the partners drew up ten principles to guide corporate practices and policies. However, these principles are vague, involving little more than boilerplate commitments to "maintain ethical business practices" and engage in "continual improvements of our environmental performance." More important, although the principles provide for "independently verified reporting requirements," they do not specify how this is to be accomplished or whether or how their findings are to be made public. Moreover, independent monitoring is voluntary. Not surprisingly, the principles have been met with considerable skepticism.[23]

A few firms, like Shell in the Niger Delta, have gone beyond the general commitments promoted by the Mining, Minerals, and Sustainable Development Project to address local environmental and social concerns directly. In Angola, where ChevronTexaco is investing $5 billion a year to produce oil, the company is working with the government to develop environmental regulations that will govern its operations. Along with its partners TotalElfFina (Total), ENI-Agip, and the Angolan state-owned oil company, ChevronTexaco has also allocated $24 million for community development projects over five years.[24] In Papua New Guinea it has worked with the World Wildlife Fund on a large-scale integrated conservation and development project that has avoided many of the negative social and environmental impacts of energy development in fragile ecosystems.[25] For its part, Shell has attempted to apply the lessons it learned in Nigeria to its development of a new gas project in Peru. Shell has signed an agreement with a local NGO to monitor the project's social and environmental impact and supported an elaborate consultation exercise to increase the company's knowledge of local issues.[26]

In Madagascar in 2004, Rio Tinto PLC hired an environmentalist to help redesign a major limonite mine that has long been opposed by British environmental groups. The company has spent eighteen years planning for the mine, trying to fashion a plan that would minimize its social and environmental impacts. However, many environmentalists still oppose the project on the grounds that few local residents will benefit from a major natural resource development project on their lands.[27] It is also generally more difficult for mining companies than for oil companies to voluntarily address environmental and community issues in developing countries because the former operate with much lower profit margins.

In West Papua, New Guinea, BP—which experienced a public relations disaster in 1997, when it used soldiers to guard a Colombian pipeline against Marxist guerrillas—has hired a team of sociologists and consultants to work with local residents to promote community development. The company, which is developing a $2 billion gas plant, is seeking to show that its "much-trumpeted embrace of corporate social responsibility extends beyond the boardroom and into the boondocks." However, in light of the long-standing tensions between the central government of Indonesia and the residents of West Papua the *Economist* observed that BP may not be able to expand production in Indonesia without harming its carefully cultivated reputation as a "responsible" oil company. Moreover there are likely to be conflicts between the government's practice of crony capitalism and the "caring capitalism" to which BP aspires. [28]

ExxonMobil's $3.5 billion 660-mile pipeline from the oil fields of Chad to Cameroon may well represent the most ambitious corporate effort to link energy exploration with human rights and community development to date. Responding to criticisms from NGOs, who hoped to turn the project into "Exxon's Nigeria"—they had placed an ad in the *New York Times* headlined, "Here's Your Chance to Invest in Corrupt Governments and Get High-Yield Rainforest Destruction at No Extra Cost"—the company agreed to work with NGOs and the World Bank to monitor the government's use of its royalty payments, essentially assuming the roles of development agency, human rights promoter, and environmental watchdog at the same time.

Under an agreement reached with the government of Chad, 10 percent of oil revenues will be held in trust, 80 percent will be earmarked for education, health, and rural development, and 5 percent will go back to the oil-producing regions. All expenditures will be supervised by a nine-person committee that includes representatives of four NGOs. In addition, 145 meetings between Exxon and several NGOs resulted in sixty changes in the pipeline's route as well as an agreement to create an environmental foundation and two national parks. The plan is groundbreaking and could influence other multinationals' operations.[29] But it has proven both expensive and time-consuming; and it is unclear if its model can or will be adopted elsewhere.

Spending on environmental and social projects, in addition to helping soften NGO criticisms and improve a company's international reputation, can be regarded as an extension of company investments in security. Yet such programs face numerous challenges. One is defining the limits of corporate responsibility. When companies contribute to health care or education projects in communities around their operations, they risk creating conflict between villages that benefit from these programs and those that do not. Moreover, such programs may raise local expectations about services or other benefits that a company is unable or unwilling to provide. In fact, the more companies do, they more they are expected to do—in some cases by local governments who then use a company's programs as an excuse to cut back on their own social expenditures. Companies must also address how to deal with a community's heightened expectations after they depart—as virtually all do when their resource development projects are completed. And, as Shell's experience in the Niger Delta suggests, even the most extensive and well-intentioned community development efforts are unlikely to adequately address local grievances, which tend to stem from long-standing conflicts between local communities and the central government as well as government corruption and repression.

As Bennett Freeman, the former U.S. deputy assistant secretary of state who developed the Voluntary Principles and who is now managing director for corporate responsibility for the public relations firm Burson-Marsteller, cautions, although multinational corporations can help, they shouldn't be viewed as the solution to all of the world's social and environmental problems; he warns that they are "stopgap measures" that are likely to be abandoned once a company departs.[30] John Kline, a professor in the School of Foreign Service at Georgetown University, sounds a similar note of caution: "Often, if you take [a community development program] as an isolated case, it seems rational and beneficial, but it's hard to project some of these things too far into the future—and companies may lack experience in areas that really have political functions."[31]

Combating Corruption

A third dimension of the efforts of major foreign investors to support human rights has focused on promoting transparency in the relations between a company and its host government. In 2002 a worldwide coalition of 200 NGOs began urging governments and businesses to endorse yet another voluntary agreement, "Publish What You Pay" (PWYP). The purpose of this code is to put pressure on reputationally sensitive oil, gas, and mining firms to prove that they are not bribing corrupt officials or diverting funds that should be used for local development purposes.[32] A few extractive firms have begun to publish their payments unilaterally, including BP and Shell. But when BP promised transparency around its payments to the government in Angola, the latter threatened to expel the company and BP was forced to back down.[33] Much of the success of PWYP is dependent on that of a parallel public effort, the Extractive Industries Transparency Initiative, whose purpose is to make host-country governments publicly accountable for royalties they receive from multinational companies. But at this writing in 2005, only ten countries have agreed to abide by its principles. While several major corporations involved in construction, energy, metals, and mining have signed a "zero-tolerance" pact against paying bribes and a number of oil companies have adopted such a policy on their own, there are no mechanisms for monitoring or enforcement.[34] Much of the impact of these policies will depend on the effectiveness of other international efforts to reduce public sector corruption.

Investment Decisions and Human Rights

While firms in extractive industries are among the most visible targets of human rights activists, companies in a number of other sectors are also under growing pressure to incorporate human rights considerations into their investment and lending decisions. Some of these pressures have led businesses to curtail their activities in countries that have become the focus of public protest.

Pressure to Divest: From South Africa to Burma

CSR and human rights have long focused their attention on practices in individual countries. During the 1970s and 1980s, many NGOs in both the United States and Britain urged companies to sever their economic ties with the Republic of South Africa, and many did so.[35] In addition, corporate withdrawals helped prompt the American government to impose trade and investment restrictions. Since the early 1990s activists have mounted a similar campaign against foreign firms with investments in Burma (which adopted the name Myanmar in 1989).[36] Controlled by a military junta since the early 1960s, the government of Burma became increasingly repressive during the 1990s. The generals voided the results of a national election, imprisoned prodemocracy activist Aung San Suu Kyi (who won the Nobel peace prize in 1991), and forcibly conscripted hundreds of thousands of Burmese, including women and children, to work on construction projects, often with little or no pay. At the same time, foreign investment grew steadily, increasing more than fourfold during the first half of the 1990s. By the middle of the decade, approximately 325 foreign firms had business links to Burma through direct investments, subsidiaries, or partnerships—in some cases with the Burmese military, whose holding company is the country's largest investor.

The largest foreign investments in Burma were for the construction of two natural gas pipelines to transport gas from the Andaman Sea, which contained an estimated 5 million cubic feet of reserves. The result of a joint venture among the national energy companies of Burma and Thailand, the U.S. firm Unocal, and the French firm Total, the $1.2 billion project began in 1996 and was completed two years later. Production began in 2000.

Unocal has invested $340 million in the pipeline, making it the largest American investor in Burma. Aware from the outset of the controversy raised by this investment, Unocal cosponsored a three-year, $6 million socioeconomic development program and employed 2,000 workers at above-market wages to construct the thirty-nine miles of pipeline that ran through Burma.

Nevertheless, the pipeline project has been widely criticized by human rights, environmental, and consumer organizations. In 1995, after a survey team was attacked, the Burmese government sent large numbers of troops to the area. According to a UN official, "arbitrary killings, beatings, rapes and confiscation of property . . . [were] most commonly occurring in the border areas where the Army [was] engaged in military operations or regional development projects." The pipeline's opponents claimed that several villages had been destroyed or relocated to clear the pipeline route and charged that a railway built to transport security troops had inflicted widespread environmental damage and employed forced labor. Environmental groups predicted that the onshore pipeline would result in widespread environmental destruction of wetlands as well as to the mangrove ecosystems, and expressed concern about the lack of adequate environmental controls by the Burmese government on the pipeline's operations.[37]

In the early 1990s a group of students joined forces with Global Exchange, an international human rights organization, to form the Free Burma Coalition. Modeled on the anti-apartheid movement, one of its primary objectives was to weaken the military government by cutting off foreign investment. By early 1997 the coalition had achieved considerable success. It was at least partially responsible for the decision of Federated Department Stores, Disney, Eddie Bauer, Levi Strauss, Liz Claiborne, Reebok, and Sears to end their business ties in Burma. They were subsequently joined by Apple Computer, Eastman Kodak, Hewlett-Packard, General Electric, and PepsiCo—following a nationwide boycott of Pepsi and the firm's fast-food franchises, Taco Bell and Pizza Hut.[38] More significantly, both Texaco and Arco, which had been granted exploration concessions for a natural gas project, withdrew their proposed investments in response to consumer and investor pressures, as did Premier Oil, UK.

Unocal, not surprisingly, remains the primary target of the Free Burma Coalition. With active chapters on more than one hundred college campuses and in more than twenty-five countries, the coalition has sponsored consumer boycotts and letter-writing campaigns, urging its members to send their mutilated gas credit cards to Unocal's CEO. It also filed several shareholder resolutions, one of which called on Unocal to adopt the International Labor Organization's Code of Conduct on Workplace Human Rights. In 2002 this resolution was supported by a record 31 percent of the shares voted.

Employing a novel tactic, the coalition filed a lawsuit under the hitherto obscure 1789 Alien Tort Claims Act on behalf of Burmese villagers, claiming they had been harmed when the army of Burma forced them to clear jungle for the company's natural gas pipeline and that companies could be held "vicariously liable" for the damage they caused.[39] This lawsuit was settled in December 2004, when Unocal agreed to pay an unspecified amount to the plaintiffs and to provide extra funds for development in areas surrounding the pipelines.[40] A similar suit is pending against Total. Both companies, however, insist that no forced labor went into the pipeline's construction and that they should not be held responsible for the conduct of the Burmese military.

It is testimony to the effectiveness of American public pressures for divestment, including a consumer boycott, that Unocal sold off its Union 76 service stations and consumer products divisions.[41] In its 1994 annual report, the company stated that it "no longer considers itself as a U.S. company," and in April 1997 it opened what it termed a "twin corporate headquarters in Malaysia" to which it posted the company's president and several senior executives.[42] Unocal's board of directors has periodically reviewed the project's social impact and continues to argue that it "represents a significant opportunity to bring sustainable, long-term benefits to the people."[43] Like Total, it has indicated that it plans to remain in Burma. Unocal has, however, responded to activists and shareholders by hiring a director of corporate responsibility, establishing an internal corporate responsibility steering team, and issuing a human rights report.

The pattern of corporate responses to pressures for divestment is similar in Burma and South Africa. In the latter there was considerable divestment by consumer goods and manufacturing companies, but none by firms involved in natural resource extraction. Moreover, a number of the American firms that left South Africa found it difficult to regain their market share after sanctions were lifted following the end of apartheid in 1993. Their competitive disadvantage vis-à-vis those firms who remained suggests that, at least in this case, corporate virtue was not rewarded. It remains to be seen whether this will also prove true in Burma, where democracy remains elusive. The country's military rulers appear indifferent to the economic losses caused by the withdrawal of some foreign investors and the restrictions of foreign trade and investment.

Moreover, not all firms are equally vulnerable to domestic pressures to change their business practices, especially when their policies are voluntary. Non-U.S.-headquartered companies have been and remain the major foreign investors in Burma. (In 1990 less than one-fifth of the foreign firms in Burma were headquartered in the United States.) One of the two controversial natural gas pipeline projects, worth $1.2 billion, is managed by the French firm TotalFina Elf, which has a 31 percent equity interest. Mitsubishi is constructing a $70 million storage facility as part of the natural gas project, which it will then lease for fifteen years. Both British American Tobacco and the courier DHL, a subsidiary of Germany's Deutsche Post, continue to do business in Burma, as do Mazda, Sony, Suzuki, Samsung, Daewoo, and Hyundai.[44] After Premier Oil of the United Kingdom sold its stake in a pipeline project following a sustained public divestment campaign, its share was purchased by Malaysia's state-owned energy firm.[45]

Beyond Burma

A number of firms have become more discriminating in their sourcing and investment decisions. According to a survey conducted by Business for Social Responsibility in 2002, many multinational firms now have lists of countries that are off-limits to sourcing, with over half employing country selection criteria that include social indicators.[46] While Burma showed up most frequently on the lists of proscribed countries, thirty other countries also appeared on at least one corporate list, notably Sudan, the only other country from which firms have recently found themselves pressured to divest.[47]

Another survey, conducted by the United Kingdom's Ashridge Centre for Business and Society, reported that human rights issues had caused 36 percent of the biggest 500 companies to abandon a proposed investment project and 19 percent to disinvest from a country.[48] (However, only fifty-two of the Fortune Global 500 responded to this survey, virtually all of which were based in Europe or the United States.) Similarly, a World Bank survey of 107 companies from the extractive, agribusiness, and manufacturing sectors found that 36 percent of those responding had withdrawn from a country because of CSR concerns. In the extractive sector a majority reported that they have chosen not to enter a country because of CSR concerns, but far fewer reported withdrawing once operations have been established. As a World Bank report explained: "To a greater extent than other sectors, the extractive sector faces high up-front capital expenditures, long-term horizons for return on investment, and steep political and social learning curves when entering each new country."[49]

The experiences of Levi Strauss reflect some of the difficulties of balancing investment and human rights considerations. In 1993, when Levi Strauss implemented its "Guidelines for Country Selection" it decided to phase out production in China.[50] According to Levi Strauss's manager of communications, the majority of participants in the company's China Policy Group had recommended staying in China, but senior managers did not think the potential benefits outweighed the risks to brand image, corporate reputation, and long-term commercial interests.[51] As the only firm ever to restrict its investments in China on human rights grounds, the company's decision attracted considerable publicity and was widely applauded by the human rights community.[52]

The company's production volume from China initially decreased by about 70 percent, from 2.6 million units to 800,000. But it then made no further cuts. Five years later, in 1998, faced with declining sales, it quietly reversed its policy. The company officially claimed that the human rights situation in China had improved, thus making it possible to find responsible suppliers. But according to Peter Jacobi, the company's president, commercial considerations drove Levi Strauss's decision. "[The] company had no choice but to engage itself more fully in China or risk losing out in the competitive game of the global apparel business," he explained, adding, "You're nowhere in Asia without being in China."[53]

Lending Decisions

Financial institutions have also found themselves under pressure to incorporate human rights concerns into their corporate strategy. Bank-Track, an alliance of fifteen organizations, including Friends of the Earth and the Rainforest Action Network, has attempted to make banks more accountable for the social consequences of their lending decisions. According to a study by KPMG and F&C Asset Management, a European investment manager with $217 billion under management, banks "are likely to continue to be drawn into the human rights debate, if not willingly then by default," because they do not want to risk being associated with human rights abuses committed by their customers.[54]

In 2003, ten major financial institutions agreed to adopt principles developed by the World Bank's International Finance Corporation for lending to infrastructure projects in developing countries.[55] Labeled the Equator Principles, they established environmental and social impact standards for project financing, ranging from environmental assessment and natural habitat protection to the protection of indigenous peoples and child labor. Borrowers that fail to comply with the loan conditions can be held in default.[56]

To date, the principles have been endorsed by twenty-eight financial institutions in fourteen countries who are collectively responsible for more than 80 percent of international project financing. Signatories include the Bank of America and Citicorp in the United States, as well as financial institutions in Germany, France, Great Britain, Australia, the Netherlands, Switzerland, Brazil, and Japan. The firms' motivations for joining have varied. Some were concerned about risk to their reputation; others, such as Citibank, were under pressure from activists who had encouraged consumers to cut up their bank credit cards; and others were seeking to position themselves as leaders in sustainable development. In some cases banks agreed to the principles in order to restore their reputations following a series of financial scandals.[57]

Under the principles, all lending projects are grouped into one of three categories, depending on the environmental and social risks associated with them. For the riskiest projects, such as dams and power plants, the banks agreed to require environmental impact assessments, public consultations, and increased transparency from the borrower. The principles were consistent with some institutions' existing practices and strengthened others'. The signatory banks hope the standards become industry norms so that they do not lose customers to competitors that are unwilling to uphold them.

Again, though, these principles have no enforcement mechanism—other than public and possibly peer pressure—or disclosure requirements, though Citibank and some others have agreed to report on their progress in implementing the agreement's provisions. When the first sixteen financial signatories met with representatives of thirteen NGOs in London in June 2004, six banks described in general terms what they had done to implement the principles and how their approach to project financing had changed since their adoption. Citibank, for example, has committed itself to work with the Rainforest Action Network to protect ecologically or socially fragile areas, and both HSBC and the Bank of America have established new guidelines for loans that affect forestry.

However, according to BankTrack, "Signatories are still funding unsustainable projects and . . . it is unclear to what extent banks are actually complying with the principles." For example, BankTrack has criticized Equator banks for funding the Baku-Tbilisi-Ceylon pipeline because it violated "ethical, legal and human rights standards."[58] A report issued by a consortium of global NGOs on the principles' first anniversary criticized signatory banks for their lack of transparency in implementing the "Triple P": the balancing of people, planets, and profits.[59] NGO officials believe progress is being made, but that there is still a long way to go.[60] However, NGO priorities are not necessarily the same as those of developing country governments. For example, many NGOs have opposed virtually every proposal to finance new dam construction in developing countries and are also against any lending for oil and gas projects. Yet many of these projects may make positive contributions to local and national development.[61] As in the case of pressures to end child labor, not all NGO demands on corporations create net social benefits.

Toward Global Norms of Corporate Citizenship?

The most ambitious effort to develop norms for global corporations is the UN-sponsored Global Compact.[62] The idea for a global compact was first proposed by UN Secretary-General Kofi Annan in a speech to the World Economic Forum in January 1999. Officially launched two years later, it represents the first effort of the UN to work with business: its goal was to fill "the governance void of the global economy" and "humanize the globalization process."[63] Its strategy is to identify a set of core principles covering human and workplace rights, corruption, and environmental responsibility and then to encourage companies to incorporate them into their global business operations.

The compact is a code of conduct but contains no certification standards. The compact "consider(s) companies to be participants engaged in a multi-stakeholder network, not members of a club that have met some performance standard to gain entry."[64] By signing on to the compact, a company publicly commits to support its principles and to attempt to abide by them. The compact had originally required signatory companies to submit examples of how they had adopted its principles, but this requirement was discontinued at the end of 2002. It now requires companies to publish their progress in living up to the compact's principles in their annual financial reports or in separate CSR reports, which are then accessible through the UN's web portal. The compact also has begun to develop plans for "delisting" inactive companies.

With 1,366 corporate participants, the Global Compact is the largest voluntary citizenship network, far exceeding, for example, the Global Reporting Initiative (387 participants) or SA8000 (353 participants).[65] Its local activities involve an additional 1,000 firms. Nearly half of the compact's membership are European firms, but only 8 percent are based in North America. Despite its considerable efforts to recruit American companies, they have not joined in large numbers. This appears to be due to three factors: fear of legal liabilities related to endorsing the compact's principles, concern about the implications of the compact's labor rights provisions, and a lower opinion of the value of the UN. In contrast, the compact has attracted substantial participation from developing countries: 147 signatories from the Philippines, 95 from India, 83 from Brazil, and 52 from Panama.

According to Georg Kell, the compact's executive director, the compact has attracted four kinds of firms. First are those companies that have been forced to adopt CSR policies owing to pressures from activists and now want to use the compact to encourage their competitors to adopt similar policies. Second are firms from developing countries who want to learn more about the potential for private-public initiatives. A third group of firms are interested in exploring future public-private initiatives, often with the assistance of international organizations. In the fourth category are those with executives "who are genuinely interested in making the world a better place" and want to encourage other firms to do likewise.[66]

The Global Compact has adopted a learning approach to redefining global CSR. To improve corporate practices and policies it sponsors learning forums where academics, executives, and NGO representatives discuss both the opportunities and challenges of global CSR. But 86 percent of the compact's signatories have not attended any international meeting, and six out of seven participants have yet to make any submissions to its online learning forum.[67] However, a recent survey reports that nearly half of the signatory companies have changed some policies in relation to the compact's ten principles and 34 percent cite the Global Compact as a significant driver of these changes. According to one manager, "Without the Compact, many projects would be happening, but only at a regional or local level. The Compact 'upsized' the issues and made them global." More than half of the survey respondents have entered into local partnership projects, incorporated human rights principles into company policies, or revised human resources policies to eliminate discrimination.[68]

For firms based in OECD countries, the compact is best understood as signaling their continued engagement with corporate citizenship, rather than a markedly new commitment, though it does appear to have promoted an increase in partnership projects between companies and international development agencies.[69] Its most likely impact will be on the human rights practices of firms from developing countries, many of whom have become participants in a global CSR network for the first time. The compact's impact on the supply of global corporate virtue has been "incremental," and some NGOs view companies' participation in the compact as "a defensive response by trans-national corporations to public pressure. By establishing this blue chip minimalism, they hope to avoid something that would lead to a more serious (and effective) means of accountability/regulation at the global level."[70]

Despite such critiques, the UN Global Compact's broad membership suggests that business norms regarding social responsibility are taking root beyond just the United States and Europe. Some firms in South Africa, Brazil, Mexico, Malaysia, and Costa Rica, among others, have begun to develop their own CSR programs.[71] Nonetheless, only a small portion of the tens of thousands of global firms have joined the compact.

Assessing the Business Case for Human Rights

A report by Amnesty International warns companies: "The increasing scrutiny of corporate behavior by the media, consumer groups, community organizations, local and international nongovernmental organizations and the immediacy of global communication leave companies with little, if any, hiding place."[72] But not all firms are equally vulnerable to public disapproval: witness the large number of global firms that have remained in Burma or that continue to be associated with human rights violations. Many extractive industry firms have no visible brand; they do not sell directly to consumers and many are headquartered in countries where civic pressures are minimal or nonexistent. When the Canadian oil company Talisman, which had a major concession in Sudan, withdrew after activist campaigns caused its stock price to plunge, the largest foreign investors in this country became firms from China, Malaysia, and India, where NGO pressures are much weaker.[73]

There is a similar international response to calls for divestment from Burma, allegations of human rights abuses in other countries, and pressure to adopt codes of conduct and transparency. U.S. and British firms have been the most responsive to pressures in their home countries, followed by a few other European firms, but trailed by Asian corporations. Consider, for example, that "the vast majority of companies listed on the CAC 40 (the main stock exchange index on the French Bourse) . . . have subsidiaries or other commercial activities in many countries directly targeted by human rights activists."[74] When the *Financial Times* Stock Exchange launched its ethical index in 2001, it excluded ten French firms on the basis of human rights criteria: 25 percent of the CAC 40. As one executive from the French firm Total explained in a 1997 interview inquiring about the firm's investments in Iraq, Iran, and Libya: "It's just that the Lord put the reserves in places that are a bit hot on political grounds. We're a bit more relaxed about such countries than some of our competitors. . . . We're certainly more comfortable than some other European oil companies. Only some Asian companies feel as free to invest as we do."[75]

Moreover, as the experience of Levi Strauss in China illustrates, companies can be financially disadvantaged by voluntary restrictions on where they do business. No global manufacturing firm can afford not to produce or sell in China as a matter of principle, and none have. Indeed, Burma and Sudan are the only countries from which many Western firms have withdrawn their investments in response to activists' demands. Yet while Sudan's human rights abuses are unique, corporate investments in natural resource development continue to expand in many countries whose human rights practices are comparable to those of Burma, such as the Asian nations of the former Soviet Union. Burma is also a small, poor country with a limited market for consumer goods, and there is no shortage of other countries to which firms can outsource low-wage manufacturing. And while an individual oil company can withdraw from a region, or decline to do business in a particular country, the number of places it can exclude is limited by the geographic location of energy resources.

The failure of companies to take human rights issues into account in making investment decisions or managing business operations poses another business risk, namely that local violence can force withdrawal from a project. Like Shell, in 1999 Texaco was forced by community protests to halt its operations in the Niger Delta, and two years later ExxonMobil shut down production at a liquefied natural gas facility in

Indonesia for several months after it was attacked by armed separatists.[76] These business risks have prompted NGOs to lobby pension funds to consider development and human rights issues in their investment decisions.

Despite these risks, there is little evidence that investors believe they will have a material impact on financial performance. Either the business risks of investments in repressive, corrupt, or unstable regimes or regions are not significant, or whatever risks some firms face are outweighed by the benefits of these investments. In short, while there may be a business case for more responsible investment or community relations policies, investors and many firms have yet to appreciate it:

> The reality is that many of the advantages of a good human rights record may not manifest themselves in the short term. . . . The costs (e.g. of developing and implementing human rights management systems) are incurred in the short term, [while] the benefits may be long term, and are, in many cases, likely to be extremely difficult to measure in financial terms. . . . Many companies . . . frequently see human rights as being at odds with short-term business requirements."[77]

Conclusion

Multinational firms face major challenges in developing and implementing human rights policies that extend beyond the employees of their subcontractors. In many respects they are in uncharted territory, under pressure to assume obligations that have historically been the responsibilities of governments or international institutions. A number of firms and banks have taken human rights issues into account in their investment decisions, others have taken steps to be more responsible corporate citizens abroad, and several banks have adopted social criteria for lending policies. But substantive changes remain limited: many standards for corporate human rights practices are ill-defined, the monitoring of particular business investments tends to be media-driven, and not all global firms face similar domestic pressure to act more virtuously.

Global firms that want to balance respect for human rights with business imperatives have few easy choices. Geir Westgaad, vice president for country analysis and social responsibility at Statoil, observes that globalization means that "what happens in an isolated area of a jungle becomes an international issue."[78] This is a lesson that Shell, BP, Premier Oil, ExxonMobil, Newmont Mining, Rio Tinto, PepsiCo, and Citbank, among others, have learned painfully. But even the most proactive investment or lending policies may not be able to avoid violence or human rights controversies in host countries, especially since local conflicts over foreign investment are often rooted in long-standing regional and ethnic tensions. And more responsible corporate practices may fail if the host government is itself repressive or corrupt or hostile or indifferent to environmental protection and community development. It does little good for a company to commit to a policy of not paying bribes if the host country government demands them. Moreover, while more irresponsible human rights practices can threaten a firm's international reputation, they can also restrict where it makes investments and loans, placing it at a competitive disadvantage if its competitors are less vulnerable to NGO and public criticism.

CHAPTER 7

Beyond the Market for Virtue

Since the 1990s, many major American and European manufacturers and retailers headquartered in the United States and Europe have adopted voluntary standards for labor conditions, environmental practices, and human rights. These new commitments have been institutionalized in corporate and industry codes, multi-stakeholder initiatives, and private standard-setting bodies, often with reporting and monitoring requirements. This complex web of "soft" law has constructed new social norms for several important dimensions of business conduct.

The market for virtue, or civil regulation, has produced important changes in corporate practices, including:

—a reduction in the employment of child labor and an improvement in health and safety conditions in many of the factories and workshops that supply clothing, athletic equipment, toys, and rugs to Western manufacturing and retail firms (see chapter 4);

—an increase in the prices some agricultural producers in developing countries—notably coffee growers—receive for their products (chapter 4);

—a reduction in the quantity of wood products sold in the United States and Europe produced from tropical, old-growth, and endangered forests (chapter 5);

—a decrease in greenhouse gas emissions or in their rate of growth (chapter 5);

—the withdrawal of many companies from Burma (chapter 6);

—the amelioration of some of the negative environmental and social impacts of natural resource development in developing countries (chapter 6).

Other examples beyond the scope of this book could be added to this list, such as lower prices for AIDS drugs in many countries and an expansion in the number of corporate-community partnerships in developing countries. In short, those who claim that in the absence of additional government regulatory requirements firms are incapable of behaving more responsibly are misinformed. The market *can* supply more virtue.

As many critics of CSR have observed, social welfare would be enhanced even more if many of these voluntary standards were made legally binding. While this may well be true, it should not be allowed to obscure the significance of the improvements that *have* taken place. It would be better if China enforced its labor laws, but even if the government fails to act, Mattel can improve conditions for some Chinese workers. It would be better if Vietnam had more stringent occupational safety and health standards, but in their absence, thanks to Nike, some workers are exposed to fewer hazards. It would be better if the Indian government provided schools for all the country's children, but at least Ikea and the Rugmark Foundation can give more Indian children access to education. It would be better if the United States imposed legally binding restrictions on emissions of greenhouse gases, but since it has been unwilling to do so, voluntary corporate programs are better than nothing.

It would be better if the United States imposed tighter restrictions on the harvesting of old-growth and endangered forests, but until that day arrives, Home Depot's procurement policies have helped protect some of those forests. It would be better if the government restricted the administration of antibiotics to cattle and chicken, but in the absence of such regulations, thanks to McDonald's, fewer Americans consume food containing these drugs. It would be better (for producers, at least) if global coffee prices were higher, but thanks to Fair Trade, at least some coffee growers are receiving additional income. It would be better if the government of Chad could be trusted to use its oil revenues responsibly, but given that it cannot, ExxonMobil's efforts to monitor its royalty payments increase the likelihood that at least some of the payments will not be squandered. It would be better if the government of Indonesia enforced adequate environmental protection standards, but since it does not, ChevronTexaco's efforts have better protected the fragile ecosystems of Papua New Guinea. In short, CSR may frequently be a second-best alternative, but second-best is still better than nothing at all.

At the same time, there remains a substantial gap between discourse and practice with respect to virtually all codes and voluntary standards.[1] The most effective voluntary agreements appear to be those governing carbon emissions, though their stringency varies widely. Codes governing labor standards have important limitations when it comes to monitoring and enforcement, and the impact of social labels, such as Fair Trade, FSC, and Rugmark, is limited by their small market shares. The effectiveness of codes, such as the Voluntary Principles on Security and Human Rights, the Equator Principles, Publish What You Pay, the UN Global Compact, and the Mining, Minerals and Sustainable Development Project, also appears to be limited, although it is hard to be sure because there are so few reporting requirements and so little independent monitoring in place. Other initiatives, such as the Cocoa Industry Protocol and the Common Code for the Coffee Community, have been established too recently to be assessed.

The shortcomings of civil regulation remain substantial:

—Many workers in factories that produce goods for Western manufacturers and retailers are not paid the wages owed to them, work for long hours in poor conditions, and lack freedom of association (chapter 4).

—Living standards have improved for only a small number of workers who produce agricultural commodities for export (chapter 4).

—The rate of tropical deforestation remains significant, and many forests in both developed and developing countries are still managed unsustainably (chapter 5).

—Greenhouse gas emissions from American and European firms continue to increase (chapter 5).

—Many corporate royalty payments continue to benefit primarily corrupt elites (chapter 6).

—Many extractive industry investments continue to be associated with environmental and human rights abuses (chapter 6).

Of course more improvements are likely, especially if reporting requirements and independent monitoring are strengthened. But they will remain incremental because there are important structural limitations to the market for virtue. One of the most important is the cost of more responsible corporate behavior. Although many corporations have increased the resources they devote to CSR, they are rarely sufficient to adequately address the problems they are intended to ameliorate. One reason CSR often appears to "pay" is not so much because its benefits are so substantial as because its costs have usually been modest. Most firms' CSR expenditures fall well within their limits of discretionary spending. Even the above-average expenditures of some companies—such as BP, Shell, Nike, HP, the Gap, Timberland, M&S, and Merck—are small in comparison with their earnings.

Consider what the world would look like if companies actually adhered to the voluntary standards described in this book. Employees of firms in developing countries who supply products for export would be treated according to the terms of the corporate and labor codes that have emerged in the United States and Europe over the past decade. Producers of agricultural commodities such as coffee, whose products are consumed in the United States and Europe, would receive prices sufficient to enable them to maintain their living standards in the face of declining global commodity prices. Forestry products consumed in the United States and Europe would be harvested from sustainably managed forests. International companies would not do business in places with pervasive human rights violations, would not engage in bribery, and would not allow their royalty payments to be misused. International banks would not make loans to environmentally problematic projects in developing countries. The amount of carbon dioxide emitted by industrial firms would stabilize or decline.

Some of these improvements would undoubtedly produce benefits for some firms. But in most cases those benefits would be outweighed by additional costs. These costs would then need to be passed on to some combination of consumers, employees, and investors. But how likely is it that consumers would accept higher prices, that employees in the United States and Europe would accept lower wages and benefits, and that shareholders would accept lower returns to support more virtuous behavior? To ask this question is to answer it. Many companies would be willing to behave more responsibly if consumers, employees, and investors were willing to bear the additional costs of their doing so. But for the most part they are not. Accordingly, achieving many of these goals through civil regulation is not practicable. The market for virtue does not clear.

What would it take, for example, for Ford to produce substantially more fuel-efficient vehicles? The answer is very simple. Ford would produce such vehicles if large numbers of consumers were willing to buy them. What would it take for BP to actually move "Beyond Petroleum"? The answer is: consumer demand for renewable energy comparable to current demand for fossil fuels. What would it take for Wal-Mart to effectively monitor its suppliers and demand adherence to its stated labor practices? The answer is: consumer willingness to pay more for more responsibly produced apparel and toys. What would it take for Shell to search for energy only in countries with good human rights records? The answer is: customer willingness to pay higher prices for gasoline from Shell. What would it take for the world's major coffee companies to pay farmers higher prices? The answer is: the willingness of large numbers of consumers to pay more for coffee.

Similarly, MBA students who say they are willing to accept lower salaries from more responsible firms are on the right track. Imagine, for example, the difference it might make to firms' incentives to act more responsibly if they could attract the managers they want at substantially lower cost. Those firms could devote additional resources to CSR without reducing profits or earnings. But realistically, the chances of this happening are slim.

In the same vein, the claim of socially responsible investment funds— that their rate of return will equal, perhaps even exceed, that of main-stream investment funds—may well be counterproductive. These funds might have a much greater impact on corporate social and environmental performance if they were more willing to also invest in companies that earned less because they had chosen to act more responsibly. Such a policy might of course also require investors to accept lower returns. But there is little evidence that the growing numbers of "ethical" investors are prepared to do so. They want to be both virtuous *and* prosperous, but unfortunately the two are not always compatible.

The popularity of the business case for CSR has fostered the illusion that CSR is "free." *But if companies were more virtuous, the costs of CSR would become much clearer.* Although few current expenditures on CSR are considered "material" by security analysts, this would change for many firms if they became significantly *more* responsible. As Simon Zadek, who has played a key role in a number of CSR initiatives, acknowledges, "Even the strongest and most progressive corporations, acting alone, will rarely be able to sustain *significantly* enhanced social and environmental performance for extended periods of time."[2] In order for corporations to make sustainable improvements in their social and environmental performance, the role of government must also change.

From Government to Civil Regulation

Civil regulation has often been linked to public policy, one frequently contributing to the other. Several corporate labor codes draw on the standards of the Core Conventions of the International Labor Organization, which date from the 1940s and have been periodically updated. Other company and industry codes refer to the 1948 Universal Declaration of Human Rights and the 1997 ILO Tripartite Declaration of Principles Concerning Multinational Enterprises and Human Rights. Many corporate codes have also been influenced by the OECD Guidelines for Multinational Enterprises, which have established voluntary standards for corporate conduct.

The first voluntary industry code governing working conditions in global apparel factories grew out of the Apparel Industry Partnership created by the Clinton administration in 1996. Two years later, the British government was instrumental in the creation of the Ethical Trading Initiative, an alliance of companies, trade unions, and NGOs that seeks to improve labor conditions in developing countries. The Voluntary Principles for Security and Human Rights were a joint initiative of several global firms and the British and American governments. The negotiations that led to the code to improve working conditions and environmental standards for coffee producers were funded by the German government. Publish What You Pay, which promotes transparency in royalty payments in extractive industries, was endorsed by ten governments in addition to several major global firms and is paralleled by the Extractive Industries Transparency Initiative, which supports government efforts to combat corruption and which in turn was influenced by American legislation. The threat of American trade sanctions helped prompt chocolate manufacturers to accept responsibility for labor conditions in the Ivory Coast. Many of the efforts of American and European corporations to reduce their greenhouse gas emissions have been made in anticipation of government regulation. The United Nations created the UN Global Compact, and the World Bank's International Finance Corporation developed the lending standards that formed the basis for the Equator Principles. At the regional level, the European Union has engaged in a series of initiatives designed to define and disseminate best CSR practices among European-based companies, though it has rejected proposals to make CSR standards legally binding. A number of European governments have also promoted CSR through policy initiatives such as legislation mandating nonfinancial reporting and requiring pension funds to consider ethical criteria in their investment decisions.

From Civil to Government Regulation

Some civil norms have become legally binding. Two important cases in the United States are discussed in this book. In the first case, voluntary corporate withdrawals from Burma were followed by the imposition of trade and investment restrictions by the American government; the former played a critical role in facilitating the enactment of the latter.

In the second case, under the provisions of the Alien Tort Claims Act of 1789, which states that "the district courts shall have original jurisdiction of any civil action by an alien for tort only, committed in violation of the law of nations or a treaty of the United States," several American corporations have been sued for human rights violations committed outside the United States, including Unocal, IBM, ExxonMobil, Chevron-Texaco, Citicorp, Coca-Cola, Ford, and Del Monte.[3] The purpose of these suits is to use "civil liability . . . [as] a credible cudgel to hammer corporate miscreants for their exploitive practices in the developing would or punish their support for repressive regimes."[4]

The lawsuit against Unocal has been settled, as discussed in chapter 6. Other cases have been dismissed or are yet to be decided. The Bush administration has strongly opposed these suits, and their future legal status is unclear. But this litigation does represent the beginning of a serious effort to hold global firms legally accountable for violating the global norms established by voluntary codes and international treaties. The effectiveness of this effort to make soft law "hard" remains to be seen, especially given the strong opposition of the American government and business community to expanding the scope of international law. However, many companies with international operations are quite concerned about their potential legal vulnerability, if not under this statute, then under similar ones.[5]

The third case in which civil norms took on the force of law involved the United States' agreement in 1999 to accept more textile exports from Cambodia if the government allowed foreign monitors to inspect Cambodian garment factories and certify that labor standards were improving.[6] This was the first time the United States made preferential access to its domestic market contingent on good labor practices. This arrangement has not been problem-free. One of its unintended consequences was to promote labor unrest as Cambodian workers organized to demand increased wages they felt were due them under the agreement. In addition, the International Labor Organization, which was supposed to supply monitors, has lacked the resources to do so effectively, forcing American firms such as Gap Inc. to bear these costs.

Nonetheless, in December 2004, with the multi-fiber trade agreement expiring—and with it Cambodia's privileged access to the American market—many American and European buyers indicated that they planned to maintain or increase their purchases from Cambodia. They regard the country's relatively strong labor standards as helping to protect them from accusations that they are exploiting workers in developing countries. This suggests that the willingness of Cambodian garment manufacturers to open their factories to independent outside inspectors may assist them in competition for orders against China, which is a more efficient producer.

In Europe the most prominent example of the transition from self-regulation to legal requirements involves global climate change. What were once voluntary policies became legally binding with the European Union's ratification of the Kyoto Treaty in 2004. Equally important, the strategy adopted by BP and Shell to reduce their own carbon emissions, namely emissions trading, has become the centerpiece of public regulatory strategies. In the area of human rights, the EU has restricted imports from Burma and gives greater market access to countries with better labor and human rights practices. Finally, the aftermath of the Brent Spar case provides another example of the movement from civil to government regulation: Greenpeace's objection to Shell's decision to dispose of obsolete oil platforms on land subsequently became enshrined in international law.

Working Together:
Corporate Social Responsibility and Regulation

The fact that a company has voluntarily adopted a particular social or environmental practice does not mean that public welfare would be enhanced if all other companies were required to do the same. In fact, the public interest might well have been better served had onshore disposal of obsolete oil platforms from the North Sea *not* been made mandatory. Likewise, were the Vietnamese government to implement Nike's restrictions on the employment of workers younger than 18, Vietnamese families would be worse off. More broadly, the interests and priorities of citizens in developing countries may or not parallel the preferences of Western NGOs. And expansions of government regulation often generate corporate rents at the expense of public welfare.

There is a role for both voluntary and legally binding standards; the two should not necessarily converge. But governments remain essential to improving corporate behavior. As a recent World Bank report observes:

> Public sector regulatory and enforcement capacity plays a critically important role in underpinning CSR. When minimum environmental and social standards are established and evenhandedly implemented by public sector actors or citizens acting on rights reflected in public sector action, market-based signals can work to reward those players who go further. Without that capacity or the necessary attention to fundamental citizens' rights, businesses face substantial difficulties in finding and maintaining appropriate boundaries for their CSR interventions.[7]

The bottom line, the report finds, is that "the voluntary CSR practices of private enterprise cannot be an effective substitute for good governance."[8] This assessment is echoed by Adam Greene of the U.S. Center for International Business: "CSR and partnerships are often 'drops in the bucket,' nibbling at the edges of major public problems. They are not the road out. The road out is a functioning government, a good court system, economic opportunity for growth."[9]

Not only is CSR not a substitute for effective government, but the effectiveness of much civil regulation depends on a strong and well-functioning public sphere. This is particularly true when it comes to corporate commitments to avoid corruption and respect human rights. In these areas, there are limits to what even the most socially committed firm can accomplish in the absence of responsible government practices and policies. The impact of corporate commitments not to pay bribes will be undermined if governments continue to demand them, while many of the ethnic tensions and violence associated with investments by extractive industries stem from public governance failures. In China, government policies have undermined the enforcement of voluntary labor codes, especially by prohibiting independent unions. The impact of voluntary corporate withdrawals from Burma and the Sudan is limited by the lack of international restrictions on foreign investment in these countries.

By working with and pressuring governments to enhance their capacity to develop and enforce their own environmental, labor, and human rights standards, Western companies can both reduce their own monitoring costs and strengthen the credibility of their codes.[10] Corporate investors, working with Western governments and international organizations, also can assist or encourage the strengthening of civil society in developing countries. This might better enable their citizens to demand their own standards for corporate conduct, without having to rely on pressures from Western activists. For their part, Western governments can assist this process by incorporating labor and environmental provisions into bilateral and regional trade agreements, giving preferential market access to governments with effective regulatory standards, and providing governments with technical and financial support, as the European Union does for its new member states.[11] The point of such policies and programs is not necessarily to codify the standards of Western firms or governments, but to assist developing countries in defining and enforcing their own regulatory standards, thus creating a level playing field for all domestic companies, not only those producing goods for Western firms targeted by activists.

Such policy initiatives can also enhance developing countries' attractiveness to foreign investors looking for locations for "responsible" purchasing. For example, Cambodian garment manufacturers are now seeking to leverage their trade agreement with the United States by carving out a niche market as Asia's labor-friendly producer, as is Vietnam following a trade agreement with the United States that incorporates provisions to promote CSR.[12] Likewise, extractive industry firms might well prefer to invest in developing countries with less corruption and responsible human rights policies.

Redefining Responsibility

The important complementary relationship between civil and government regulation suggests that the definition of a responsible corporation needs to be expanded. Corporate responsibility should be about more than going "beyond compliance"; it must also include efforts to raise compliance standards. In fact, the most critical dimension of corporate responsibility may well be a company's impact on public policy.[13] A company's political activities typically have far broader social consequences than its own practices. Yet relatively few of the demands raised by activists or social investors have addressed business-government relations.[14] Corporate political positions are usually not included in the criteria employed by SRI. Nor are they included in the criteria for the numerous awards that recognize virtuous companies. Too many discussions of CSR, especially in the business community, ignore the importance of government. Those who tout the business benefits and social accomplishments of CSR too often overlook the critical connections among corporate responsibility, corporate political activity, and public policy.[15]

As Brookings Institution scholar Ann Florini writes, "We talk about governance over firms, but business also influences global rules and regulation in negative and positive ways. This dynamic should not be separate from the CSR conversation. It is a two-way process."[16] Consequently, *the definition of corporate social responsibility needs to be redefined to include the responsibilities of business to strengthen civil society and the capacity of governments to require that all firms act more responsibly.* On its own, CSR can facilitate responsible regulation by demonstrating that some social benefits can be produced in a cost-effective manner. But simply providing a good example is not enough. Responsible firms also need to support public policies that establish minimum standards for their less virtuous competitors—not just to create a level playing field, but because such requirements are frequently necessary to accomplish the underlying goals of CSR. As Jeffrey Hollender of Seventh Generation, one of the few executives to explicitly acknowledge the limits of voluntary standards, observes:

> While there are still valid market forces inducing companies to be better corporate citizens, those market forces alone are rarely adequate to effect necessary change. Market forces, when they work, often produce cheaper and more innovative solutions to social and environmental problems, but that in and of itself will not provide an acceptable solution to the problems we face.[17]

Climate change in the United States provides a perfect example of how civil regulation can reinforce and facilitate government regulation. If many companies believe that greenhouse gas emissions should be reduced and that it is possible to do so efficiently—as they apparently do—then these same companies should support national legislation that forces all firms to reduce their greenhouse gas emissions in an efficient and cost-effective manner.[18] Otherwise, self-regulation will remain largely ineffective. For this reason, a firm that supports the establishment of minimum regulatory standards—but has not reduced its own emissions—is arguably more virtuous than one that has voluntarily cut back greenhouse gas emissions but opposes additional regulatory requirements.

There are other examples. If Home Depot wants to improve forestry practices, why not support legislation requiring all forests in the United States and Canada to be managed more responsibly? If Ikea wants to reduce the use of child labor in the production of rugs, why not propose an EU human rights label for this product? If Starbucks wants to improve conditions for coffee producers, why not support an international agreement to stabilize coffee prices? If Ford wants to manufacture and market more fuel-efficient vehicles, why doesn't it support public policies that would increase the market for these vehicles? If Interface believes our current industrial practices are unsustainable, and there is insufficient demand for its "greener" carpet products, why not support regulations to promote carpet recycling?

Unfortunately, too few firms have undertaken or supported such political initiatives, in part because they are hesitant to promote expansions of government regulatory requirements. Yet "soft" civil and "hard" government regulation can and should be reinforcing. For example, uniform legal disclosure and reporting requirements for the global practices of Western firms and their suppliers could strengthen both civil regulation and the capacity of developing country governments to monitor firm behavior. Even in developed countries, additional mandatory disclosure requirements for corporate nonfinancial performance could improve the effectiveness of both civil and government regulation by making corporate practices more transparent.[19]

If companies are serious about acting more responsibly, then they need to reexamine their relationship to government as well as improve their own practices. And those who want corporations to be more virtuous should expect firms to act more responsibly on both dimensions. Civil and government regulation both have a legitimate role to play in improving public welfare. The former reflects the potential of the market for virtue; the latter recognizes its limits.

Notes

Chapter One

1. The term "virtue," while typically employed in ethical discourse, is also used in a few other studies of CSR. See, for example, Michelle Micheletti, *Political Virtue and Shopping: Individuals, Consumerism, and Collective Action* (New York: Palgrave Macmillan, 2003); and David Henderson, *Misguided Virtue: False Notions of Corporate Social Responsibility* (London: Institute of Economic Affairs, 2001). My use of the term "market for virtue" is roughly similar to that of Thomas Dunfee in his article "The Marketplace of Morality: First Steps toward a Theory of Moral Agency," *Business Ethics Quarterly* 8, no. 1 (1998) 147–45.

2. Hollender is CEO of Seventh Generation, a company that produces natural products for the home. Quote is from the dust jacket of his book, Jeffrey Hollender and Stephen Fenichell, *What Matters Most: How a Small Group of Pioneers Is Teaching Social Responsibility to Big Business, and Why Big Business Is Listening* (New York: Basic Books, 2004). Joel Bakan, *The Corporation: The Pathological Pursuit of Profit and Power* (New York: Free Press, 2004), p. 28; and Martin Wolf, "Sleep-Walking with the Enemy," *Financial Times*, May 16, 2001, p. 21.

3. The term "civil regulation" is taken from Simon Zadek, *The Civil Corporation: The New Economy of Corporate Citizenship* (London: Earthscan, 2001).

4. "The Good Company," *Economist*, January 22, 2005, p. 3.

5. John Ruggie, "Reconstituting the Global Public Domain: Issues, Actors and Practices," Faculty Research Working Paper (Cambridge, Mass.: John F. Kennedy School of Government, July 2004), p. 21.

6. This phenomenon is explored in Micheletti, *Political Virtue and Shopping*; and in David Vogel, *Lobbying the Corporation: Citizen Challenges to Business Authority* (New York: Basic Books, 1978).

7. See, for example, J. Howard, J. Nash, and J. Ehrenfeld, "Standard Setting or Smokescreen? Implementation of a Voluntary Environmental Code," *California Management Review* (Winter 2000): 63–82.

8. For an influential criticism of CSR on the grounds that its social costs often exceed its benefits, see Ethan Kaplan, "The Corporate Ethics Crusade," *Foreign Affairs* (September–October 2001): 105–19.

9. For an overview of the strategies of activists who lobbied the corporation during the 1960s and 1970s in the United States, see Vogel, *Lobbying the Corporation*.

10. "Two-Faced Capitalism," *Economist*, January 24, 2004, p. 53.

11. See, for example, John Elkington, *Cannibals with Forks* (Gabriola Island, B.C: New Society, 1998); David Grayson and Adrian Hodges, *Everybody's Business: Managing Risks and Opportunities in Today's Global Society* (London: DK, 2002); Steve Hilton and Giles Gibbons, *Good Business: Your World Needs You* (New York: Texere, 2002); Zadek, *The Civil Corporation*; and Henderson, *Misguided Virtue*. For reports, see Christian Aid, *"Behind the Mask: The Real Face of CSR*, January 2004 (www.christian-aid.org.uk); Jem Bendell, Tim Concannon, Rupesh Shah, Wayne Visser, and Mark Young, *2003 Lifeworth Annual Review of Corporate Responsibility* (Sheffield, England: Lifeworth, with Greenleaf Publishing and the New Academy of Business, 2004) (www.lifeworth.com).

12. See Ariel Colonomos and Javier Santiso, "Vive La France! French Multinationals and the Global Genealogy of Corporate Responsibility," Fondation nationale des sciences politiques (Sciences Po), June 2004; also Michel Capron and Françoise Quairel-Lanoizelee, *Mythes et réalités de l'entreprise responsable* (Paris: Decouverte, 2004).

13. "Europe Outshines U.S. in Business Ethics," *Financial Times,* February 19, 2002, p. 9. See also Susan Ariel Aaronson and James T. Reeves, *Corporate Responsibility in the Global Village: The Role of Public Policy* (Washington: National Policy Association, 2002).

14. This is the central claim of David C. Korten, *When Corporations Rule the World* (Bloomfield, Conn.: Kumarian, 2001).

15. See Ronnie Lipschutz and Cathleen Fogel, "'Regulation for the Rest of Us?' Global Civil Society and the Privatization of Transnational Regulation," in *The Emergence of Private Authority in Global Governance*, edited by Rodney Bruce Hall and Thomas Biersteker (Cambridge University Press, 2002), p. 129. There is a large scholarly literature on the growing importance of private authority, especially at the international level. See, for example, A. Claire Cutler, Virginia Haufler, and Tony Porter, eds., *Private Authority and International Affairs* (State University of New York Press, 1999); and Paul Wapner, "Politics beyond the State: Environmental Activism and World Civic Politics," *World Politics* (April 1985): 311–41; Benjamin Cashore, "Legitimacy and the Privatization of Environmental Governance: How Non-State Market-Driven (NSMD) Governance Systems Gain Rule-Making Authority," *Governance* (October 2002): 403–529; Virginia Haufler, *A Public Role for the Private Sector: Industry Self-Regulation in a Global Economy* (Washington: Carnegie Endowment for International Peace,

2000); Christoph Knill and Dirk Lehmkuhl, "Internationalization and Changing Patterns of Governance," *Governance* (January 2002): pp. 41–63.

16. For a sophisticated and comprehensive analysis of the role of "soft" regulation in governing global firms, see John J. Kirton and Michael J. Trebilcock, eds., *Hard Choices, Soft Law: Voluntary Standards in Global Trade, Environment, and Social Governance* (Brookfield, Vt.: Ashgate, 2004).

17. The term "trading up" refers to the role of product standards by governments in strengthening the regulatory standards of their trading partners. See David Vogel, *Trading Up: Consumers and Environmental Regulation in a Global Economy* (Harvard University Press, 1995).

18. See, for example, Naomi Klein, *No Logo* (London: Flamingo, 2000).

19. Jeremy Moon, "The Social Responsibility of Business and New Governance," *Government and Opposition* 37, no. 3 (2002): 385–408.

20. See www.iblf.org; www.blihr.org; www.bitc.org.uk; www.bsr.org; www.conference-board.org.

21. Arthur D. Little, *The Business Case for Corporate Citizenship* (www.weforum.org/site/homepublic.ncf), p. 8, italics added.

22. Wayne Norman and Chris MacDonald, "Getting to the Bottom of the 'Triple Bottom Line,'" *Business Ethics Quarterly* 14, no. 2 (2004): 245.

23. Julian Marshall and Michael Toffel, "Framing the Elusive Concept of Sustainability: A Sustainability Hierarchy," *Environment, Science and Technology* 39, no. 3 (2005): 673.

24. Among those publications are: Elkington, *Cannibals with Forks*; Ira A. Jackson and Jane Nelson, *Profits with Principles: Seven Strategies for Delivering Value with Values* (New York: Currency/Doubleday, 2004); R. Edward Freeman, Jessica Pierce, and Richard H. Dodd, *Environmentalism and the New Logic of Business: How Firms Can Be Profitable and Leave Our Children a Living Planet* (Oxford University Press, 2002); Chris Laszlo, *The Sustainable Company: How to Create Lasting Value through Social and Environmental Performance* (Washington: Island Press, 2003); Marc Benioff, *Compassionate Capitalism: How Corporations Can Make Doing Good an Integral Part of Doing Well* (Franklin Lakes, N.J.: Career Press, 2004); Lynn Sharp Paine, *Value Shift: Why Companies Must Merge Social and Financial Imperatives to Achieve Superior Performance* (New York: McGraw-Hill, 2003).

25. Michael Hopkins, *The Planetary Bargain: Corporate Social Responsibility Matters* (London: Earthscan, 2003), p. xii.

26. Neil Chamberlain, *The Limits of Corporate Responsibility* (New York: Basic Books, 1973), p. 4.

27. Milton Moskowitz, "What Has CSR Really Accomplished?" *Business Ethics* (May/June and July/August 2002): 4.

28. www.christian-aid.org.uk; David Korten, *When Corporations Rule the World* (Hartford, Conn.: Kumarian, 1997).

29. For the claim that firms have been *too* responsive to pressures from NGOs, see Benjamin Hunt, *The Timid Corporation: Why Business Is Terrified of Taking Risks* (Hoboken, N.J.: John Wiley, 2003), esp. chap. 2: "Self-Regulation: Entrenching Caution." See also Henderson, *Misguided Virtue*.

30. Pranay Gupte, "Arthur Laffer: Corporate Social Responsibility Detrimental to Stockholders," *New York Sun*, January 19, 2005, p. 11.

31. This is a central theme of the *Economist* article, "The Good Company."

32. See, for example, Hollender and Fenichell, *What Matters Most*; and Ray C. Anderson, *Mid-Course Correction, toward a Sustainable Enterprise: The Interface Model* (White River Junction, Vt.: Chelsea Green, 1998).

33. According to one study, the total compensation of the top five executives of publicly traded companies in the United States was $260 billion between 1993 and 2002, increasing as a percentage of total corporate income from 5.7 to just under 10 percent. Jeff Madrick, "Economic Scene," *New York Times*, October 28, 2004, p. C2.

Chapter Two

1. See Jules Cohn, *The Conscience of the Corporation: Business and Urban Affairs,1967–1970* (Johns Hopkins University Press, 1971), p. 4.

2. See James W. McKie, "Changing Views," in *Social Responsibility and the Business Predicament*, edited by James W. McKie (Brookings, 1974), p. 32.

3. Cohn, *The Conscience of the Corporation*, p. 7.

4. Milton Friedman, "The Social Responsibly of Business Is to Increase Profits," *New York Times Magazine*, September 13, 1970, pp. 32–33.

5. Christine Arena, *Cause for Success: Ten Companies That Have Put Profits Second and Come in First* (Novato, Calif.: New World Library, 2004); Bob Willard, *The Sustainability Advantage: Seven Business Case Benefits of a Triple Bottom Line* (Gabriola Island, B.C.: New Society, 2002); Charles O. Holliday Jr., Stephan Schmidheiny, and Philip Watts, *Walking the Talk: The Business Case for Sustainable Development* (Sheffield, England: Greenleaf, 2002); Malcolm McIntosh, Deborah Leipziger, Keith Jones, and Gill Coleman, *Corporate Citizenship: Successful Strategies for Responsible Companies* (London: Financial Times, 1998); Tedd Saunders and Loretta McGovern, *The Bottom Line of Green Is Black: Strategies for Creating Profitable and Environmentally Sound Businesses* (HarperSanFrancisco, 1993); and Ira Jackson and Jane Nelson, *Profits with Principles: Seven Strategies for Delivering Value with Values* (New York: Currency/Doubleday, 2004).

6. Chris Laszlo, *The Sustainable Company: How to Create Lasting Value through Social and Environmental Performance* (Washington: Island Press, 2003), p. xxiii; Sandra Waddock, *Leading Corporate Citizens: Vision, Values, Value-Added* (New York: McGraw-Hill, 2002), p. xvii. Mary Scott and Howard Rothman, *Companies with a Conscience: Intimate Portraits of Twelve Firms That Make a Difference* (New York: Citadel, 1992); Kevin T. Jackson, *Building Reputational Capital: Strategies for Integrity and Fair Play That Improve the Bottom Line* (Oxford University Press, 2004); Marc Gunther, *Faith and Fortune: The Quiet Revolution to Reform American Business*, p. 43.

7. Stuart Hart, "Beyond Greening: Strategies for a Sustainable World," *Harvard Business Review* (January–February, 1997): 67–68, 76.

8. Amory Lovins, L. Hunter Lovins, and Paul Hawken, "A Road Map for Natural Capitalism," *Harvard Business Review* (May 1999): 158.

9. Jane Simms, "Business: Corporate Social Responsibility—You Know It Makes Sense," *Accountancy* 130, no. 1311 (2002): 48–50.

10. Stan Friedman, "Corporate America's Social Conscience," *Fortune*, Special Advertising Section, May 16, 2003.

11. Wayne Norman and Chris MacDonald, "Getting to the Bottom of 'Triple Bottom Line,'" *Business Ethics Quarterly* 14, no. 2 (2004): 245.

12. See Willard, *The Sustainability Advantage*, p. 3.

13. Michael Porter and Mark Kramer, "The Competitive Advantage of Corporate Philanthropy," *Harvard Business Review* (December 2002): 67.

14. Craig Smith, "The New Corporate Philanthropy," *Harvard Business Review* (May–June 1994): 106.

15. See Richard Steckel, Robin Simons, Jeffrey Simons, and Norman Tanen, *Making Money While Making a Difference* (Homewood, Ill.: High Tide Press, 1999), p. 105.

16. Ibid., p. 5.

17. Porter and Kramer, "The Competitive Advantage of Corporate Philanthropy," p. 57.

18. Hollender and Fenichell, *What Matters Most*, p. 6.

19. Quoted in Gunther, *Faith and Fortune*, p. 42.

20. Quoted in Hollender and Fenichell, *What Matters Most*, p. 163.

21. www.UNglobalcompact.org/content/NewsDocs/WhoCaresWins.

22. The presumed financial benefits of ethical investing are also reflected in many book titles; see, for example, Amy Domini, *Socially Responsible Investing: Making a Difference and Making Money* (Chicago: Dearborn Trade, 2001); and Peter Kinder, Steven Lyderberg, and Amy Domini, *Investing for Good: Making Money While Being Socially Responsible* (New York: HarperBusiness, 1993). Other examples are Hall Brill, Jack A. Brill, and Cliff Feigenbaum, *Investing with Your Values: Making Money and Making a Difference* (Gabriola Island, B.C.: New Society, 2000), which "shows you how to put your money to work to support your ethical beliefs while earning returns that are as good or better than those earned by traditional investments." It "explains . . . how to unlock the power of investments to accomplish the dual goal of growing a nest egg and improving the world" (first page of book, n.p.); Peter Camejo's *The SRI Advantage* is subtitled *Why Socially Responsible Investing Has Outperformed Financially* (Gabriola Island, B.C.: New Society, 2002); and Amy Domini with Peter Kinder, *Ethical Investing: How to Make Profitable Investments without Sacrificing Your Principles* (Reading, Mass.: Addison-Wesley, 1986).

23. Michael Porter and Claas van der Linde, "Green and Competitive: Ending the Stalemate," *Harvard Business Review* (October 1995): 120–34.

24. One of those was the Seminar on the Business Case for CSR, European Commission, Enterprise Directorate-General, Brussels, June 17, 2004.

25. See Joshua Daniel Margolis and James Patrick Walsh, *People and Profits? The Search for a Link between a Company's Social and Financial Performance* (Mahwah, N.J.: Lawrence Erlbaum, 2001), for the most comprehensive list of these studies.

26. Ibid., pp. 4–5.

27. For descriptions and analyses of relationships between firms and NGOs, see Dennis Rondinelli and Ted London, "How Corporations and Environmental Groups Cooperate: Assessing Cross-Sector Alliances and Collaborations," *Academy of Management Executive* 17, no. 1 (2003): 61–76; and Michael Yaziji, "Turning Gadflies into Allies," *Harvard Business Review* (February 2004): 112–15.

28. Quoted in Leonard Silk and David Vogel, *Ethics and Profits: The Crisis of Confidence in American Business* (New York: Simon and Schuster, 1976), p. 145.

29. Walter Lippmann, *Drift and Mastery* (Englewood Cliffs, N.J.: Prentice-Hall, 1961, originally published 1914), pp. 22, 23.

30. A Standard Oil executive speaking in the early 1960s, ibid., p. 134.

31. Marina v. N. Whitman, *New World, New Rules: The Changing Role of the American Corporation* (Boston: Harvard Business School Press, 1999), p. 7.

32. Ibid., p. 11.

33. Duncan Norton-Taylor, "The Private World of the Class of '66," *Fortune*, February 1966, p. 13D.

34. "Why Business Faces Campus Ire," *Business Week*, August 9, 1967, p. 74.

35. Gordon Fich, "Students in Business: What Do They Think about It? Why?" *Vital Issues*, March 1969, p. 1.

36. David Vogel, *Fluctuating Fortunes: The Political Power of Business in America* (New York: Basic Books, 1989), pp. 54–55.

37. According to a British study, the average SRI investor was middle-aged and worked in a managerial or professional occupation. His or her income and education were higher than those of the public as a whole. Russell Sparkes, *Socially Responsible Investment* (New York: John Wiley, 2002), p. 77.

38. Cohen quoted in Hollender and Fenichell, *What Matters Most*, p. 263; see also Carmel McConnell, *Change Activist: How to Make Big Things Happen* (New York: Prentice-Hall, 2001). Its author, formerly a radical activist, is now a management consultant. The theme of her book is that you can make good money and still stay true to your values. Roddick quoted in McConnell, *Change Activist*, p. 12. And see, for example, Peter Kinder, "Values and Money," KLD Research & Analytics (www.kld.com/resources/papers/values [2004]).

39. Roger Cowe, "From First Tuesday to Green Tuesday," *Financial Times*, May 20, 2004, p. 8.

40. See Margolis and Walsh, *People and Profits?* for a list and summary of twelve "reviews of reviews," pp. 20– 24.

41. Stuart Hart and Gautam Ahuja, "Does It Pay to Be Green?" *Business Strategy and the Environment* 5, no. 1 (1996): 30–37.

42. Glen Dowell, Stuart Hart, and Bernard Yeung, "Do Corporate Global Environmental Standards Create or Destroy Market Value?" *Management Science* 46, no. 8 (1999): 1059–74.

43. Michael Russo and Paul Fouts, "A Resource-Based Perspective on Corporate Environmental Performance," *Academy of Management Journal* 40, no. 3 (1997): 534–59.

44. Dinah Koehler, "Capital Markets and Corporate Environmental Perfor-

mance—Research in the United States" INSEAD, Fontainebleau, France, p. 11. See also Khaled Elsayed and David Paton, "The Impact of Environmental Performance on Firm Performance: Static and Dynamic Panel Date Evidence," Nottingham University Business School, October 2003.

45. Donald Reed, *Green Shareholder Value: Hype or Hit?* (Washington: World Resources Institute, 1998).

46. Margolis and Walsh, *People and Profits?* p. 8.

47. For a comprehensive and thoughtful assessment of the literature on the financial impact of environmental performance that reaches a different conclusion, namely that environmental leaders tend to outperform the stock market, see Frank Dixon, "Financial Markets and Corporate Environmental Results," in *Environmental Performance Measurement*, edited by Daniel Esty and Peter K. Cornelius (Oxford University Press, 2002), pp. 54–65.

48. Margolis and Walsh, *People and Profits?* p. 8.

49. See Brad Brown, "Do Stock Market Investors Reward Companies with Reputations for Social Performance?" *Corporate Reputation Review* 1, no. 2 (1996): 275–76; and Alan Richardson, Michael Welker, and Ian Hutchison, "Managing Capital Market Reactions to Corporate Social Responsibility," *IJMR* (March 1999): 38, for critical analyses of this measure. For a debate on its usefulness, see Research Forum, *Business and Society Review* 34, no. 2 (August 1995): 197–240.

50. See Anne Ilinitch, Naomi Soderstrom, and Tom Thomas, "Measuring Corporate Environmental Performance," *Journal of Accounting and Public Policy* 17 (1998): 383–408.

51. Abigail McWilliams and Donald Siegel, "Corporate Social Responsibility and Financial Performance: Correlations for Misspecification," *Strategic Management Journal* 21, no. 8 (2000): 608. The study they critique is Sandra Waddock and S. Graves, "The Corporate Social Performance–Financial Performance Link," *Strategic Management Journal* 18, no. 4 (1997): 305–8.

52. Jennifer J. Griffen and John Mahon, "The Corporate Social Performance and Corporate Financial Performance Debate: Twenty-Five Years of Incomparable Research," *Business and Society* (March 1997): 12.

53. See ibid., pp. 7, 20–24; and John Mahon and Jennifer J. Griffen, "Painting a Portrait," *Business and* Society (March 1999): p. 130,

54. Margolis and Walsh, *People and Profits?* p. 13.

55. Ronald Roman, Sefa Hayibor, and Bradley Agle, "The Relationship between Social and Financial Performance," *Business and Society* 38, no. 1 (March 1999): 121.

56. As one recent scholarly article put it after an extensive literature review, "As findings about the positive relationships between CFP (corporate financial performance) and CSR become more widely known, managers may be more likely to pursue CSR as part of their strategy for attaining high CFP." Mark Orlitzky, Frank Schmidt, and Sara Rynes, "Corporate Social and Financial Performance: A Meta-Analysis," *Organization Studies* 24, no. 2 (2003): 426.

57. Every book written by an executive whose firm is widely recognized for its CSR initiatives urges other managers to follow his company's example. See, for

example, Ray C. Anderson, *Mid-Course Correction: Toward a Sustainable Enterprise* (White River Junction, Vt.: Chelsea Green, 1998); Charles Holliday, Stephan Schmidheiny, and Philip Watts, *Walking the Talk: The Business Case for Sustainable Development*; and Hollender and Fenichell, *What Matters Most*.

58. Dan diBartolomeo and Lloyd Kurtz, "Managing Risk Exposures of Socially Screened Portfolios," Northfield Information Services, September 9, 1999 (www.northinfo.com), p. 8. Another study notes that the DSI also had different macroeconomic exposures than the S&P 500. Lloyd Kurtz and Dan diBartolomeo, "Socially Screened Portfolios: An Attribution Analysis of Relative Performance," *Journal of Investing* (Fall 1996): 35–41.

59. For a detailed discussion of the composition of this index and its performance, see Alois Flatz, "Corporate Sustainability and Financial Indexes," in *Environmental Performance Measurement*, edited by Daniel Esty and Peter K. Cornelius (Oxford University Press, 2002), pp. 66–81.

60. See, for example, Alan Gregory, John Matatko, and Robert Luther, "Ethical Unit Trust Financial Performance: Small Company Size Effects and Fund Size Effects," *Journal of Business Finance & Accounting* (June 1997): 705–23, which found that the most important reason why a group of British unit trusts (mutual funds) outperformed matched pairs of funds was that the former were most heavily invested in smaller firms, which performed better during the time period of their analysis. Similarly, an unpublished paper by Kelly Young and Dennis Proffitt, "Socially Responsible Mutual Funds: Recent Performance and Other Issues Relating to Portfolio Choice," Grand Canyon University, College of Business and Professional Studies, p. 17, reports that while the returns of most SRI funds were comparable to traditional funds of the same type, all size categories of growth funds had significantly lower returns, largely because the "typical SRI fund is over invested in high-tech industry."

61. Russell Sparkes, *Socially Responsible Investment* (New York: John Wiley & Sons, 2002), p. 270.

62. Abrahm Lustgarten, "Lean, Mean—and Green?" *Fortune*, July 26, 2004, p. 210.

63. James Glassman, "Good for the Soul, Works for the Wallet," *Washington Post*, May 25, 2003, p. F1.

64. See, for example, Young and Proffitt, "Socially Responsible Mutual Funds: Recent Performance and Other Issues Relating to Portfolio Choice"; Alicia Munnell and Annika Sunden, "Social Investing: Pension Plans Should Just Say 'No,'" paper prepared for the conference "Cost and Benefits: 'Socially Responsible' Investing and Pension Funds" (Washington: American Enterprise Institute, June 7, 2004), p. 7. This is also the conclusion of the two studies considered by the Socially Responsible Investment Forum to represent "the most rigorous insights and quantitative studies of socially screened funds' performance" (2003 Report on Socially Responsible Investing Trends in the U.S., Social Investment Forum, p. 44); Bernell Stone, John Guerard Jr., Mustafa Gultekin, and Greg Adams, "Socially Responsible Investment Screening: Strong Evidence of No Significant Cost for Activity Managed Portfolios," *Journal of Investing* (forthcoming);

and Rob Bauer, Kees Koedijk, and Roger Otten, "International Evidence on Ethical Mutual Fund Performance and Investment Style," Discussion Paper (London: Centre for Economic Policy Research, January 2002). For a list of the extensive literature on this subject, see Appendix 3 of the 2003 Report on Socially Responsible Investing Trends.

65. See, for example, Camejo, *The SRI Advantage*; and Jeroen Derwall, Nadja Gunster, Rob Bauer, and Kees Koedijk, "The Eco-Efficiency Premium Puzzle" (www.erim.eir.ni).

66. Susannah Goodman, Jonas Kron, and Tim Little, *The Environmental Fiduciary* (Oakland, Calif.: Rose Foundation for Communities and the Environment), http:///p. 2.

67. Joanne Rickness and Paul Williams, "A Descriptive Study of Social Responsibility Mutual Funds," *Accounting Organizations and Society* 13, no. 4 (1998): 397.

68. For this criticism, as well as a series of more wide-ranging criticisms of SRI, see Jon Entine, "The Myth of Social Investing," *Organization & Environment* (September 2003): 1–17.

69. Paul Hawken and the Natural Capital Institute, *Socially Responsible Investing* (www.naturalcapital.org/images/NCI[October 2004]); the quotes are from p. 17.

70. James C. Collins and Jerry I. Porras, *Built to Last: Successful Habits of Visionary Companies* (New York: Harper Business, 1994), pp. 2, 3.

71. For a list of the most socially responsible firms of the 1970s, see the corporations included in Thornton Bradshaw and David Vogel, eds., *Corporations and Their Critics: Issues and Answers to the Problems of Corporate Social Responsibility* (New York: McGraw-Hill, 1981).

72. Peter Landers and Joann Lublin, "Merck's Big Bet on Research by Its Scientists Comes Up Short," *Wall Street Journal*, November 28, 1993, p. 1; see also "Face Value: The Acceptable Face of Capitalism," *Economist*, December 14, 2002, p. 61.

73. Alison Maitland, "Winner's New Leaders Face a 'Healthy Challenge,'" *Financial Times*, July 8, 2004, p. 1.

74. Jonathon Porritt, "Does Philip Green Understand?" (letter to the editor), *Financial Times*, July 9, 2004, p. 14.

75. Simon Zadek, "Doing Good and Doing Well: Making the Business Case for Corporate Citizenship" (New York: Conference Board, 2000), p. 19.

76. Michael Skapinker, "Why Corporate Laggards Should Not Win Ethics Awards," *Financial Times*, July 21, 2004, p. 8.

77. Martin Dickson, "Good, Not Great," *Financial Times*, July 7, 2004, p. 20.

78. Sara Silver, "How to Grow a Good Name on Green Bananas," *Financial Times*, November 26, 2004, p. 8. See also J. Gary Taylor and Patricia Scharlin, *Smart Alliance* (Yale University Press, 2004).

79. Rogelio Oliva and James Quinn, "Interface's Evergreen Services Agreement," Harvard Business School case 9-603-112, July 4, 2003, p. 5.

Chapter Three

1. Dale Kurchiner, "5 Ways Ethical Business Creates Fatter Profits," *Business Ethics* (March/April 1996), p. 21.

2. Cone Communications Study, Boston, Mass., 1995.

3. Dara O'Rourke, "Opportunities and Obstacles for Corporate Responsibility Reporting in Developing Countries," World Bank/International Finance Corporation, March 2004, p. 22 (www.worldbank.org).

4. Cambridge Reports, Roper Center for Public Opinion Research, July 1989; Pew Research Center, July 2003.

5. Stephen Garone, "The Link between Corporate Citizenship and Financial Performance," Conference Board, Research Report 1234-99-RR, p. 9.

6. Quoted in Phil Macnaghten and John Urry, *Contested Natures* (Thousand Oaks, Calif.: Sage, 1998), p. 83; Garone, "The Link between Corporate Citizenship and Financial Performance," p. 9.

7. "Human Rights," *Economist*, June 3, 1995, p. 59.

8. Amy Cortese, "The New Accountability: Tracking the Social Costs," *New York Times*, March 24, 2002, pp. 3, 4.

9. Craig Smith, "Corporate Social Responsibility: Whether or How?" *California Management Review* (Summer 2003): 61–62. See also Sandra Waddock, "What Will It Take to Create a Tipping Point for Corporate Responsibility?" Boston College, Carroll School of Management, pp. 5–6.

10. Quoted in Smith, "Corporate Social Responsibility," p. 62.

11. Bob Willard, *The Sustainability Advantage: Seven Business Case Benefits of a Triple Bottom Line* (Gabriola Island, B.C.: New Society, 2002), p. 111.

12. Michel Capron and Françoise Quairel-Lanoizelee, *Mythes et réalités de l'entreprise responsable* (Paris: La Decouverte, 2004), p. 57.

13. Dara O'Rourke, "Opportunities and Obstacles for Corporate Social Reporting in Developing Countries," World Bank/International Finance Corporation, March 2004, p. 22.

14. Thomas Blue Bjorner, Lars Garn Hansen, and Clifford S. Russell, "Environmental Labeling and Consumers' Choice: An Empirical Analysis of the Effect of the Nordic Swan," *Journal of Environmental Economics and Management* 47 (2004): 411–34.

15. O'Rourke, "Opportunities and Obstacles," p. 6.

16. Deborah Doane, "Beyond Corporate Social Responsibility," *Futures, the Journal of Policy, Planning and Futures Studies* 37, nos. 2–3 (2004): 5.

17. Dara O'Rourke, "Market Movements: Advocacy Strategies to Influence Global Production and Consumption," University of California, Berkeley, Department of Environmental Science, Policy, and Management, p. 8.

18. The few attempts to develop ethical brands for apparel products in the United States have had little impact. For an extensive discussion of this issue, see Monica Prasad, Howard Kimendorf, Rachael Meyer, and Ian Robinson, "Consumers of the World Unite: A Market-Based Response to Sweatshops," *Labor Studies Journal* 29, no. 3 (2004): 57–79.

19. Sara Silver, "How to Grow a Good Name on Green Bananas," *Financial Times*, November 14, 2004, p. 8.

20. Roger Cowe, "Improving Quality of Life and Profits," *Financial Times,* August 13, 2002, p. 12.

21. Robert Frank, *What Price the Moral High Ground? Ethical Dilemmas in Competitive Environments* (Princeton University Press, 2004), p. 66.

22. Jane Simms, "Business: Corporate Social Responsibility—You Know It Makes Sense," *Accountancy* 130, no. 1311 (2002): 48–50.

23. For lists of boycotts, see Michelle Micheletti, *Political Virtue and Shopping: Individuals, Consumerism, and Collective Action* (New York: Palgrave Macmillan, 2003), pp. 84–86; and Wallace N. Davidson III, Dan L. Worrell, and Abuzar El-Jerrym, "Influencing Managers to Change Unpopular Corporate Behavior through Boycotts and Divestures: A Stock Market Test," *Business and Society* 34, no. 2 (1995): 147–70. For a broader overview and analysis of boycotts, though now somewhat dated, see N. Craig Smith, *Morality and the Market: Consumer Pressure for Corporate Accountability* (London: Routledge, 1990).

24. Simon Zadek, *The Civil Corporation: The New Economy of Corporate Citizenship* (London: Earthscan, 2001), p. 61.

25. Joel Makower, *Beyond the Bottom Line: Putting Corporate Responsibility to Work for Your Business and the World* (New York: Simon and Schuster, 1994), p. 105.

26. Michael Skapinker and Alison Maitland, "Does Caring Boost the Bottom Line?" *Financial Times,* March 3, 2002.

27. Richard Tomkins, "When Caring Is a Good Investment," *Financial Times,* October 5, 2001.

28. "The 100 Top Brands," *Business Week,* August 2, 2004, pp. 76, 69.

29. Donald J. Reed, *Stalking the Elusive Business Case for Corporate Sustainability* (Washington: World Resources Institute, 2001), p. 15.

30. Curt Weeden, *Corporate Social Investing: The Breakthrough Strategy for Giving and Getting Corporate Contributions* (San Francisco: Berrett-Koehler, 1998), p. 32.

31. "2003 Corporate Reputation Watch Survey," Hill Knowlton and Korn/Ferry International Forbes CEO Forum, October 1, 2003 (www.corporate_reputation_watch.com), pp. 6, 7.

32. Alison Maitland, "Bitter Taste of Success," *Financial Times,* March 11, 2002.

33. "Living with the Enemy," *Economist,* August 9, 2003, p. 50.

34. Simon Zadek, "Doing Good and Doing Well: Making the Business Case for Corporate Citizenship," Conference Board Research Report 1282-00RR, p. 17.

35. Quoted in David Levy, "Business and the Evolution of the Climate Regime: The Dynamics of Corporate Strategies," in *The Business of Global Environmental Governance,* edited by David Levy and Peter Newell (MIT Press, 2005), p. 85.

36. Fiona Harvey, "A Good Name Can Pay Big Dividends," *Financial Times,* November 19, 2004, p. 5.

37. Richard Steckel, Robin Simons, Jeffrey Simons, and Norman Taner, *Making Money while Making a Difference* (Homewood, Ill.: High Tide Press, 1999), pp. 11, 12.

38. Makower, *Beyond the Bottom Line,* p. 105.

39. J. A. Chatman, "Improving Interactional Organizational Research: A

Model of Person-Organization Fit," *Academy of Management Review* 14 (1989): 333–49; the latter point is a central finding of James C. Collins and Jerry I. Porras, *Built to Last: Successful Habits of Visionary Companies* (New York: Harper Business Essentials, 1994).

40. See, for example, Daniel Greening and Daniel Turban, "Corporate Social Performance as a Competitive Advantage in Attracting a Quality Workplace," *Business and Society* 39, no. 3 (September 2000): 254–80; T. N. Bauer and L. Aiman-Smith, "Green Career Choices: The Influence of Ecological Stance on Recruiting," *Journal of Business and Psychology* 10 (1996): 445–58; and Daniel Turban and Daniel Greening, "Corporate Social Performance and Organizational Attractiveness to Prospective Employees," *Academy of Management Journal* 41, no. 3 (June 1997): 658–72.

41. Institute for Global Ethics Newsletter, August 2, 2004 (www.globalethics.org).

42. Ann Harrington, "By the Numbers," *Fortune*, April 19, 2004, p. 38.

43. Simon London, "Benevolence and the Bottom Line," *Financial Times*, July 14, 2004, p. 8.

44. Joseph Perteira, "Doing Good and Doing Well at Timberland," *New York Times*, September 9, 2003, p. B1.

45. The Shell and Novo Nordisk reports are from Vicky Kemp, *To Whose Profit?* (Godalming, Surrey, U.K.: World Wildlife Fund, 2001), p. 25.

46. Both of the preceding quotes are from World Economic Forum, "Values and Value: Communicating the Strategic Importance of Corporate Citizenship to Investors," survey of CEOs, CFOs, and investment relations officers, Geneva, 2003 (www.weforum.org).

47. Chris Tuppen, "The BT Business Case for CSR," presented at the seminar "The Business Case for CSR," European Commission, Brussels, June 17, 2004.

48. See Alison Maitland, "Business Bows to Growing Pressures," FT Responsible Business, *Financial Times*, November 29, 2004, p. 1.

49. See Alison Maitland, "Health Is a Serious Business, but So Is Choice," *Financial Times*, June 28, 2004, p. 6.

50. See Bethany McLean and Peter Elkind, *The Smartest Guys in the Room: The Amazing Rise and Scandalous Fall of Enron* (New York: Portfolio, 2003).

51. "Why Nike Has Broken into a Sweat," *Financial Times*, March 7, 2002, p. 13.

52. "Living with the Enemy," *Economist*, August 9, 2003, p. 49.

53. Quoted in David Vogel, *Lobbying the Corporation: Citizen Challenges to Business Authority* (New York: Basic Books, 1978), p. 48.

54. Steckel and others, *Making Money while Making a Difference*, p. 33.

55. See Alsop, *The 18 Immutable Laws of Corporate Reputation*, p. 70; and Marc Gunther, *Faith and Fortune: The Quiet Revolution to Reform American Business* (New York: Crown Business, 2004), p. 35.

56. Jeffrey Hollender and Stephen Fenichell, *What Matters Most: How a Small Group of Pioneers Is Teaching Social Responsibility to Big Business, and Why Big Business Is Listening* (New York: Basic Books, 2004), p. 47.

57. "Corporate Responsibility and Investor Confidence Survey," conducted for Calvert, November 18, 2003, p. 6 (www.harrisinteractive.com).

58. See Smith, "Corporate Social Responsibility," p. 63.

59. European Sustainable and Responsible Investment Forum, *Socially Responsible Investment among European Institutional Investors*, 2003 Report (Paris, September 2003), p. 10.

60. Stephanie Le Page, "L'investissement socialement responsable fait son nid," *Les Echos*, January 23–24, 2004, p. 15.

61. Garone, "The Link between Corporate Citizenship and Financial Performance," p. 7.

62. Juan Somavia, "Introduction," *Natural Resources Forum* 28, no. 4 (2004): 253.

63. CSR Europe, "The European Survey on Socially Responsible Investment and the Financial Community" (Brussels, 2001).

64. R. Henkel, A. Kraus, and others, "The Effect of Green Investments on Corporate Behavior," *Journal of Finance and Quantitative Analysis* 36, no. 4 (2001): 431–49.

65. Siew Hon Teoh, Ivo Welch, and C. Paul Wazzan, "The Effect of Socially Activist Investment Policies on the Financial Markets: Evidence from the South Africa Boycott," *Journal of Business* 72, no. 1 (1999): 38, 39.

66. Ronald Kahn, Claes Lekander, and Tom Leimkuhler, "Just Say No? The Investment Implications of Tobacco Divestiture," *Journal of Investing* (Winter 1997): 62–70.

67. "Sin Stocks Rock?" Lifeworth annual review of corporate responsibility, 2002 (www.lifeworth.net).

68. See Dan Ahrens, *Investing in Vice: The Recession-Proof Portfolio of Booze, Bets, Bombs and Butts* (New York: St. Martin's, 2004).

69. Teoh, Welch, and Wazzan, "The Effect of Socially Activist Investment Policies," p. 37; see also Martin B. Meznar, Douglas Nigh, and Chuck C. Y. Kwok, "Effect of Announcements of Withdrawal from South Africa on Stockholder Wealth," *Academy of Management Journal* 37, no. 6 (1994): 1633–48; Peter Wright and Stephen P. Ferris, "Agency Conflict and Corporate Strategy: The Effect of Divestment on Corporate Value," *Strategic Management Journal* 18, no. 1 (1997): 77–83; and Martin B. Meznar, Douglas Nigh, and Chuck C. Y. Kwok, "Announcement of Withdrawal from South Africa Revisited: Making Sense of Contradictory Event Study Findings," *Academy of Management Journal* 41, no. 6 (1998): 715–30.

70. Sarah Murray, "Moving on beyond Plain Philanthropy," *Financial Times*, December 10, 2002, p. II; Kate Burgess, "Why Ethical Indices Still Have Their Critics," *Financial Times*, December 10, 2002, p. IV.

71. Global Environmental Management Initiative, *Clear Advantage: Building Shareholder Value* (Washington, 2004), p. 14.

72. Somavia, "Introduction," p. 253.

73. See Burgess, "Why Ethical Indices Still Have Their Critics," p. IV.

74. FTSE4Good, "Human Rights Standards Raised for FTSE4Good Index," Press release, April 10, 2003.

75. Quoted in Oliver Balch, "Raising the Bar of Performance," *Financial Times*, November 29, 2004, p. 7.

76. Balch, "Raising the Bar," p. 7.

77. "'Best' Behavior," *Economist*, July 14, 2001, p. 71.

78. 2003 Report on Socially Responsible Investing Trends in the United States, Social Investment Forum, December 2003, p. 16 (www.socialinvest.org).

79. Eric Chol, "Les usines du Sud sous surveillance," *L'Express*, October 16, 2003, p. 79.

80. World Economic Forum, "Values and Value."

81. Hewson Baltzell, "Refuting Media Bias against SRI," *Business Ethics* (Fall 2003): 15.

82. Frank Dixon, "Financial Markets and Corporate Environmental Results," in *Environmental Performance Measurement: The Global Report 2001–2002*, edited by Daniel Esty and Peter K. Cornelius (Oxford University Press, 2002), p. 62.

83. Quoted in David Grayson and Adrian Hodges, *Everybody's Business: Managing Risks and Opportunities in Today's Global Society* (New York: DK Publishing, 2002), p. 78.

84. Steven Haywood, "The New Corporate Balance Sheet," *Environmental Policy Outlook*, October 2, 2002, p. 4 (www.aei.org/publications).

85. Alison Maitland, "Scandals Draw Attention to 'Superficial' Measures," *Financial Times*, December 10, 2002, p. 10.

86. World Economic Forum, "Values and Value."

87. Ibid.

88. Roger Cowe, "Transparency Issue Can Be Easily Clouded," *Financial Times*, November 29, 2004, p. 6.

89. www.accountability.org.uk.

90. Maef Woods, "The Global Reporting Initiative," *CPA Journal* (June 2003): 7. Since 1995 a number of European governments have enacted legislation requiring increased corporate nonfinancial disclosures. Danish companies are required to report on their environmental impact. Norwegian companies are required to include environmental information in their annual reports; similar requirements exist for large companies in Sweden. In 1996 both Belgian companies and the subsidiaries of foreign corporations were required to issue reports on their social performance. Dutch legislation requires more than 200 firms to report on their environmental activities. France requires listed companies to describe the social, environmental, and financial outcomes of their activities, and Australia enacted legislation requiring firms listed on the Australian Stock Exchange to issue an annual sustainability report. The British government requires companies to report social, environmental, and ethical risks that may affect the interests of shareholders. However, these disclosure requirements remain vague. Unlike company financial statements, corporate nonfinancial disclosures are usually not audited, and while compliance with these government disclosure requirements has increased, it remains uneven. No firm has yet been prosecuted for noncompliance or for reporting misleading, incomplete, or unsubstantiated information.

91. Roger Cowe, "Spotlight Set to Fall on Effects of Big Business," *Financial Times*, November 3, 2003.

92. Alison Maitland, "Truants, Nerds and Supersonics," *Financial Times*,

November 18, 2002, p. 9. For the *Economist's* most recent evaluation of company social reports, see "Wood for the Trees," *Economist*, November 6, 2004, p. 64.

93. "Topside Down in CSR," *Reguletter*, November 2004, p. 10.

94. "Does It Add Value?" *Economist*, November 13, 2004, p. 81.

95. Mark Turner, "Appealing to Money Men," *FT Business and Development*, June 24, 2004, p. 3.

96. Woods, "The Global Reporting Initiative," p. 7. For another effort to standardize CSR reporting, see "Principles for Global Corporate Responsibility: Bench Marks for Measuring Business Performance," Steering Group of Global Principles Network, 2003 (www.bench-marks.org).

97. See Nicholas Franco, "Corporate Environmental Disclosure: Opportunities to Harness Market Forces to Improve Corporate Financial Performance," Conference on Environmental Law, Keystone, Colo., March 8–11, 2001.

98. Wayne Norman and Chris MacDonald, "Getting to the Bottom of 'Triple Bottom Line,'" *Business Ethics Quarterly* 14, no. 2 (April 2004): 249.

99. Marc Gunther, "Tree Huggers, Soy Lovers, and Profits," *Fortune*, June 23, 2003, p. 104.

100. Oaul Koku, Aigbe Akhigbe, and Thomas Springer, "The Financial Impact of Boycotts and Threats of Boycott," *Journal of Business Research* 40, no. 1 (1997): 15–20.

101. Quoted in Zadek, *The Civil Corporation*, p. 61.

102. Curt Weeden, *Corporate Social Investing: The Breakthrough Strategy for Giving and Getting Corporate Contributions* (San Francisco: Berrett-Koehler, 1998), p. 32.

103. www.accountability.org.uk.

104. Hollender and Fenichell, *What Matters Most*, p. 211.

105. Quoted in ibid., p. 232.

106. Howard Rothman, "Under Pressure," *Business Ethics* (September/October 1996): 15.

107. Quoted in ibid., p. 233.

108. Riva Atlas, "Firm That Was Hit Hard on 9/11 Grows Anew," *New York Times*, September 10, 2004, p. C4.

109. The quotation is from Ann Zimmerman, "Costco's Dilemma: Be Kind to Its Workers, or Wall Street," *Wall Street Journal*, March 26, 2004, p. B1; see also Stanley Homes and Wendy Zellner, "The Costco Way: Higher Wages Mean Higher Profits: But Try Telling Wall Street," *Business Week*, April 12, 2004, pp. 76–77.

Chapter Four

1. For useful overviews of private sector initiatives to address labor practices, see Janelle Diller, "A Social Conscience in the Global Marketplace? Labour Dimensions of Codes of Conduct, Social Labeling and Investor Initiatives," *International Labour Review* 138, no. 2 (1999): 99–129; and *Rising above Sweatshops*, edited by Laura Hartman, Denis Arnold, and Richard Wokutch (Westport, Conn.: Praeger, 2003).

2. Jennifer Burns and Debora Spar, "Hitting the Wall: Nike and International

Labor Practices," Harvard Business School case 9-700-047, September 15, 2000, p. 2.

3. Laura Hartman and Richard Wokutch, "Nike, Inc.: Corporate Responsibility and Workplace Standard Initiatives in Vietnam," in *Rising above Sweatshops*, edited by Hartman, Arnold, and Wokutch, p. 149.

4. Quoted in Philip Rosenzweig, "International Sourcing in Athletic Footwear: Nike and Reebok," Harvard Business School case N-394-289, July 14, 1994, pp. 6–7.

5. Burns and Spar, "Hitting the Wall," p. 6.

6. Quoted in ibid.

7. Ibid., p. 7.

8. Ibid., p. 10.

9. Steven Greenhouse, "Nike Shoe Plant Is Called Unsafe for Workers," *New York Times*, November 8, 1997, p. A1.

10. Burns and Spar, "Hitting the Wall," p. 10.

11. Russell Sparks, *Socially Responsible Investment* (New York: John Wiley, 2002), quoted on p. 187.

12. William Echikson, "It's Europe's Turn to Sweat about Sweatshops," *Business Week*, July 19, 1999, p. 96.

13. Burns and Spar, "Hitting the Wall," p. 11.

14. John Cushman, "Nike Pledges to End Child Labor and Apply U.S. Rules Abroad," *New York Times*, May 23, 1998, p. C1.

15. Dara O'Rourke, "Outsourcing Regulation: Analyzing Nongovernmental Systems of Labor Standards and Monitoring," *Policy Studies Journal* 31, no. 1 (2003): 10.

16. Simon Zadek, "The Path to Corporate Responsibility," *Harvard Business Review* (December 2004): 129.

17. Michel Skapinker, "Why Nike Has Broken into a Sweat," *Financial Times*, March 7, 2002, p. 13.

18. Daniel Litvin, *Empires of Profit: Commerce, Conquest and Corporate Responsibility* (New York: Texere, 2003), p. 246.

19. For a detailed discussion and analysis of the impact of NGO and media pressures on Nike's workplace health standards, see Dara O'Rourke, *Community-Driven Regulation: Balancing Development and the Environment in Vietnam* (MIT Press, 2004), chap. 6.

20. Aaron Bernstein, "Floor under Foreign Factories," *Business Week*, November 9, 1998, p. 126.

21. Steven Greenhouse, "Anti-Sweatshop Movement Achieving Gains Overseas," *New York Times*, January 1, 2000, p. A10; see also Bob Herbert, "Nike Blinks," *New York Times*, May 21, 1998, p. A33.

22. Hartman and Wokutch, "Nike," pp. 150–58.

23. Denis Arnold and Laura Hartman, "What's Wrong with Pro-Sweatshop Arguments?" University of Tennessee, n.d., p. 12.

24. Aaron Bernstein, "The New Nike," *Business Week*, September 20, 2004, p. 86.

25. Eric Dash, "Founder of Nike to Hand Off Job to a New Chief," *New York Times*, November 19, 2004, p. C6.

26. Bernstein, "The New Nike," p. 81.

27. John Obendorfer, "The Nike Decision Treads on Dangerous Grounds," *Financial Times*, October 14, 2003, p. 19.

28. Jarol Manheim, *The Death of a Thousand Cuts: Corporate Campaigns and the Contemporary Attack on the Corporation* (Mahwah, N.J.: Lawrence Erlbaum, 2001), p. 107.

29. For a discussion of Chiquita's efforts to improve the condition of banana producers in Central America, see Tara Radin, "Chiquita Brands International, Inc.: Values-Based Management and Corporate Responsibility in Latin America," in *Rising above Sweatshops*, edited by Hartman, Arnold, and Wokutch, pp. 353–85.

30. Jill Esbenshade, *Monitoring Sweatshops: Workers, Consumers, and the Global Apparel Industry* (Temple University Press, 2004), p. 135.

31. Quoted in Alison Maitland, "Big Brands Come Clean on Sweatshop Labour," *Financial Times*, June 10, 2003, p. 10. See also Aaron Bernstein, "Sweatshops: Finally, Airing the Dirty Linen," *Business Week*, June 23, 2003, p. 100.

32. Michael Santoro, "Philosophy Applied I: How Nongovernmental Organizations and Multinational Enterprise Can Work Together to Protect Global Labor Rights," in *Rising above Sweatshops*, edited by Hartman, Arnold, and Wokutch, pp. 108, 109.

33. For a critical appraisal of the accomplishments and limitations of the student anti-sweatshop movement, see Jeffrey Isaac, "Thinking about the Sweatshop Movement," *Dissent* (Fall 2001): 100–12.

34. Elliot Schrage, "Promoting International Worker Rights through Private Voluntary Initiatives," a Report to the U.S. Department of State on Behalf of the University of Iowa Center for Human Rights, January 2004, p. 105.

35. Helle Jorgensen, Peder Pruzzan-Jorgensen, Margaret Junjk, and Aron Cramer, "Strengthening Implementation of Corporate Social Responsibility in Global Supply Chains," World Bank Group—Corporate Social Responsibility Practice, October 2003, p. 6.

36. For a discussion of FTI and its impact on British supermarkets, see Susanne Friedberg, *French Beans and Food Scares: Culture and Commerce in an Anxious Age* (Oxford University Press, 2004), pp. 89–190.

37. Theodore H. Moran, *Beyond Sweatshops: Foreign Direct Investment and Globalization in Developing Countries* (Brookings, 2002), p. 92.

38. www.cleanclothes.org (2005).

39. Michel Capron and Françoise Quairel-Lanoizelee, *Mythes et réalités de l'entreprise responsable*, p. 65.

40. Echikson, "It's Europe's Turn," p. 96.

41. Moran, *Beyond Sweatshops*, p. 92.

42. Eric Chol, "Les usines du Sud sous surveillance," *L'Express*, October 16, 2003, pp. 78–79.

43. Claude Fussler, Aron Cramer, and Sebastian van der Vegt, eds., *Raising the Bar: Creating Value with the United Nations Global Compact* (Sheffield, England: Greenleaf, 2004) p. 176.

44. Echikson, "It's Europe's Turn," p. 96.

45. Edward Luce, "Ikea's Grown-Up Plan to Tackle Child Labor," *Financial Times*, September 15, 2004, p. 7.

46. Howard Reitz and Lynn Sharp Paine, "Charles Veillon, S.A. (B)," Harvard Business School case 9-398-010, October 17, 1997.

47. Charis Gresser and Sophia Tickell, *Mugged: Poverty in Your Coffee Cup* (London: Oxfam International, 2002), p. 9.

48. Hugh Williamson, "Coffee Industry to Seal Pact on Better Working Conditions," *Financial Times*, September 10, 2004, p. 5.

49. Schrage, "Promoting International Worker Rights," pp. 135–36, 141.

50. Michael Peel, "Bitter Chocolate for Children," *Financial Times*, December 21, 2004, p. 12.

51. Quotes are from Schrage, "Promoting International Worker Rights," pp. 145, 148.

52. Kate Raworth, *Trading Away Our Rights* (London: Oxfam International 2004), p. 56.

53. Ans Kolk and Rob Van Tulder, "The Effectiveness of Self-Regulation: Corporate Codes of Conduct and Child Labour," *European Management Journal* (June 2002): 268.

54. O'Rourke, "Outsourcing Regulation," p. 23.

55. Sarah Murray, "Social Issues Gain in Importance," *Financial Times*, Special Report on Responsible Business, November 29, 2004, p. 2.

56. Quoted in Peter Goodman and Phillip Pan, "The Cost of Falling Prices," *Washington Post National Weekly Edition*, February 16–22, 2004, p. 19.

57. See Dara O'Rourke, *Smoke from a Hired Gun: A Critique of Nike's Labor and Environmental Auditing* (San Francisco: Transnational Resource and Action Center, 1997); and "Monitoring the Monitors: A Critique of Pricewaterhouse-Coopers's Labor Monitoring," White Paper, September 28, 2000.

58. See Santoro, "Philosophy Applied," p. 105.

59. For a detailed discussion of Mattel's labor practices, in whose design and implementation the author participated, see S. Prakash Sethi, *Setting Global Standards: Guidelines for Creating Codes of Conduct in Multinational Corporations* (New York: John Wiley, 2003), pp. 239–72.

60. Kapstein, "The Corporate Ethics Crusade," *Foreign Affairs* (September/October 2001): 115.

61. Kimberly Ann Elliott and Richard Freeman, *Can Labor Standards Improve under Globalization?* (Washington: Institute for International Economics, 2003), p. 43.

62. See Bernstein, "Sweatshops," p. 100.

63. Jorgensen and others, "Strengthening Implementation," p. 20.

64. Ibid., p. 16. This assessment is echoed by Ann Florini, *The Coming Democracy: New Rules for Running a New World* (Brookings, 2005), pp. 109–10.

65. Steven Greenhouse, "A Push to Better Labor's Lot in Bangladesh," *New York Times*, September 27, 2002, p. C2.

66. Aaron Bernstein, "Sweatshop Reform: How to Solve the Standoff," *Business Week*, May 3, 1999, p. 187.

67. Robert Pollin, Justine Burns, and James Heinz, "Global Apparel Produc-

tion and Sweatshop Labour: Can Raising Retail Prices Finance Living Wages?" *Cambridge Journal of Economics* 28, no. 2 (2004): 154, 164.

68. Joseph Pereira, "Reebok, Adidas, Nike Aim to Bring Back the $100-Plus Sneaker," *Wall Street Journal*, November 10, 2004, p. D1.

69. See Moran, *Beyond Sweatshops*, p. 91.

70. Raworth, *Trading away Our Rights*, p. 57.

71. *Play Fair at the Olympics* (Oxford: Oxfam, 2004), pp. 38, 39.

72. Raworth, *Trading away Our Rights*, p. 54.

73. *Play Fair*, p. 36.

74. Ibid., p. 28.

75. Skapinker, "Why Nike Has Broken into a Sweat," p. 13.

76. See Santoro, "Philosophy Applied," p. 106.

77. Jorgensen and others, "Strengthening Implementation," p. 28.

78. Ibid., p. 25.

79. Raworth, *Trading away Our Rights*," p. 50.

80. For more detailed information on the results of the company audits made public on the FLA website, see Bernstein, "Sweatshops," pp. 100–101.

81. Alison Maitland, "Brands Can Find the Going Rough," *Financial Times*, Special Report on Responsible Business, November 29, 2004, p. 6.

82. Schrage, "Promoting International Worker Rights," pp. 51, 56.

83. Elliott and Freeman, *Can Labor Standards Improve?* p. 114.

84. Elisabeth Malkin, "Cleanup at the Maquiladora," *Business Week*, July 29, 1996, p. 48.

85. Kolk and Tulder, "The Effectiveness of Self-Regulation," pp. 266, 261.

86. Schrage, "Promoting International Worker Rights," p. 171.

87. Kolk and Tulder, "The Effectiveness of Self-Regulation," p. 269.

88. Kapstein, "The Corporate Ethics Crusade," p. 110.

89. "Human Rights," *Economist*, June 3, 1995 p. 59.

90. Robert Crawford and Olivier Cadot, "Soccer Balls Made for Children by Children: Child Labor in Pakistan," INSEAD case, Fontainebleau, France, 1999, p. 14.

91. Friedberg, *French Beans*, p. 187.

92. Crawford and Cadot, "Soccer Balls," p. 14.

93. David Murphy and Jem Bendell, "New Partnerships for Sustainable Development," in *The Greening of Business in Developing Countries*, edited by Peter Utting (London: Zed Books, 2002), p. 237.

94. Robert Luibicic, "Corporate Codes of Conduct and Product Labeling Schemes: The Limits and Possibilities of Promoting International Labor Rights through Private Initiatives," *Law and Policy in International Business* (Fall 1998): 140.

95. Dara O'Rourke, "Market Movements," University of California, Berkeley, Department of Environmental Science, Policy, and Management, p. 18.

96. Arnold and Hartman, "What's Wrong with Pro-Sweatshop Arguments?" pp. 10–11.

97. Greenhouse, "Anti-Sweatshop Movement."

98. Steven Greenhouse, "A Hip-Hop Star's Fashion Line Is Tagged with a Sweatshop Label," *New York Times*, October 28, 2003, p. B1.

99. Bernstein, "Sweatshops," p. 100.

100. Jeff Ballinger, "The New Free-Trade Heel," *Harper's*, August 1992, p. 64.

101. Bernstein, "Sweatshop Reform," *Business Week*, May 3, 1999, p. 188.

102. See Ian Maitland, "The Great Non-Debate over International Sweatshops," *British Academy of Management Annual Conference Proceedings,* September 1997, pp. 240–65.

103. Jenny Strasburg, "Gap Inc. Agrees to Union Factory," *San Francisco Chronicle*, April 20, 2004, p. C4.

104. O'Rourke, "Outsourcing Regulation," p. 21.

105. David Gonzalez, "Latin Sweatshops Pressed by U.S. Campus Power," *New York Times*, April 4, 2003, p. A3; see also Mischa Gaus, "The Maturing Movement against Sweatshops," *In These Times*, February 16, 2004, pp. 36, 52.

106. "Human Rights," *Economist*, June 3, 1995 p. 59.

107. Pierre McDonagh, "Communicative Campaigns to Effect Anti-Slavery and Fair Trade," *European Journal of Marketing* 36, nos. 5/6 (2002): 649–52.

108. "Human Rights," *Economist*, June 23, 1995, p. 58.

109. www.rugmark.org.

110. This section is based on "2003 Report on Fair Trade Trends in the U.S., Canada & the Pacific Rim" (www.fairtradefederation.com).

111. Margaret Levi and April Linton, "Fair Trade: A Cup at a Time?" *Politics and Society* 31, no. 3, (2003): 419.

112. See Marc Gunther, *Faith and Fortune* (New York: Crown Business, 2004), p. 116.

113. Rob Walker, "Brewed Awakening?" *New York Times Magazine*, June 6, 2004, p. 38.

114. Levi and Linton, "Fair Trade," p. 419.

115. Steve Stecklow and Erin White, "What Price Virtue?" *Wall Street Journal*, June 8, 2004, p. A1.

116. Gresser and Tickell, *Mugged*, pp. 40, 41.

117. Levi and Linton, "Fair Trade," p. 417; see also Schrage, "Promoting International Worker Rights," p. 81.

118. Gresser and Tickell, *Mugged*, p. 40.

119. Levi and Linton, "Fair Trade," p. 420.

120. Ibid., p. 421.

121. O'Rourke, "Outsourcing Regulation," p. 22.

122. Chiquita has established an extensive program to improve the conditions under which bananas are produced in Central America. While primarily designed to affect environmental conditions, the company's programs also affect working conditions. See J. Gary Taylor and Patricia J. Scharlin, *Smart Alliance: How a Global Corporation and Environmental Activists Transformed a Tarnished Brand* (Yale University Press 2004).

123. "Sweatshop Wars," *Economist*, February 27, 1999 p. 63.

124. Noreena Hartz, "Corporations on the Front Line," *Corporate Governance* 12, no. 2 (2004): 204.

125. Quoted in Greenhouse, "Anti-Sweatshop Movement."

126. Marc Gunther, "Money and Morals at GE," *Fortune*, November 15, 2004, p. 178.

127. Sarah Murray, "More than a Round Table Conference," *Financial Times*, Special Report on Responsible Business, November 29, 2004, p. 4. For criticisms of working conditions in the electronics sector, see "Clean Up Your Computer," a CAFOD report (www.cafod.uk/policy [July 28, 2004]).

128. Deborah Leipziger, *The Corporate Responsibility Code Book* (Sheffield, England: Greenleaf, 2003), p. 349.

Chapter Five

1. For an excellent critical analysis of this concept and the various ways it has been defined, see Julian Marshall and Michael Toffel, "Framing the Elusive Concept of Sustainability: A Sustainability Hierarchy," *Environmental Science and Technology* 39, no. 3 (2005): 673–82.

2. This account is primarily based on U. Steger and others, "The Brent Spar Platform Controversy" (A) (B) (C), International Institute for Management Development (IMD) case OIE 170, 171, 072, August 8, 2000.

3. Ragnar Lofstedt and Ortwin Renn, "The Brent Spar Controversy: An Example of Risk Communication Gone Wrong," *Risk Analysis* 17, no. 2 (1997): 132.

4. Benjamin Hunt, *The Timid Corporation: Why Business Is Terrified of Taking Risks* (Hoboken, N.J.: John Wiley, 2003), p. 69,

5. Steger and others, "The Brent Spar," Case (B), p. 9.

6. Ibid.

7. See ibid., p. 2.

8. Ibid., p. 3.

9. Quoted in Hunt, *The Timid Corporation*, p. 71.

10. Jeffrey Hollender and Stephen Fenichell, *What Matters Most: How a Small Group of Pioneers Is Teaching Social Responsibility to Big Business, and Why Big Business Is Listening* (New York: Basic Books, 2004), p. 55.

11. Margaret Keck and Kathryn Sikkink, *Activists beyond Borders: Advocacy Networks in International Politics* (Cornell University Press, 1988), p. 160.

12. David Murphy and Jem Bendell, "New Partnerships for Sustainable Development," in *The Greening of Business in Developing Countries*, edited by Peter Utting (London: Zed Books), p. 218.

13. Ibid.

14. Ibid., pp. 3, 4.

15. Marc Gunther, "The Mosquito in the Tent," *Fortune*, May 31, 2004, p. 162.

16. Jim Carlton, "Once Targeted by Protestors, Home Depot Plays Green Role," *Wall Street Journal*, August 6, 2004, p. 1.

17. Gunther, "The Mosquito," p. 162.

18. Marc Gunther, *Faith and Fortune* (New York: Crown Business, 2004), p. 206.

19. Benjamin Cashore, "Legitimacy and the Privatization of Environmental Governance: How Non-State Market-Driven (NSMD) Governance Systems Gain Rule-Making Authority," *Governance* 15, no. 4 (2002): 514. See also Benjamin Cashore, Graeme Auld, and Deanna Newsom, *Governing through Markets: Forest Certifi-*

cation and the Emergence of Non-State Authority (Yale University Press, 2004), for a detailed comparative analysis of the dynamics of private forest certification.

20. Joseph Domask, "From Boycotts to Global Partnerships: NGO's, the Private Sector and the Struggle to Protect the World's Forests," in *Globalization and NGOs: Transforming Business, Government, and Society*, edited by Jonathan Doh and Hildy Teegen (Westport, Conn.: Praeger, 2003), p. 168.

21. For detailed comparisons of the major forest certification schemes, see Saskia Ozinga, *Behind the Logo: An Environmental and Social Assessment of Forest Certification Schemes* (Moreton-in-Marsh, U.K.: Fern, May 2001) (www.fern.org); and Stephen Bass and others, *Certification's Impacts on Forests, Stakeholders and Supply Chains,* a report of the International Institute for Environment and Development (IIED) project Instruments for Sustainable Private Sector Forestry (Hertfordshire, U.K.: Earthport, May 2001).

22. Domask, "From Boycotts to Global Partnerships," pp. 171–72.

23. Bass, *Certification's Impacts,*" p. 43. For an analysis of why the United States has proven to be a relatively infertile ground for the FSC, see Benjamin Cashore, Graeme Auld, and Deanna Newsom, "The United States' Race to Certify Sustainable Forestry: Non-State Environmental Governance and the Competition for Policy-Making Authority," *Business and Politics* 5, no. 3 (2003): 219–60.

24. Bass, *Certification's Impacts,* p. 43.

25. Domask, "From Boycotts to Global Partnerships," p. 179.

26. Charles O. Holliday Jr., Stephan Schmidheiny, and Philip Watts, *Walking the Talk: The Business Case for Sustainable Development* (San Francisco: Berrett-Koehler, 2002), p. 178.

27. For a case study of a family-owned firm in California that has successfully developed a green marketing strategy, see Magali Delmas, Erica Plambeck, and Monifa Porter, Hayward Lumber Company, Stanford Graduate School of Business case, OIT–38, August 25, 2004.

28. An important shortcoming of *Governing through Markets* by Cashore, Auld, and Newsom—an otherwise comprehensive book on FSC—is that it does not assess the FSC's impact on forestry practices.

29. Domask, "From Boycotts to Global Partnerships," p. 165.

30. Peter Dauvergne, *Shadows in the Forest: Japan and the Politics of Timber in Southeast Asia* (MIT Press, 1997), p. 2. Dauvergne paints a devastating portrait of Southeast Asian timber practices. His more recent study, *Loggers and Degradation in the Asia-Pacific* (Cambridge University Press, 2001), reports changes in rhetoric but no improvement in environmental practices.

31. Murphy and Bendell, "New Partnerships," p. 221.

32. Holliday, *Walking the Talk,* p. 179.

33. Bass, *Certification's Impacts,* p. 86.

34. See Sarah Roberts, Kirsti Thornber, and Nick Robins, "Domino Effect," *Tomorrow Magazine,* September–October 2000, pp. 35, 36.

35. Simon Counsell and Kim Terje Loraas, *Trading in Credibility: The Myth and Reality of the Forest Certification Council* (London: Rainforest Foundation, 2002) (www.rainforestfoundationuk.org).

36. Ibid., p. 22.

37. Forest Stewardship Council, "An FSC Analysis of the Rainforest Foundation Report 'Trading in Credibility'" (Bonn, Germany: FSC, 2002), p. 8.

38. See Cashore, "Legitimacy," p. 519.

39. Danny Hakim, "Talking Green vs. Making Green," *New York Times*, March 28, 2002, p. C1.

40. www.sierraclub.org/global_warming/cleancars/cafe/ford.asp[February 25, 1999].

41. Danny Hakim, "Ford Stresses Business, but Disappoints Environmentalists," *New York Times*, August 20, 2002, p. C4..

42. Timothy Luke, "SUVS and the Greening of Ford," *Organization & Environment*, September 2001, p. 317.

43. Sierra Club, "Ford Motors' 100th Birthday" (www.sierraclub.org/pressroom/media).

44. Hakim, "Talking Green," p. C2.

45. Tim Bust, "Ford Takes Revamp Back to Its Roots," *Financial Times*, February 4, 2002, p. X.

46. Kathleen Kerwin, "How to Market a Groundbreaker," *Business Week*, October 18, 2004, p. 104.

47. Keith Naughton, "Seeing Green," *Newsweek*, December 13, 2004, p. 42.

48. See Forest Reinhardt and Emily Richman, "Global Climate Change and BP Amoco," Harvard Business School case 9-700-106, February 28, 2001, p. 9.

49. Darcy Frey, "How Green Is BP?" *New York Times Magazine*, December 2, 2002, section 6, p. 99.

50. David Victor and Joshua House, "BP's Emissions Trading System," Stanford University, Department of Political Science, September 2004, p. 16.

51. Reinhardt and Richman, "Global Climate Change," p. 9.

52. Ibid., p. 29.

53. Neela Banerjee, "BP Pulls out of a Campaign to Open up Alaska Area," *New York Times*, November 26, 2002, section C, p. 4.

54. Frey, "How Green Is BP?" p. 99.

55. Ibid., p. 99.

56. Cait Murphy, "Is BP beyond Petroleum? Hardly," *Fortune*, September 20, 2002, p. 44.

57. Paul Driessen, *Eco-Imperialism* (Bellevue, Wash.: Free Enterprise Press, 2003), p. 116.

58. Quoted in ibid.

59. See Frey, "How Green Is BP?" p. 99.

60. ww.exxonmobil.com/Corporate/Newsroom/Publications[2004].

61. Steven Hayward, "The New Corporate Balance Sheet," *Environmental Policy Outlook*, October 1, 2002, p. 6 (www.aei.org/publications). In fact, through February 2005, this assessment proved half right: while the shares of both BP and ExxonMobil increased by a similar percentage, Shell's performed more poorly.

62. Claudia H. Deutsch, "Together at Last," *New York Times*, September 9, 2001, p. C1.

63. Tara Weingarten, Julie Halpert, and Joan Raymond, "The Unstoppable SUV," *Newsweek*, July 2, 2001, p. 42.

64. Michael Ellis, "GM Touts Big Engine despite Hybrid Clamor," *Business Reuters*, January 10, 2005 (www.reuters.com).

65. On P&G see Roger Cowe, "Improving Quality of Life and Profits," *Financial Times*, August 13, 2002, p. 12; on Interface and Coca-Cola, see Michelle Conlin, "From Plundered to Protector," *Business Week*, July 19, 2004, p. 61; on Dupont, see Carey, "Global Warming," *Business Week*, August 16, 2004, p. 62; and "Green-Roots Greenery," *Economist*, January 18, 2003, p. 35; on Federal Express and UPS, see Marc Gunther, "Tree Huggers, Soy Lovers, and Profits," *Fortune*, June 23, 2003, p. 99; and on Motorola, Alcoa, and Waste Management, see A. Revkin, "U.S. Is Pressuring Industries to Cut Greenhouse Gas Emissions," *New York Times*, January 20, 2003, p. A1.

66. www.socialfunds.com/news/article [November 1, 2000].

67. Goddard quoted in Katherine Ellison, "Burn Oil, Then Help a School; It All Evens Out," *Fortune*, July 2, 2002, p. 39; see also Mark Thomsen, "IBM, Johnson & Johnson and Polaroid Aim to Save Money by Saving the Environment" (socialfunds.com/news/article.cgi/article 452 [December 15, 2000].

68. www.Chicagoclimateexchange.com/about/program.

69. For an informative discussion of state policy regulations, see Barry Rabe, *Statehouse and Greenhouse* (Brookings, 2004); see also John Carey, "Global Warming," p. 62.

70. Fiona Harvey, "Making a Dash for Green Growth," *FT Sustainable Business*, October 14, 2004, p. 6.

71. See, for example, John Berger, *Charging Ahead: The Business of Renewable Energy and What It Means for America* (New York: Henry Holt, 1997).

72. Coalition for Environmentally Responsible Economies, "Value at Risk: Climate Change and the Future of Governance" (Boston: CERES Sustainability Governance Project, April 2002), p. i.

73. "Survey: Ignoring Climate Changes Poses Big Financial Risk," *BizWeek*, February 17, 2003.

74. See Robert Monks, Anthony Miller, and Jacqueline Cook, "Shareholder Activism on Environmental Issues: A Study of Proposals at Large U.S. Corporations (2000–2003)," *Natural Resources Forum* 28, no. 4 (2004): 317–30.

75. Guy Gugliotta and Eric Pianin, "Bush Plans on Global Warming Alter Little," *Washington Post*, January 1, 2004, p. A1.

76. David Victor, *Climate Change* (New York: Council on Foreign Relations, 2004), p. 27.

77. Gugliotta and Pianin, "Bush Plans on Global Warming Alter Little." p. A1.

78. For a comprehensive study of the wide variation in the response of global firms to climate change, see Ans Kolk, "Business Responses to Climate Change: Identifying Emergent Strategies," *California Management Review* 47, no. 3 (2005): 6–20.

79. Vanessa Houlder, "Swiss Re Changes the Climate," *Financial Times*, April 17, 2004, p. 10.

80. ens-news/ens/July2003/2003-07-09-11. The report gave the highest scores to BP, Royal Dutch Shell, and Dupont, and its lowest to ChevronTexaco, ConocoPhillips, Exxon Mobil, DaimlerChrysler, and General Electric.

81. For a description of voluntary corporate agreements on climate change in Europe, see *Voluntary Environmental Agreements,* edited by Patrick ten Brink (Sheffield, England: Greenleaf, 2002), part C, pp. 255-341.

82. See Thomas Lyon and John Maxwell, *Corporate Environmentalism and Public Policy* (Cambridge University Press, 2004); and Neil Gunningham, Robert Kagan, and Dorothy Thornton, *Shades of Green: Business, Regulation, and Environment* (Stanford University Press, 2003).

83. See, for example, Bob Willard, *The Sustainability Advantage: Seven Business Case Benefits of a Triple Bottom Line* (Gabriola Island, B.C.: New Society, 2002); Bob Doppelt, *Leading Change towards Sustainabilty: A Change-Management Guide for Business, Government and Civil Society* (Sheffield, England: Greenleaf, 2003); Tedd Saunders, *The Bottom Line of Green Is Black: Strategies for Creating Environmentally Sound Businesses* (HarperSanFrancisco, 1993); Chris Laszlo, *The Sustainable Company: How to Create Lasting Value through Social and Environmental Performance* (Washington: Island Press, 2003); Brian Nattrass and Mary Altomare, *The Natural Step for Business: Wealth, Ecology, and the Evolutionary Corporation* (Gabriola Island, B.C.: New Society, 2001); John Elkington, *Cannibals with Forks: The Triple Bottom Line of 21st Century Business* (Gabriola Island, B.C.: New Society, 1998); Charles Holliday Jr., Stephan Schmidheiny, and Philip Watts, *Walking the Talk: The Business Case for Sustainable Development* (Sheffield, England: Greenleaf, 2002).

84. For a discussion of green consumerism in Sweden, see Michele Micheletti, *Political Virtue and Shopping: Individuals, Consumerism, and Collective Action* (New York: Palgrave Macmillan, 2003), pp. 119-49. For two somewhat dated discussions of green consumerism, see John Elkington, Julie Hailes, and Joel Makower, *The Green Consumer* (New York: Penguin, 1990); and Sandra Vandermerwe and Michael D. Oliff, "Consumers Drive Corporations Green," *Long Range Planning* 23, no. 6 (1990): 10-60.

85. See Michelle Conlin, "From Plunder to Protector," *Business Week,* July 19, 2004, p. 60.

86. Forest Reinhardt, *Down to Earth: Applying Business Principles to Environmental Management* (Harvard Business School Press, 2000), p. 22. Reinhardt's study is unique among books on environmental management in that it presents case studies of business failures as well as successes.

87. Quoted in Dale Murphy, *The Structure of Regulatory Competition* (Oxford University Press, 2004), p. 178.

88. Jill Ginsberg, "Choosing the Right Green Marketing Strategy," *MIT Sloan Management Review* (Fall 2004): 79.

89. Richard MacLean, "The Search for Deep Green," *Environmental Protection* 15, no. 3 (2004): 1.

90. Vanessa Houlder, "An Increased Sense of Urgency," *Financial Times,* Special Report on Business and Development, June 24, 2004, p. 11.

91. For a summary of international voluntary environmental codes, see Petra Christmann and Glen Taylor, "Globalization and the Environment: Strategies for International Voluntary Environmental Initiatives," *Academy of Management Executive* 16, no. 3 (2002): 121-35.

92. Jeffrey Rayport and George Lodge, "Responsible Care," Harvard Business School case 9 -391-135, March 18, 1991.

93. For the most recent description of the industry's own assessment of the codes' impact, see the fourth status report, International Council of Chemical Associations, www.icca-chem.org. A study by Andrew King and Michael Lenox, "Industry Self-Regulation without Sanctions: The Chemical Industry's Responsible Care Program," *Academy of Management Journal* 43, no. 4 (2000): 698–716, found that Responsible Care has had no impact on the environmental performance of chemical firms in the United States. See also Jennifer Howard, Jennifer Nash, and John Ehrenfeld, "Standard or Smokescreen?" *California Management Review* 42, no. 2 (2000): 63–82. However, a broader study, Neil Gunningham, "Environment, Self-Regulation, and the Chemical Industry: Assessing Responsible Care," *Law & Policy* 17, no. 1 (1995): 59–109, found some improvements in the United States, Canada, and Australia. For an analysis of RC's impact in two developing countries, see Ronie Garcia-Johnson, *Exporting Environmentalism: U.S. Multinational Chemicals Corporations in Brazil and Mexico* (MIT Press, 2000).

94. "Corporations: Number of ISO 14001 Companies" (Earthtrends.wri.org/text/environmental governance).

95. For an exhaustive review of the literature on the environmental impact of ISO 14001, see Michael Toffel, "Resolving Information Asymmetries in Supply Chains: Are Certified Voluntary Programs Effective?" University of California, Berkeley, Haas School of Business, November 2004. Toffel's study, which examines the impact of ISO 14001 on compliance in the United States, found only a modest impact. However, Matthew Potoski and Aseem Prakash ("Covenants with Weak Swords: ISO 14001 and Firms' Environmental Performance," Iowa State University, Department of Political Science, September 2004), found more a positive impact in the United States. There is little research on the impact of ISO 14001 on environmental performance in developing countries.

96. Michael Toffel, "Evaluating Suppliers' Production Practices: The Role of Voluntary Programs," University of California, Berkeley, Haas School of Business, October 2004, pp. 10, 11.

97. Glen Dowell, Stuart Hart, and Bernard Yeung, "Do Corporate Global Environmental Standards Create or Destroy Market Value?" *Management Science* 46, no. 8 (2000): 1059–74; see also Petra Christmann, "Multinational Companies and the Natural Environment: Determinants of Global Environmental Policy Standardization," *Academy of Management Journal* 47, no. 5 (2004): 747–60.

Chapter Six

1. See Alison Maitland, "Human Rights Weigh Heavier with Investors," *Financial Times*, April 6, 2000, p. 15.

2. David White, "Shell Tries to Repair Troubled Delta Relations," *Financial Times*, February 24, 2004, p. 5.

3. Joshua Hammer, "Nigeria Crude," *Harper's*, June 1996, pp. 58–61.

4. Paul Lewis, "After Nigeria Represses, Shell Defends Its Record," *New York Times International*, February 13, 1996, p. A1.

5. David Murphy and Jem Bendell, "New Partnerships for Sustainable Development," in *The Greening of Business in Developing Countries*, edited by Peter Utting (London: Zed Books, 2002), p. 227.

6. Lewis, "After Nigeria," p. A1.

7. Murphy and Bendell, "New Partnerships," p. 227.

8. Ibid.

9. Geoffrey Chandler, "The Evolution of the Business and Human Rights Debate," in *Business and Human Rights,* edited by Rory Sullivan (Sheffield, England: Greenleaf, 2003), p. 24.

10. Peter Frankental and Frances House, *Human Rights: Is It Any of Your Business?* (London: Amnesty International and the Prince of Wales Business Leadership Forum, 2000), p. 96.

11. Peter Maas, "Road to Hell," *New Republic,* January 31, 2005, p. 16.

12. See Frankental and House, *Human Rights,* p. 96; and Daniel Litvin, *Empires of Profit* (New York: Texere, 2003), p. 259.

13. Michael Peel, "Shell Faces New Ogoni Dilemma in South Nigeria," *Financial Times,* September 14, 2004, p. 5.

14. Christian Aid, *"Behind the Mask: The Real Face of CSR"* (London, 2004), p. 2.

15. Chandler, "The Evolution," p. 24.

16. Ibid., p. 25.

17. Frankenthal and House, *Human Rights,* pp. 82–106.

18. According to the Business and Human Rights Resource Center, twenty-six companies have developed policies that refer to the UDHR, and an additional twelve have made policy commitments to human rights, but without explicitly referring to the UDHR. Rory Sullivan and Nina Seppala, "From the Inside Looking Out," in *Business and Human Rights*, edited by Sullivan, p. 107

19. Bennett Freeman and Genoveva Uriz, "Managing Risk and Building Trust," in *Business and Human Rights*, edited by Sullivan, pp. 242–59.

20. Ibid., p. 249.

21. This paragraph is based on Freeman and Uriz, "Managing Risk," pp. 247–48.

22. "Sociologists before Geologists," *Economist,* June 27, 2002, p. 59. The company has also been the subject of a lawsuit filed by villagers who claim that the firm's mercury emissions have adversely affected their health. They are seeking $543 million in damages. The company claims that its emission standards fall within American regulatory guidelines, a contention that has been disputed. Jane Perlez, "Mining Giant Told It Put Toxic Vapors into Indonesia's Air," December 22, 2004, *New York Times* p. A12.

23. S. Prakash Sethi, "The Effectiveness of Industry-Based Codes in Serving Public Interest," *Transnational Corporations* (forthcoming).

24. Daphne Eviatar, "Africa's Oil Tycoons," *The Nation,* April 12, 2004, pp. 11–16.

25. Jared Diamond, *Collapse: How Societies Choose to Fail or Succeed* (New York: Viking, 2005), pp. 442–52.

26. Murphy and Bendell, "New Partnerships," p. 228.

27. Deborah Ball, "Ex-Activist Finds Grass Is Greener on Corporate Side," *Wall Street Journal*, November 17, 2004, p. A12.

28. "Sociologists before Geologists," p. 59.

29. See Jerry Useem, "Exxon's African Adventure," *Fortune*, April 15, 2002, p. 102.

30. Alison Maitland, "Business Bows to Growing Pressures," *Financial Times*, Special Report on Responsible Business, November 29, 2004, p. 2.

31. Quoted in Sarah Murray, "Take a Good Look at the Local Issues," *Financial Times*, Special Report on Business and Development, June 30, 2004, p. 14.

32. Dara O'Rourke, "Opportunities and Obstacles for Corporate Social Responsibility Reporting in Developing Countries," a report prepared for the Corporate Social Responsibly Practice of the World Bank Group (World Bank/International Finance Corporation, March 2004), p. 19.

33. "Gearing Up: From Corporate Responsibility to Good Governance and Scalable Solutions," in *Sustainability—The Global Compact* (London: Sustainability Ltd., June 2004), p. 30.

34. Glenn R. Simpson, "Multinational Companies Unite to Fight Bribery," *Wall Street Journal*, January 25, 2005, p. A2.

35. For a detailed discussion of these citizen pressures on business, see David Vogel, *Lobbying the Corporation* (New York: Basic Books, 1976), chap. 5.

36. See Judith White, "Globalization, Divestment and Human Rights in Burma," *Journal of Corporate Citizenship* (Summer 2004): 47–65.

37. Lane La Mure and Debora Spar, "The Burma Pipeline," Harvard Business School Case 9 0 798-079 (revised March 3, 2000,) pp. 8, 9.

38. White, "Globalization, Divestment," p. 56.

39. Paul Magnusson, "Making a Federal Case out of Overseas Abuses," *Business Week*, November 25, 2002, p. 78.

40. Edward Alden and Doug Cameron, "Unocal Settles Burma Abuse Case," *Financial Times*, December 14, 2004, p. 6.

41. White, "Globalization," p. 54.

42. Jarol Manheim, *The Death of a Thousand Cuts* (Mahwah, N.J.: Lawrence Erlbaum, 2001), p. 106.

43. See Debora Spar and Lane La Mure, "The Power of Activism: Assessing the Impact of NGOs on Global Business," *California Management Review* (Spring 2003): 86.

44. White, "Globalization," p. 53.

45. "Forced Labour and Other Customs," *Economist*, December 18, 2004, p. 54.

46. Dara O'Rourke, "Opportunities and Obstacles for Corporate Social Reporting," p. 3.

47. For a discussion of investor and NGO pressures on firms in Canada, the United States, and Europe not to invest in the Sudan, see Russell Sparkes, *Socially Responsible Investment* (Hoboken, N.J.: John Wiley, 2002), pp. 187–91.

48. Maitland, "Human Rights Weigh Heavier with Investors."

49. J. Berman and T. Webb, "Race to the Top: Attracting and Enabling Global Sustainable Business" (World Bank Group—Corporate Social Responsibility Practice, October 2003), p. 15.

50. For a detailed discussion of Levi Strauss's guidelines and its decision to disengage from China, see Jane Katz and Lynn Sharp Paine, "Levis Strauss & Co.: Global Sourcing (A) and (B)," Harvard Business School case 9-395-127, February 27, 1997; and 9-395-128, March 10, 1995.

51. See Karl Schoenberger, *Levi's Children* (New York: Grove Press, 2000), p. 123.

52. Louise Kehoe, "Bold Fashion Statement," *Financial Times*, May 8/9, 1993, p. 9.

53. Schoenberger, *Levi's Children*, p. 125.

54. See Alison Maitland, "An Investment in Human Rights," *Financial Times*, October 28, 2004, p. 10.

55. Michael Phillips and Mitchell Pacelle, "Major Banks Will Adhere to Environmental Standards," *Wall Street Journal*, June 4, 2003, pp. A1, A10.

56. www.equator-principles.com/ngo.

57. See Demetri Sevastopulo and Vanessa Houlder, "'Greening' of Financial Sector Gathering Speed," *Financial Times*, June 4, 2004, p. 6.

58. Quoted in ibid.

59. William Baue, "Are the Equator Principles Sincere or Spin?" (www.socialfunds.com [June 4, 2004]).

60. See Sevastopulo and Houlder, "Greening."

61. Sebastian Mallaby, "NGOs: Fighting Poverty, Hurting the Poor," *Foreign Policy* (September/October 2004): 50–58.

62. The two most comprehensive accounts of the Global Compact are *Raising the Bar*, edited by Claude Fussler, Aron Cramer, and Sebastian ven der Vegt (Sheffield, England: Greenleaf, 2004); and *Learning to Talk*, edited by Malcolm McIntosh, Sandra Waddock, and Georg Kell (Sheffield, England: Greenleaf, 2004). See also John Gerard Ruggie, "Reconstituting the Global Public Domain—Issues, Actors, and Practices," *European Journal of International Relations* 10, no. 4 (2004): 499–531.

63. Georg Kell and David Levin, "The Global Compact Network," in *Learning to Talk*, edited by McIntosh, Waddock, and Kell, p. 44.

64. Ibid., p. 62.

65. McKinsey and Company, survey results reported in "Assessing the Global Compact's Impact," 2004, p. 2.

66. See Mark Turner, "Effort to Bury Mistrust," *Financial Times*, Special Report on Business and Development, June 24, 2004, p. 4.

67. McKinsey and Co., "Assessing the Global Compact's Impact," p. 16.

68. McKinsey and Co., "Assessing the Global Compact's Impact," pp. 16, 6, 3.

69. Ibid., p. 3.

70. Turner, "Effort to Bury Mistrust," p. 4.

71. See *The Greening of Business*, edited by Utting.

72. See Alan Cowell, "A Call to Put Social Issues on Corporate Agendas," *New York Times*, April 6, 2000, p. C4.

73. Ruggie, "Reconstituting the Global Public Domain," p. 524.

74. Ariel Colonomos and Javier Santiso, "Vive la France!" Paris, Sciences Po, p. 19.

75. Quoted in Sparkes, *Socially Responsible Investment*, p. 185.

76. Freeman and Uriz, "Managing Risk," p. 247.

77. Sullivan and Seppala, "From the Inside Looking Out," p. 112.

78. Murray, "When Exploration Rights Meet Human Rights," *Financial Times*, March 15, 2002, p. 12.

Chapter Seven

1. See Dara O'Rourke, *Community-Driven Regulation* (MIT Press, 2004), p. 189.

2. Simon Zadek, *Tomorrow's History* (Sheffield, England: Greenleaf, 2004), p. 210; italics in original.

3. Robert Bork, "Judicial Imperialism," *Wall Street Journal*, June 17, 2003.

4. Elliot J. Schrage, "Judging Corporate Accountability in the Global Economy," *Columbia Journal of Transnational Law* 42 (2003): 153–76; see also Steven Ratner, "Corporations and Human Rights: A Theory of Legal Responsibility," *Yale Law Journal* (December 2001): 443–545.

5. See Alison Maitland, "Compliance Bound to Be Binding" *Financial Times*, February 22, 2002, p. 10. See also Paul Magnusson, "Making a Federal Case of Overseas Abuses," *Business Week*, November 25, 2002, p. 78.

6. Frederick Balfour and Sheri Prasso, "Bumps in the Road to Labor Reform," *Business Week International Edition*, September 11, 2000, p. 28; and Amy Kazmin, "Garment Buyers Prefer Cambodia," *Financial Times*, December 4, 2004, p. 9.

7. Halina Ward, "Public Sector Roles in Strengthening Corporate Social Responsibility: Taking Stock" (World Bank–International Finance Corporation, January 2004), p. 7.

8. Ibid.

9. "Leadership, Accountability and Partnership: Critical Trends and Issues in Corporate Social Responsibility" (Cambridge, Mass.: Kennedy School of Government Corporate Social Responsibility Initiative, March 4, 2004), p. 7.

10. For an analysis of the relationship between corporate and government environmental standards in Vietnam, see O'Rourke, *Community-Driven Regulation*.

11. For a useful discussion of the way trade policies can promote CSR in developing countries, see Susan Ariel Aaronson, "A Match Worth Making: Linking Trade Policies with Voluntary Corporate Social Responsibility Initiatives," Globalization Brief (Washington: Frank Hawkins Kenan Institute for Private Enterprise, Washington Center, June 2004) (www.csrpolicies.org).

12. See James Brooke, "A Year of Worry for Cambodia's Garment Makers," *New York Times*, January 24, 2004, p. B1.

13. Robert Reich is one of the few writers on CSR who has explicitly addressed this issue. While his solution, namely that corporations should play no role in affecting public policy, may be unrealistic, he has identified an important dimension of CSR that is too often ignored. Robert B. Reich, "The New Meaning of Corporate Social Responsibility," *California Management Review* (Winter 1998): 8–17.

14. For one of the few efforts to do so, see Frank Dixon, "SRI Takes on System Change," *Business Ethics* (Winter 2004): 15–16. Dixon labels his approach, which includes an assessment of corporate political activity, "Total Corporate Responsibility." Some other activists have begun to consider corporate tax payments as a dimension of CSR. According to John Christensen, "Corporate responsibility must begin with paying your normal dues to the societies in which you operate." Roger Cowe, "Tax Avoidance Is Rising Up the Ethical Agenda," *Financial Times*, November 19, 2004, Special Report, p. 2. See also Vanessa Houlder, "The Tax Avoidance Story as a Morality Tale," *Financial Times*, November 23, 2004, p. 7.

15. Notable exceptions are Susan Ariel Aaronson and James T. Reeves, *Corporate Responsibility in the Global Village: The Role of Public Policy* (Washington: National Policy Association, 2002); and Jeremy Moon, "Government as a Driver of Corporate Social Responsibility," International Centre for Corporate Responsibility Research Paper Series (www.nottingham.ac.uk/business/ICCR).

16. Quoted in "Leadership, Accountability," p. 7.

17. Jeffrey Hollender and Stephen Fenichell, *What Matters Most: How a Small Group of Pioneers Is Teaching Social Responsibility to Big Business, and Why Big Business Is Listening* (New York: Basic Books, 2004), p. 94.

18. For a sophisticated analysis of the relationship between private and public environmental policies, which also discusses the issue of global climate change, see Thomas P. Lyon, "'Green' Firms Bearing Gifts," *Regulation* (Fall 2003): 36–40.

19. For a discussion of the critical role of transparency in improving corporate social performance, see Ann Florini, "Business and Global Governance: The Growing Role of Corporate Codes of Conduct," *Brookings Review* (Spring 2003): 4–8.

Index

Abbott, 41
ABN-AMRO, 66
Accenture, 58
AccountAbility, 66, 68, 71
AccountAbility Forum, 7–8
ACLU. *See* American Civil Liberties Union
Activists and activism: activist funds, 65; attacks on firms, 93; audits and, 91; banking and lending and, 155; BP and, 126; Burma and, 150, 159; climate change, 130; as consumers, 52; expectations of, 114; in Europe, 86; forestry issues, 49, 120; human rights and, 139; Nike and, 80; Shell oil platform and, 112–14; Sudan and, 159; Talisman and, 158; targeting by, 54, 73; views of wages, 100. *See also* American Civil Liberties Union
Adelphia, 38
Adidas, 79, 84
Adidas-Solomon, 87, 97
Advertising. *See* Marketing and advertising
AFL-CIO. *See* American Federation of Labor-Congress of Industrial Organizations
Africa, 88–89, 96

Agriculture and agricultural products: child labor and, 87, 96, 98; codes of conduct and, 87–89, 107; social labeling and, 76–77; voluntary standards and, 85, 90, 165. *See also* Cocoa industry; Coffee industry
AIDS, 42
Airwalk, 79
Alcan, 128–29, 132
Alcoa, 128, 130, 132, 146
Alcohol, 39
Alien Tort Claims Act (*1789*), 152, 168
Amazon books, 6
American Civil Liberties Union (ACLU), 81–82
American Electric Power, 64, 129
American Express (AmEx), 21, 41
American Federation of Labor-Congress of Industrial Organizations (AFL-CIO), 84
American Forest & Paper Association, 118
AmEx. *See* American Express
Amnesty International, 83, 158
AMRC. *See* Asia Monitor Resources Center
Anderson, Ray, 44
Anglo-American, 146

Angola, 22, 147, 149
Animal testing, 50
Annan, Kofi, 156
Antiwar movement, 7, 24
ANWR. *See* Arctic National Wildlife Refuge
Apparel industry, 94–96, 101, 107, 154, 168. *See also* Gap Inc.; Levi Strauss; Nike; Reebok
Apparel Industry Partnership, 10, 78, 83–84, 167
Apple Computer, 151
Arco, 151
Arctic National Wildlife Refuge (ANWR), 125
Ariel Appreciation, 37
Arthur D. Little, 11, 58
Ashridge Centre for Business and Society, 153
Asia Monitor Resources Center (AMRC), 91
Aspen Institute, 66
Association of British Assurers, 66–67
Athletic footwear and apparel, 93–94. *See also* Nike
Atlantic Richfield, 18, 42
Aung San Suu Kyi, 150
Australia, 155
Automobile industry, 137. *See also* Sport utility vehicles; individual manufacturers
AVE. *See* Foreign Trade Association of German Retailers, 83
Avon, 55
Azar, Jack, 131

Baby boomers, 27–28
Bain, 57
Bakan, Joel, 2
Baku-Tbilisi-Ceylon pipeline, 156
Ballinger, Jeffrey, 81
B&Q, 115
Bangladesh, 92, 98
Bank of America, 155
Banks and banking, 139, 154–56, 160, 161, 165

Bank Sarisan, 66
BankTrack, 154, 156
Bayer, 129
BBC, 80
Behind the Mask: The Real Face of Corporate Social Responsibility (Christian Aid), 12
Belgium, 66, 104
Ben and Jerry's Homemade, 28, 43–44, 50, 71, 73
Berle, Adolf Augustus, 25
Beyond Petroleum campaign, 53
Bhopal (India), 137
BHP Billiton, 146
Birkenstock, 72
BMW, 57
Body Shop: business strategies of, 28, 57; ETI and, 85; financial results of, 43, 55; management of, 71; market for, 50, 134; SA8000 and, 83
Boeing, 41
Booz Allen Hamilton, 57
Borneo, 114–15
Botswana, 42
Bottom Line of Green Is Black, The (Saunders and McGovern), 19–20
Boycotts. *See* Consumer issues
BP: Atlantic Richfield and, 42; CSR and, 2, 52, 53, 54, 55, 165; emissions trading by, 169; employment issues, 58; environmental issues, 1, 5, 123–26, 127, 128–29, 132, 133, 135–36; financial results of, 44; human rights issues, 144, 145, 145–46; name change of, 125–26; public pressures on, 121, 165; PWYP agreements, 149; solar power of, 125, 126; in West Papua, New Guinea, 147–48
BP Amoco, 123
BP Pension, 66
Brazil, 88, 120, 155, 157, 158
Breast cancer, 55–56
Brent Spar. *See* Shell
Bridgeway Ultra Small Company Tax Advantage, 37

Bristol-Myers Squibb, 63
British American Tobacco, 58–59
British Columbia (Canada), 120
British Petroleum. *See* BP
British Telecommunications (BT), 58
Broughton, Martin, 58–59
Browne, John, 53, 123, 124
BT. *See* British Telecommunications
Building Reputational Capital (Jackson), 20
Built to Last (Collins and Porras), 41
Burkina Faso, 88
Burma (Myanmar): government in, 151, 152–53; human rights issues in, 2; investment in, 61; oil pipelines in, 150–52; PepsiCo in, 51; pressure to divest and, 150–52, 159; trade and investment restrictions in, 168, 169, 170; Union Oil in, 5, 51; withdrawal of companies from, 2, 139, 140, 162
Burson-Marsteller, 149
Bush (George W.) administration, 131, 168
Business. *See* Corporations
Business Charter for Sustainable Development, 136
Business Ethics, 12, 72
Business for Social Responsibility, 11, 153
Business in the Community, 11, 42
Business Leaders Initiative on Human Rights, 11
Business schools, 6–7, 28, 56, 58–59, 166. *See also* Universities
Business Week, 7, 53, 78, 79, 122

CAC 40, 159
Cadbury Schweppes, 89, 90
CAFE. *See* Coffee and Farmer Equity
Cafedirect, 104, 105
California Public Employees Retirement System (Calpers), 63
Calvert Asset Management, 22
Calvert Fund, 37
Calvert Group, 40, 63; Social Index, 63; Social Investment Balanced A, 37; Social Investment Fund, 22

Cambodia, 97, 168–69, 171
Cambridge Associates, 66
Cameroon, 148
Canada, 120, 132, 172. *See also* North America
C&A, 53, 72, 73, 86, 87, 90, 91
Cantor Fitzgerald, 72
Carbon dioxide (CO_2). *See* Environmental issues
Carpet industry. *See* Ikea; Interface; Rugmark
Carrefour, 53, 73, 86–87, 106
Casino, 87
Caterpillar, 131
Cause for Success (Arena), 19
Celestial Seasonings, 28, 57, 72
Center for Environmental Leadership, 127
Central America, 50, 83, 88
CERES. *See* Coalition for Environmentally Responsible Economies
Chad, 148, 163
Chamberlain, Neil, 12
Chase Manhattan Bank, 18, 19
Chemical industry, 136–37
Chevron, 145
ChevronTexaco, 54, 130, 146, 147, 163, 168. *See also* Texaco
Chicago Climate Exchange, 129
Chile, 116
China: AMRC and, 91; child labor in, 97; competition from, 94; ETI and, 86; exports of, 85, 95; government policies in, 170; investment in Canada, 158; labor conditions in, 163; Levi Strauss in, 154, 159; Nike in, 77, 81; production in, 169; SA8000 and, 83; unions in, 83, 101
Chiquita Brands International, 2, 43, 50, 83
Chocolate. *See* Cocoa industry; Hershey; Mars
Christian Aid, 12, 144
Christian Industrial Committee, 91
Chrysler, 54
Ciba, 135

Circuit City, 41
Citibank, 2, 155
Citicorp, 41, 155, 168
Cities. *See* Urban affairs
Citigroup, 51, 57, 59
Civil liability, 168
Civil regulation. *See* Corporate social
    responsibility
Civil rights movement, 7
Clean Clothes Campaign, 86
Climate. *See* Environmental issues;
    Globalization and global issues
Climate Change Action Plan (*1993*), 131
Climate Group, 132
Climate Leaders, 131
Climate Savers, 129
Clinton (Bill) administration, 10, 78, 82,
    83, 167
CO_2 (carbon dioxide). *See* Environmental issues
Coalition for Environmentally Responsible Economies (CERES), 69, 130,
    132, 136
Coca-Cola, 57, 128, 168
Cocoa industry, 88–89, 96
Cocoa Industry Protocol, 89
Code of Conduct on Workplace Human
    Rights, 152
Codes of conduct: adoption of voluntary
    standards, 162; in agriculture,
    87–89; carbon reduction programs,
    128–30; consumer effects and,
    165–66; derivation of corporate
    codes, 166–67; effectiveness of, 76,
    94, 96–102, 106–07, 109, 164, 165,
    170; European voluntary codes,
    85–87; in forestry, 117–21; global
    standards and, 136–37; human rights
    and, 139–40; popularity and use of,
    34, 75; social labeling and, 102–06;
    strategies of civil regulation and, 6;
    UN Global Compact, 8, 156–57;
    U.S. voluntary codes, 82–85
Coffee and Farmer Equity (CAFE), 88
Coffee industry, 87–88, 103–06, 162,
    163, 166, 167, 172

Cohen, Ben, 28
Collins, James, 41
Colombia, 144, 146, 147
Combs, Sean, 99
Committee for Economic Development,
    19
Common Code for the Coffee Community, 88, 164
Companies with a Conscience (Scott and
    Rothman), 20
Competition. *See* Economic issues
Cone Communications, 47
Conference Board, 11, 62
Congo, 120
Connolly, J. W., 135
Conoco, 145
Conservation International, 88
Consumer issues: automobiles, 127–28;
    boycotts, 47, 48, 51–52, 70–71, 89,
    103, 114, 115, 116, 142, 151; CSR
    and, 47–49, 52, 165–66; environmental factors, 116, 119, 122, 123,
    127–28, 134; ethical premiums, 49,
    50, 102, 135; gap between intentions
    and actions, 52; green marketing,
    134–36; purchasing and labor practices, 76, 80, 93; purchasing and
    prices, 93–94, 135
Control Data, 18, 42
Co-operative Bank, 50, 57
Coop Italia, 50
Core Conventions of the International
    Labor Organization, 166–67
Corporate Citizenship (McIntosh,
    Leipziger, Jones, and Coleman), 19
Corporate Citizenship Initiative, 67
Corporate social responsibility (CSR):
    business changes and, 1–3, 15, 75,
    148–49, 162, 163; civil regulation
    and, 3, 6, 9, 13, 15, 46–47, 49, 73,
    94, 109, 112–14, 164, 165, 166–71;
    company reputation and, 54, 76;
    costs of compliance, 92–96; critics
    and criticisms of, 12–13, 163; definitions and concepts of, 4–6, 171–73;
    economic factors, 3, 8, 11–12,

16–17, 19–24, 29–35, 46, 73, 76, 94–96, 108–09, 162–63, 164–64, 170, 172; employees and, 56–60, 73; European views of, 23; financial-market constraints on, 71–72; history of, 7; human rights and, 139–61; limitations of, 138, 139–40; marketing and advertising of, 48–51, 56; measurement, monitoring, and enforcement of, 16, 30, 75–76, 84–87, 89–96, 97, 99, 139–40, 164, 170; network, 68; old-style corporate responsibility, 17–19; public policy and, 171–73; R&D and, 32; reporting of, 67–70; resurgence and growth of, 6–12, 16–17, 26–29; risk management and, 43; role and effects of, 3–4, 7, 8–10, 11, 14–15, 40–45, 54, 109, 139–40, 156, 162–63; social labeling, 8, 48–49, 102–06, 164; sourcing and investment decisions and, 153–56; Voluntary Principles on Security and Human Rights, 145–46. *See also* Consumer issues; Developing countries; Environmental issues; Fair Trade and Fair Trade labeling; Investment issues; UN Global Compact; *individual corporations*
Corporate virtue. *See* Corporate social responsibility
Corporation of London, 66
Corporations: activist attacks on, 93; brands of, 53, 76, 102, 105, 107; business case for human rights, 158–60; business environments and, 24–29; corruption and, 149–50; corporate philanthropy and foundations, 17–19, 21, 26, 55–56, 57; CSR and, 10–13, 39, 73; employees of, 56–60, 72; executives of, 14, 53, 59, 67, 68–69, 132, 135–36, 157, 166, 178n33; fraud and illegal activities, 14; governance and management of, 9, 13, 14, 19, 20–21, 25–26, 38–39, 65, 74, 132, 133, 166; industrial organization, 24–26; marketing and

advertising by, 21, 33, 48–51, 56, 134–36; measurement of financial performance, 30; multinational businesses, 8–9; owners of, 25; political influence of, 10, 171; public versus private companies, 71–72; redefining responsibility of, 171–73; regulation of, 9–10, 133–34; reporting by, 39, 67–69; reputations of, 53, 54–56; roles of, 10, 12–13, 23–24; strategies of, 34–35, 73–74; transparency in conduct of, 22–23; triple bottom line of, 11, 67. *See also* Codes of conduct; Environmental issues; Investment issues; Labor issues; *individual corporations*
Corruption, 149–50, 161, 165, 167, 170
Costa Rica, 86, 158
Costco, 72
Council on Economic Priorities, 82
Council on Foundations, 21
CSR. *See* Corporate social responsibility
Cummins Engine, 18, 42, 44

Dartmouth College, 78–79
Dayton-Hudson, 18, 42
Del Monte, 168
Denmark, 104
Developing countries: agricultural producers in, 162; banks and banking for, 154–56; civil regulation in, 9; civil society in, 170–71; consumer issues of, 49; CSR in, 7, 75–77, 139, 144, 163, 169; doing business and investing in, 153–54, 171; environmental issues in, 111, 119–20, 136, 138, 163; extractive industries in, 140, 144–53; FT certification and, 105; ISO *14001* and, 137; monitoring and enforcement of workplace standards in, 82–96; promoting sustainable development, 146–50; UN Global Compact and, 157, 158; Western governments and, 170–71; working conditions in, 75–109, 110, 111. *See also* Nike; Shell; *individual countries*

Disney. *See* Walt Disney
DJSI World. *See* Dow Jones Sustainability World Index
Dogwood Alliance, 116
Dole Food Products, 83
Domini, 28; *400* Social Index, 35–36; Social Equity Fund, 35
Domini, Amy, 28
Dominican Republic, 101
Dow Chemical, 6, 24, 51–52, 59, 129
Dow Corning, 129
Dow Jones: Global Index, 36; Sustainability Index, 11; Sustainability World Index (DJSI World), 35, 36, 42, 64
Dreyfus, 66
Dreyfus Premier Third Century, 37
Drift and Mastery (Lippmann), 25
Dubois, Pablo, 105–06
Dunkin' Donuts, 105
Dupont, 128–29, 130, 132, 135–36

Earthscan, 8
Eastman Kodak, 151
Economic issues: capitalism and virtue, 3–4; child labor, 97; civil regulation and, 9; competition, 26, 29, 34, 43, 44, 56, 93, 95–96, 109, 135; costs of audits and compliance, 91–96; CSR, 3, 8, 11–12, 16–17, 19–24, 29–35, 108–09, 165–66; eco-marketing, 8; ethics and profits, 29–35; global capitalism, 9; global poverty and inequality, 13; living standards, 164, 165; managerial capitalism, 26; politicization of the market, 4; reduction of greenhouse gases, 130, 131–32; social and environmental factors, 136; socioeconomic class, 50; social investing, 62–63
Economist, 3, 7, 147
Economist Intelligence Unit, 68–69
EcoPledge, 116
Eddie Bauer, 84, 151
Edwards, Lee, 125
Eileen Fisher, 72, 91

Eitel, Maria, 59
Ellis Island (N.Y.), 21
El Salvador, 87, 91–92, 101
Emissions. *See* BP; Environmental issues
Employment issues. *See* Corporations; Labor issues
Energy Star, 131
ENI-Agip, 147
Enron, 5, 38–39, 59
Environmental Defense Fund, 124, 128–29
Environmental issues: biodiversity, 119; carbon dioxide, 124–25, 129, 131, 165; climate change, 64, 111, 121–38; coffee industry and, 88; complexity of, 110; corporate concerns, 1–2, 5, 20, 22, 59, 110–11, 126–38; CSR and, 14, 47; eco-labeling and -marketing, 8, 48–49; emissions trading, 129, 169; energy, 123–26, 142–43, 146–48, 150–53, 156, 159; firm performance and, 29–30, 128–38; forestry, 111, 114–21, 133, 136, 155, 162, 163, 164, 165; greenhouse emissions, 123–27, 127, 128–29, 131, 162, 164, 167, 172; investing and investments, 36–37, 38, 61; lessons learned, 126–28; NGOs and, 24, 111, 114, 116, 122; ocean dumping, 113; shareholder resolutions and, 64–65. *See also* BP; Burma; Ford; Shell; Sustainability
Environmental Protection Agency (EPA), 131, 138
Environmental Trading System (BP), 125
Environmental summit (Rio de Janeiro; *1992*), 11
EPA. *See* Environmental Protection Agency
Equator Principles, 155–56, 164, 167
Erasmus University, 37
Ernst & Young, 79, 90
Esprit, 28
Estée Lauder, 55

Ethical Trading Initiative (ETI), 85, 98,167
Ethiopia, 105
Ethnic issues, 145–46, 161, 170
ETI. *See* Ethical Trading Initiative
Europe: boycotts in, 51; business environment in, 24; Clean Clothes Campaign in, 86; company codes, 86–87; CSR in, 6, 8, 23, 47, 48, 52, 167; employment issues, 58; energy issues, 124; environment and climate issues in, 132, 133, 136, 169; Fair Trade certification in, 103, 104; forestry issues in, 114–15, 118, 120, 121, 136; investment in, 10, 61, 64; ISO *14001*, 137; new business environments, 27; reporting in, 68, 188n91; voluntary codes in, 85–87. *See also* Shell; individual countries
European Sustainable and Responsible Investment Forum, 61
European Union, 2, 6, 23, 104, 124, 167, 169, 171. *See also* Europe; *individual countries*
Extractive industries, 140, 144–50, 153–54, 158, 164, 171. *See also* Nigeria; Petroleum; *individual companies*
Extractive Industries Transparency Initiative, 149, 167
ExxonMobil: in Chad and Cameroon, 148, 163; CSR and, 54; employee issues, 58; environmental issues and, 55, 130–31; financial results, 127; human rights violations and, 168; in Indonesia, 159–60; in SRI portfolios, 40; Voluntary Principles on Security and Human Rights and, 145
Exxon Valdez, 55

Factories. *See* Labor issues; Manufacturing
Fair Labor Association (FLA), 82, 83–84, 87, 90, 92, 96
Fair Trade and Fair Trade labeling: Chiquita and, 50; coffee industry

and, 1, 8, 49, 54, 103–05, 121; effects of, 105–06, 163, 164; market for virtue and, 76
Fairtrade Labeling Organization International, 103
Faith and Fortune: The Quiet Revolution to Reform American Business (Gunther), 20
F&C Asset Management, 154
Fannie Mae, 41
Federal Express, 128
Federated Department Stores, 151
Fédération des Entreprises du Commerce et de la Distribution, 86
Fédération International de Football Association, 86
Financial Times (*FT*): chief executives, 53; CSR, 7, 43, 67; environmental issues, 136; Nigeria and Shell, 143–44; SRI indexes, 61; Starbucks, 54; Stock Exchange, 159
Fiorina, Carly, 44
First Tuesday, 28
5 percent club, 18
FLA. *See* Fair Labor Association
Flatz, Alois, 36
Florini, Ann, 172
Foot Locker, 93
Ford: boycotts and protests of, 51, 52, 54; Chicago Climate Exchange and, 129; CSR goals of, 121–23, 127–28; electric cars, 134–35; environmental issues, 135–36, 165, 173; evaluations of, 41; human rights violations and, 168
Ford, William Clay, Jr., 121–22, 127–28
Foreign Trade Association of German Retailers (AVE), 83
Forest and trade networks (FTNs), 119
Forest Ethics, 116
Forestry. *See* Environmental issues
Forest Stewardship Council (FSC), 49, 117–19, 120–21, 164
Fortune magazine, 7, 27, 30, 31, 57, 70, 126
Fortune *500* companies, 40, 68, 117

Fortune Global 500 companies, 97, 153
Fortune Global 100 companies, 68
Forum for the Future, 66
Foul Ball campaign, 97
France: business firms in, 159; CSR in,
    8; financial institutions in, 155; Fair
    Trade in, 104; investment issues, 61,
    65, 66; supermarkets in, 107; views
    of child labor, 47
Franklin Research and Development
    Corporation, 29, 83
Frank, Robert, 50
Free Burma Coalition, 151–52
Freeman, Bennett, 149
Freeport McMoRan, 145, 146
Friedman, Milton, 19, 26
Friends of the Earth, 154
FSC. See Forest Stewardship Council
FT. See Financial Times
FTNs. See Forest and trade networks
FTSE International, 64; All Share Index,
    36; 4Good Index, 35, 36, 63, 64;
    FTSE Group, 64

Gabon, 115–16
Galeries Lafayette, 87
GAO. See General Accounting Office
Gap Inc.: audits and auditing, 91–92; in
    Cambodia, 168–69; compliance by,
    96; CSR and, 54, 73, 165; FLA and,
    84; public criticism of, 52, 53, 107;
    sourcing by, 90; unions and, 101
Garment industry, 89
Gates Foundation, 42, 55
GE. See General Electric
General Accounting Office (GAO), 132
General Dynamics, 63
General Electric (GE), 41, 57, 151
General Motors (GM), 54, 128, 131,
    134
Genetic modification, 51
Germany: coffee industry in, 88; finan-
    cial institutions in, 155; forestry
    issues, 114, 119; investment issues in,
    66; Rugmark in, 8, 102, 103
Gifford, Kathie Lee, 78

Gillette, 41, 64–65
Global Citizenship Initiative, 11, 65–66
Global Climate Coalition, 123
Global Compact. See UN Global Com-
    pact
Global Exchange, 104, 151
Globalization and global issues: business
    networks, 28; climate change, 64,
    111, 121–38, 169; corporate
    response to, 12; critiques and critics
    of, 8; CSR, 157; economic factors, 9,
    13; environmental factors, 112,
    128–29, 137–38; human rights and,
    160–61; international corporate
    reporting, 69; legal accountability
    and, 168; meaning of globalization,
    160; norms of corporate citizenship,
    156–58; regulatory privatization, 9;
    SRI funds, 61; standards, 136–38.
    See also UN Global Compact
Global Reporting Initiative (GRI), 8,
    22–23, 69, 157
Goddard, Jim, 129
Goldman Sachs, 28, 57
Good to Great (Collins and Porras), 41
Government regulation, 9–10, 166–73
Great Britain: CSR and, 7–8, 10, 47, 48,
    107; energy issues, 124; ethical con-
    sumerism in, 8, 47, 134; ETI and, 85;
    Fair Trade coffee in, 103–04, 105;
    financial institutions in, 155; forestry
    issues, 114, 115, 118; investment in,
    36, 61; pension funds in, 66;
    response to activists in, 159; Shell
    and, 112, 142; supermarkets in, 107
Green and Black, 50
Greene, Adam, 170
Greening. See Environmental issues
Greenleaf, 8
Green Lights, 131
Greenpeace, 88, 112–14, 141, 169
GRI. See Global Reporting Initiative
Gulf of Mexico, 113–14
Guo Nian Garment, 91

Halliburton, 40

Hallmark, 116
H&M, 73, 86, 87, 98
Hart, Stuart, 20
Harvard Business Review, 20
Harvard Business School, 27, 79–80
Hasbro, 85
Hawken, Paul, 20, 40
Healthcare, 38
Heinz, USA, 135
Henderson, Judy, 22–23
Hennes & Mauritz. *See* H&M
Hershey, 53, 88, 89
Hertie, 103
Hewlett-Packard (HP): in Burma, 151;
   Climate Group and, 132; CSR and,
   44, 73, 165; DJSI World and, 64;
   forestry issues, 116; ISO *14001* and,
   137; public views of, 5, 41
Hollender, Jeffrey, 2, 72, 172
Howard, Steve, 132
Home Base, 115
Home Depot: CSR and, 73; employee
   issues, 64; forestry issues, 1, 115–16,
   118, 119, 172; procurement policies
   of, 163; public pressure and, 53
Honda, 128
Honduras, 78, 95, 97, 99, 101
Hong Kong, 90
Hopkins, Michael, 12
HP. *See* Hewlett-Packard
HSBC, 155
Human rights, 64, 102, 139–61, 168, 170

IBM, 41, 57, 116, 129, 130, 132, 168
Ikea: child labor and, 1, 172–73; CSR
   and, 44, 73, 98, 163; forestry issues,
   118; private ownership of, 72; public
   criticism of, 53, 107; supplier social
   performance and, 87
ILO. *See* International Labor Organization
ILO Tripartite Declaration of Principles
   Concerning Multinational Enterprises and Human Rights, 167
India, 87, 95, 96, 102–03, 157, 158,
   163

Indonesia: ChevronTexaco in, 163; BP
   in, 145–46, 147; forestry issues, 115,
   120; Freeport McMoRan in, 146;
   Home Depot in, 115; Nike in,
   77–79, 81; unions in, 101; working
   conditions in, 95, 100
Innovest, 37; Strategic Value Advisors,
   66
Insight Investments and Accountability,
   42
Intel, 128
Interface, 44, 73, 128, 129, 134,
   135–36, 173
International Business Leaders Forum,
   11
International Cocoa Organization, 89
International Coffee Organization, 106
International Council of Toy Industries,
   85
International Finance Corporation, 155,
   167
International Institute of Tropical Agri-
   culture, 89
International Labor Organization (ILO),
   62, 83, 86, 97, 152, 168–69
International Maritime Organization,
   113
International Organization for Standardization (ISO), 137
International Paper, 129
International Textile Workers Association, 83
International Union of Foodworkers, 88
Internet, 6, 9
Intersport, 93
Investment issues: corporate financial
   performance, 30; corporate philanthropy, 17–18; CSR and, 17, 25–26,
   33, 46–47, 60–72, 167; divestment,
   63, 150–54; environmental factors,
   122; financial-market effects on CSR,
   71–72; human rights and, 160–61;
   impact of social investing, 61–65,
   170; mainstreaming SRI, 65–67;
   management objectives, 26; mutual
   funds, 60, 61, 182n60; pension

funds, 66; reporting, 39, 67–70; screening, 37, 39, 40, 60, 61, 62, 65, 66; shareholder pressures and resolutions, 64–65, 71, 72; socially responsible investing, 6, 8, 21–24, 27–28, 35–45, 60–63, 69–71, 166; unethical and vice funds, 22, 63. *See also* Corporate social responsibility
Ireland, 120
ISO. *See* International Organization for Standardization
ISO *14001* standard, 137–38
Italy, 66
Ivory Coast, 88–89, 167

Jacobi, Peter, 154
Japan, 94, 103, 119–20, 136, 155
J. C. Penney, 95, 97
Johnson & Johnson, 41, 55, 57, 129
Jordan, Michael, 78, 99–100
Journal of Corporate Citizenship, 8

Karstadt, 103
Kell, Georg, 157
Kimberly-Clark, 41
Kinder Lyderberg Domini (KLD) Research & Analytics, 30, 31, 35
Kinder, Peter, 28
Kinko's, 116, 118, 119
KLD. *See* Kinder Lyderberg Domini Research & Analytics
Kline, John, 149
Knight, Phil, 77, 79–80
Korea, 94, 97
Korten, David, 12
KPMG, 21, 68, 90, 154
Kraft Foods, 88, 105
Kroger, 41
Kyoto Treaty (*2004*), 124, 129, 169

Labor issues: in apparel factories, 49; child labor, 1, 5, 47, 49, 51, 75, 76–77, 78, 85, 87, 88–89, 96–100, 102, 107, 109, 162, 172; collective bargaining, 65; in contemporary CSR, 7, 22, 32, 59, 164; costs of compliance, 92–93, 95; employment discrimination, 64; forced labor, 150, 151, 152; foreign labor abuses, 77–78; freedom of association, 75, 100–01, 107–08, 164; monitoring, 1, 75, 82–85, 107; overtime, 95–96, 100, 107–08; paternalistic policies, 26, 42; prison labor, 85; production deadlines and, 95–96; public awareness of, 102; shareholder resolutions and, 64; social labeling and, 102–06; supplier working conditions, 75; sweatshops, 47, 53, 55, 59, 76, 79, 80, 81, 83, 109; unions, 83, 85, 88, 100–01; U.S. preferential access and, 168–69; wages and compensation, 75, 76, 81, 83, 88, 92–93, 96, 99–100, 107–08; working conditions, 99, 164. *See also* Fair Labor Association; individual corporations
Lafarge, 132
Laffer, Arthur, 12
Lance Armstrong Foundation, 55
Laszlo, Chris, 20
Latin America, 120
Leading Corporate Citizens (Waddock), 20
Leclarc, 87
Levi Strauss: in Burma, 151; child labor, 98; in China, 59, 154, 159; competition and, 94; CSR and, 18, 42, 44, 49, 72, 73; employee issues, 58; financial results of, 44; FLA and, 84; Guidelines for Country Selection, 154; wages and compensation, 100; working conditions, 99
Life magazine, 78
Liggett Group, 124
Lippmann, Walter, 25
Liz Claiborne, 84, 91, 99, 107, 151
Lockheed Martin, 63
London Principles of Sustainable Finance, 66
London Stock Exchange, 63
Los Angeles Times, 123–24
Lovins, Amory, 20

Lovins, L. Hunter, 20
Lowe's, 116, 118, 119
Lutz, Bob, 128
Luxembourg, 103

Madagascar, 147
Malaysia, 114–15, 120, 152, 158
Mali, 88
M&S. *See* Marks & Spencer
Manufacturing: audits of, 90–91; child
 labor in, 96; environmental issues,
 138; manufacturing codes, 90, 107;
 monitoring of, 107; outsourcing,
 89–90, 94, 159; sustainable manu-
 facturing, 122–23. *See also individ-
 ual corporations*
Margolis, Joshua Daniel, 23–24, 30, 32
Marketing and advertising, 21, 33,
 49–51. *See also* Corporate social
 responsibility; Corporations
Marks & Spencer (M&S), 42–43, 44,
 55, 73, 85, 87, 165
Marriott, 41
Mars, 53, 73, 88, 89
Mattel, 53, 85, 91, 99, 107, 163
MBAs. *See* Business schools
McDonald's, 2, 5, 53, 73, 85, 163
McKinsey, 57
McWilliams, Abigail, 32
Means, Gardiner Coit, 25
Media, 109, 112–13, 122, 123–24, 142,
 160
Mellon Capital Management, 66
Merck: CSR and, 73, 165; financial
 results of, 44; public views of, 41;
 river blindness drug, 42, 57, 59;
 Vioxx drug withdrawal, 55
Merck, George, 42
Mexico, 101, 117, 158
Microsoft, 40, 55
Military and defense contractors, 39–40,
 63
Millstone coffee, 105
Mining, Minerals, and Sustainable
 Development Project, 146–47, 164
Mitsubishi, 146

Monoprix, 87
Monsanto, 5, 51
Morocco, 96
Moskowitz, Milton, 12
Motorola, 41, 128, 129
Mozambique, 22
Multinational organizations, 9, 149,
 160
Mutual funds. *See* Investment issues
Myanmar. *See* Burma

Napalm. *See* Dow Chemical
National Breast Cancer Awareness
 Month, 56
National Labor Committee, 91
Natural gas, 124–25
Nature magazine, 113
Nepal, 102–03
Nestlé, 71, 88, 89
Netherlands: Clean Clothes Campaign
 in, 86; Fair Trade in, 8, 103, 104;
 financial institutions in, 155; forestry
 issues, 114, 115; Voluntary Principles
 on Security and Human Rights and,
 145
Net Impact, 28
New Balance, 79
New Industrial State (Galbraith), 25
Newmont Mining, 145
Newport Mining, 146
Newsweek magazine, 128
New York Times, 19, 122, 126, 148
NGOs. *See* Nongovernmental organiza-
 tions
Nigeria, 51, 65, 140–44, 146, 148–49.
 See also Saro-Wira, Ken
Nike: auditing and monitoring of, 1, 91;
 boycotts and protests against, 6, 51;
 child labor and, 97, 98; civil campaigns against, 71, 73, 78–79, 93,
 107; code of conduct of, 80–81; com-
 munity development programs, 81;
 CSR and, 77–82, 95, 165; environmental issues, 129; financial performance of, 79–80, 81; FLA
 participation, 84; Foul Ball campaign,

97; outsourcing and sourcing by, 94, 95, 107; OSHA standards and, 99; public awareness of, 52; wages and compensation, 99–100; working conditions, 53, 55, 59, 99, 163

Nivea, 55

Nongovernmental organizations (NGOs): activism by, 9–10, 24, 54, 92, 116, 122; auditing by, 84, 91; banks and banking and, 155, 156; environmental issues and, 111, 114, 116, 122, 138; ExxonMobil and, 148; human rights issues, 145, 160; ISO *14001* and, 137; SA*8000* and, 83; targeting of corporations by, 7, 52–53, 107, 109; UN Global Compact and, 158; Voluntary Principles on Security and Human Rights and, 145; WRC and, 84. *See also individual organizations*

Noranda, 146

Nordic Swan, 48

Nordstrom, 41, 84

Norsk Hydro, 144, 145

North America, 103, 115, 120, 121, 132, 136, 157. *See also* Canada; United States

Norway, 145

Novo Nordisk, 58

Nuclear power, 39, 63

Nucor, 41

Occidental Petroleum, 145, 146

Occupational Health and Safety Administration (OSHA), 99

OECD. *See* Organization for Economic Cooperation and Development

OECD Guidelines for Multinational Enterprises, 167

Office Depot, 116, 117

Oil. *See* BP; ExxonMobil; Shell

Ontario (Canada), 120, 132

Ontario Power Generation, 128–29

Organization for Economic Cooperation and Development (OECD), 6, 89, 158

Oromiya Coffee Farmers Co-operative Union, 105

O'Rourke, Dara, 90

OSHA. *See* Occupational Health and Safety Administration

Oslo-Paris Commission, 113

Otto Versand, 83, 103

Oulton, Will, 64

Outsourcing. *See* Manufacturing

Overath, Dieter, 88

Oxfam International, 88, 94, 95, 104

Pakistan, 78, 97, 98, 102–03

Panama, 157

Papua New Guinea, 145–46, 147, 163

Parnassus Equity Income, 37

Parnassus Fund, 37

Partnerships for Climate Action, 128–29

Patagonia, 28, 44, 50, 57, 72, 73, 84, 135–36

Pax World Balanced, 37

Pax World Fund, 22

Pechiney, 128–29, 132

PepsiCo, 2, 51, 151

Perkins, George, 25

Peru, 147

Petroleum. *See* BP; ExxonMobil; Shell

Phelps Dodge, 146

Philip Morris, 41, 58. *See also* Tobacco and tobacco industry

Philippines, 157

Phillips-Van Heusen, 84

Pitney Bowes, 41

Pizza Hut, 151

Placer Dome, 146

Planetary Bargain, The (Hopkins), 12

Polaroid, 42, 129

Political issues: corporations and political activity, 6; product production, 52; social investment, 22, 23; U.S. political strategies, 7

Polls. *See* Research studies

Porras, Jerry, 41

Porter, Michael, 21, 23

Portugal, 22

Posner, Michael, 84

Premier Oil, 144, 151
PricewaterhouseCoopers, 20, 67, 90, 91
Pricketter, Glenn, 127
Princeton University, 17
Procter & Gamble, 41, 54, 105, 128
Production. *See* Manufacturing
Profits with Principles (Jackson and Nelson), 20
Property, 25
Publish What You Pay (PWYP), 149, 164, 167

Rainforest Action Network (RAN), 59, 115–16, 154, 155
Rainforest Alliance, 43
Rainforest Foundation, 120
RAN. *See* Rainforest Action Network
R&D. *See* Research and development
Raytheon, 131
RC. *See* Responsible Care
Reebok: auditing and monitoring of, 91; in Burma, 151; environmental issues, 64–65; FLA and, 84; "Foul Ball" campaign and, 97; SA*8000* and, 83; working conditions, 71, 99
Reese, Robert, 89
Regulation. *See* Corporate social responsibility; Government regulation
Research and development (R&D), 32
Research studies: of audits and monitoring, 92; of banks and banking, 154; of boycotts, 70–71; of child labor, 97; of commercial audits, 90–91; of consumers and CSR, 47–49, 52–53, 54, 93; of CSR reporting, 68–69; of employees and CSR, 56–57; of CSR and profits, 25–35, 73, 95; of eco-efficient investments, 37; halo effect in, 48; of investors and CSR, 60–61, 62, 67, 71; of ISO *14001*, 137; of multinational firms, 153; of Nike, 78–80; of the UN Global Compact, 157–58
Responsible Care (RC), 136–37
Revlon, 55
Rice, Jerry, 78

Rio Environmental Summit (Rio de Janeiro; *1992*), 10–11
Rio Tinto, 144, 145, 146, 147
River blindness. *See* Merck
Roanoke Electric Steel Corporation, 129
Rockefeller, David, 18, 19
Rockefeller Philanthropy Advisors, 130
Roddick, Anita, 28, 43, 71
Roper polls, 52
Ruggie, John, 3
Rugmark and Rugmark Foundation, 8, 49, 76, 96–97, 102–03, 163, 164

SA*8000*, 83, 91, 94, 157
Safeway, 54
Safeway Stores UK, 85
SAI. *See* Social Accountability International
Sainsbury, 53, 54, 85
S&P *500*, 35–36, 37, 63
SANE BP, 126
Sara Lee, 88, 105
Saran Wrap, 51–52
Saro-Wira, Ken, 65, 141–42, 144. *See also* Nigeria
Sarawak, 114–15
SCAM, 118–19
Schroders, 66
Sean John, 99
Sears, 54, 151
Security, 145–46
September *11, 2001*, 72
Seventh Generation, 28, 44, 50, 72, 73, 134
Shareholders. *See* Investment issues
Shell: boycotts and protests against, 6, 51, 53; Brent Spar oil platform disposal, 5, 51, 111, 112–14, 123, 136, 144, 169; civil campaigns against, 71, 73, 111; CSR and, 44, 52, 54, 165; emissions trading by, 169; employment issues, 57–58; environmental issues, 55, 128–29, 132; financial results of, 44; human rights issues, 140–44, 145, 166; investment issues, 1, 39, 65; in Nigeria, 51,

140–44, 146, 147, 148–49, 159; in
Peru, 147; PWYP agreements, 149;
solar power of, 127
Shell Solar, 127
Shorebank, 57
Siegel, Donald, 32
Sierra Club, 121, 122
Silicon Valley, 27
Slavery, 89
Smith, Craig, 48
Soccer ball production, 78, 97, 98, 107
Social Accountability International
(SAI), 82, 83, 90, 91, 100. See also
SA8000
Social entrepreneurship, 13
Social Investment Forum, 37, 60–61
Social mutual funds. See Investment
issues
Solar power, 125, 126, 127
Somavia, Juan, 62
Sony, 41
South Africa, 7, 22, 55, 63, 86, 150,
152
South Korea, 77
South Pacific, 120
Sporting goods industry, 94–96, 97. See
also Nike; Reebok
Sport utility vehicles (SUVs), 51, 52,
122, 123, 128. See also Ford
SRI (socially responsible investing). See
Investment issues
Sri Lanka, 95, 96
Standard Oil of New Jersey, 17–18
Standards, 82–96, 99, 136–38, 162,
164, 165, 170
Staples, 53, 64, 116–17, 119
Starbucks: CAFE and, 88; CSR and, 73;
environmental issues and, 54; Fair
Trade and, 1, 104, 173; financial
results of, 44; public criticism of, 107
Starkist, 135
State Street Global Advisors, 37
Statoil, 144, 145
Statue of Liberty, 21
ST Microelectronics, 130
Stonyfield Farm, 28, 44

Sudan, 6, 153, 158, 159, 170
Sumitomo, 146
Suncor Energy, 129
Surveys. See Research studies
Sustainability: corporate issues, 20, 53,
67, 133; CSR and, 13; defining of,
110; Dow Jones Sustainability Index,
11; employee issues, 57–58; forestry
issues, 49; promoting sustainable
development, 146–50; reporting of,
68; voluntary codes and, 165
SustainAbility, 68
Sustainability Advantage, The (Willard),
19
Sustainability Asset Management
Group, 35
Sustainable Company, The (Laszlo), 20
Sustainable Forestry Initiative, 118
SUVs. See Sport utility vehicles
Swartz, Jeffrey, 57
Sweden, 66, 86, 87, 119
Swiss Re, 132
Switzerland, 103, 104, 155
Syngenta, 96

Taco Bell, 151
Taiwan, 77, 94
Talisman, 158
Target, 54
Tchibo, 88
Tellus Institute, 69
Tesco, 85
Texaco, 145, 151, 159. See also
ChevronTexaco
Texas Homecare, 115
Textile industry, 97
Thailand, 81, 99, 120, 150
3M, 41, 116
Timberland, 2, 57, 73, 83, 91, 165
Tobacco and tobacco industry, 39, 58,
61, 63, 11, 124
Togo, 88
Tom's of Maine, 28
TotalElfFina, 147. See also Total
Total, 150, 152, 159. See also TotalElf-
Fina

Toy Industries of Europe, 85
Toy Industry Association of America, 85
Toyota, 128
Toys. *See* Mattel; Toys "R" Us; Wal-Mart
Toys "R" Us, 83, 85
Trade and trade policies, 9, 89, 167, 171
Transfair, 88, 105
Tuck School of Business, 78–79
Turner Construction, 118
Tylenol. *See* Johnson & Johnson

UAW. *See* United Automobile, Aerospace and Agricultural Implement Workers of America
UDHR. *See* Universal Declaration of Human Rights
UN Global Compact, 8, 11, 23, 66, 139, 156–58, 164, 167. *See also* Globalization and global issues
UNICEF, 88–89
Unilever, 43–44, 50, 53, 71
Union Carbide, 55
Union Oil, 5, 51
Union 76, 152
United Automobile, Aerospace and Agricultural Implement Workers of America (UAW), 122
United Fruit Company, 43
United Kingdom. *See* Great Britain
United Nations (UN), 6, 156–57. *See also* UN Global Compact; UNICEF
United Nations Environmental Program, 66, 69
United Parcel Service (UPS), 128
United States (U.S.): consumer purchasing in, 48; CSR in, 7, 9–10; environmental and climate issues, 131, 131, 132, 133, 136, 163, 172; Fair Trade coffee in, 104, 105; forestry issues, 115, 116, 117, 118, 120, 121, 172; investment in, 8, 36, 37, 60, 61; Kyoto treaty, 129; new business environments, 24–29; ocean disposal by, 113; response to activists in, 159; Rugmark carpets and, 103; trade

sanctions by, 167; UN Global Compact in, 157; workplace standards in developing countries and, 82–85. *See also* North America
United Students Against Sweatshops, 84
United Way, 18
Universal Declaration of Human Rights (UDHR; UN; *1948*), 144, 167
Universities: FLA affiliations, 84; investment by, 22; student attitudes and pressures, 26–27, 59, 79, 101, 151; teaching by, 24, 28; university-logo goods, 83–84, 93, 101; WRC and, 84–85. *See also* Business schools; *individual colleges and universities*
University of Iowa, 97
Unocal, 65, 150, 151–52, 168
UPS. *See* United Parcel Service
Urban affairs, 18–19
Uruguay Round (WTO agreement), 95
U.S. Center for International Business, 170
U.S. Steel, 25, 131

Vagelos, Roy, 57
VanCity Savings Credit, 50
Veillon, 87
Verité, 91
Vietnam, 77, 79, 81, 163, 169, 171
Vietnam War, 22, 24, 51–52
Vioxx. *See* Merck
Voluntary Principles on Security and Human Rights (*2000*), 145–46, 149, 164, 167

Waddock, Sandra, 20
Walgreens, 41
Walker, Frank, 48
Walker Group, 47
Walker Information, 48
Walking the Talk (Holliday, Schmidheiny, and Watts), 19
Wall Street Journal, 7, 36, 54, 124
Wal-Mart: boycotts and protests against, 52; CSR and, 106; environmental issues, 55; evaluation of, 5, 41; FLA

and, 84; investment issues, 40; labor
issues, 64, 72, 85, 165–66; sourcing
by, 89–90; success of, 93; unioniza-
tion of, 101
Walsh, James Patrick, 23–24, 30, 32
Walt Disney: audits and auditing, 91;
boycotts and protests against, 52, 53;
contract terminations, 92; CSR and,
73; evaluations and criticisms of, 41,
107; FLA and, 84; labor issues, 85;
sourcing by, 89
Washington Post, 129
Washington Times, 126
Waste Management, 128
Wells Fargo, 41
Western Mining Corporation, 146
Westgaad, Geir, 160
West Papua (Indonesia), 146
West Papua, New Guinea, 147
White Paper on Corporate Social
Responsibility (EU), 23
WH Smith, 85
Wild Oats, 105
Wolf, Martin, 2
Worker Rights Consortium (WRC), 82,

84–85, 101
Working Assets, 72
Working conditions. *See* Labor issues
World Bank, 92, 148, 153, 154, 155,
167, 170
World Business Council for Sustainable
Development, 10–11, 66
WorldCom, 38
World Economic Forum, 65–66, 67,
132, 156
World Resources Institute, 53, 66
World Trade Organization (WTO), 9, 95
World Wildlife Fund (WWF), 118, 129,
137–38, 147
WRC. *See* Worker Rights Consortium

Xerox, 131

Young, Andrew, 78

Zadek, Simon, 166
Zambia, 86, 98
Zimbabwe, 86
Zurich Scudder, 66